THE CONDUCT OF PHILANTHROPY

Frontispiece. William Richard Sutton (*c.* 1837–1900)

The Conduct of Philanthropy

William Sutton Trust 1900–2000

PATRICIA L. GARSIDE

THE ATHLONE PRESS
LONDON & NEW BRUNSWICK, NJ

First published in 2000 by
THE ATHLONE PRESS
1 Park Drive, London NW11 7SG
and New Brunswick, New Jersey

British Library Cataloguing in Publication Data
A catalogue record for this book is available from the British Library

ISBN 0 485 11531 X   HB

Library of Congress Cataloging-in-Publication Data

Garside, Patricia L.
  The conduct of philanthropy : the William Sutton Trust, 1900–2000 / Patricia L. Garside.
    p.   cm.
  Includes bibliographical references and index.
  ISBN 0-485-11531-X (hb : alk. paper)
  1. William Sutton Trust--History. 2. Housing trusts--Great Britain--History. I. Title.

HD7333.A3 G36 1999
363.5'83--dc21

                                                          99-047609

Distributed in The United States, Canada and South America by
Transaction Publishers
390 Campus Drive
Somerset, New Jersey 08873

Typeset by Acorn Bookwork, Salisbury
Printed and bound in Great Britain by
Cambridge University Press

For

John

Contents

Foreword

Upon reaching an age of venerability many organisations have a desire to pause, reflect and record their story. On achieving a centenary the desire often becomes irresistible. This book is just such a response.

The story starts with William Richard Sutton, carrier, astute investor and successful London businessman, who died in May 1900. The executors of his Will after overcoming challenges and difficulties succeeded in creating the Sutton Model Dwellings Trust (now the William Sutton Trust). The Trust has grown and prospered without interruption since, and it still pursues the original aims to this day. Many thousands of people of slender means and in need of homes have benefited from its work over the years.

A number of accounts of the Trust's history have been written. One of these, published in 1982, was compiled by two former senior members of the Trust's staff. This gave a fascinating detailed account of progressive development with mention of individuals who had special influence on the Trust's direction and it has been a most useful source of reference in the preparation of this latest book. However, where this new book differs is in the examination of the Trust in relation to its social context and period. The reader is presented with a discussion of the evolution of social housing in the twentieth century and the part the William Sutton Trust has played in this.

Several years ago, the Trustees decided to commission Professor Garside to write a two-stage history – firstly, to mark the centenary of William Sutton's will made in 1894, and secondly, that of William Sutton's death in 1900. *Building a Legacy: William Sutton and his Housing Trust*, published in 1994, focused on the life of William Sutton himself. This book now goes on to assess the work and impact of the William Sutton Trust over its first century.

Philip Mayo, who chaired the Trustees' Board when the project was set up in 1993, steered the small working party in the initial stages of planning and coordination. The working party, led subsequently by Christine Davies, actively participated in the project throughout and was an important sounding board for ideas. Michael Rose, Professor of Social History at Manchester University, acted as independent advisor. They are all to be congratulated on translating the original idea into practical achievements.

Of course the major contribution has been that of the author, Professor Patricia Garside. The depth of research and her scholarship are embedded in this work. Many of her findings are new even to those who know the background of the Trust well. She is to be congratulated on completing a memorable book which has been so demanding in its production. Thanks are also due to the many people who contributed to the project and cannot be mentioned individually here. The efforts of committees are frequently ridiculed, here is an example to counter some of the cliches.

Apart from acknowledging the contribution of so many people my aim is to commend to you the story that follows. Regardless of your knowledge of twentieth century housing more revelations await you.

John Farrant
Chairman of the Trustees, The William Sutton Trust
February 1999

Preface

I would like to thank the William Sutton Trustees for asking me to write this book. It has been a most absorbing and compelling task. I think the results will be of interest to those who have been involved with the Trust as tenants, employees, partners or competitors. The book shows, though, that the history of the Trust also has wide significance. Its experience in twentieth century housing provision leads to a reconsideration of the conduct of the voluntary sector, local and central government and the private market.

My work has been shared with the Trust throughout and in a variety of ways. I have found its support exemplary. The mechanism of a working party with oversight of the project operated extremely well. I am grateful for the willingness of working party members to engage actively with the research. Michael Rose acted as academic advisor and his independent involvement was an invaluable asset. Needless to say, the views (and the failings) of the book are my own.

Sections of the book have previously been presented in papers at academic conferences, *Urban History Group*, (April 1996), *European Association of Urban Historians, Third International Conference on Urban History* (August 1996), and the *Conference to Mark the Centenary of Seebohm Rowntree's First Study of Poverty in York* (March 1998). I acknowledge the value of the contributions made by discussants and participants in these sessions. Some early results of the research were published (with Susannah Morris) in *Building a Legacy: William Sutton and His Housing Trust* (The William Sutton Trust, 1994).

I particularly want to thank the research assistants who worked on individual elements of the book – Susannah Morris, Jessica Datta and Michael Wardle. They each made a significant contribution, digging deeply into their allotted tasks and emerging with unexpected material of exceptional quality. They and I received painstaking and valuable assistance from the staff of the following libraries – the London Metropolitan Archives, where most of the records of the William Sutton Trust are deposited, the Public Record Office, the House of Lords Record Office, the City of London School, the United Grand Lodge of England, the reference and local history libraries in the London Boroughs of Chelsea, Finsbury, Islington, Kensington, Lambeth, Lewisham, Southwark, and Tower Hamlets, and in Birmingham, Brighton, Croydon, Hertfordshire, Hull, Leeds, Liverpool, Manchester, Morden, Newcastle, Plymouth and Salford. Tenants and members of staff of the William Sutton Trust also made invaluable contributions to the research. Their interviews, in particular, became at times all too engrossing! Generous help was also received from Reginald Sutton, Derek Burns, and Jonathan Barry. Technical staff at the University of Salford and at the William Sutton Trust, especially Chris Tivey and Fred Rothwell, readily offered their expert advice.

The beginning of my research for this book was interrupted by illness. I would like to acknowledge the help I received from academic colleagues and from the Trust's working party in getting back to work. I am very grateful to them all. I want also to thank my family, especially Thomas and Ruth, and my close friends for their resourcefulness and concern. Above all, it was John, my husband, who saw us through a very difficult time. Despite my passion for history, he did not allow it to overwhelm his commitment to the future. It seems fitting to dedicate this book to him. I do so with much love and appreciation.

University of Salford

List of Illustrations

Figures

Tables

CHAPTER 1

The Philanthropy of William Sutton

Centenaries often provide the occasion for reevaluation and reflection. The hundredth anniversary of the death of William Richard Sutton, carrier, brewer and property developer in the City of London presents one such opportunity. William Sutton died on 20 May 1900, a self-made multimillionaire who showed no philanthropic impulses while he lived. Nevertheless, he left virtually the whole of his fortune to provide housing for the poor in London and other 'populous places' in England. The Sutton Model Dwellings Trust, as it was originally known, was endowed with more than £2 million (about £77 million at 1997 prices).[1] The Trust was by far the wealthiest foundation among the philanthropic housing societies. Its initial assets were four times as large as those of its nearest rival, the Peabody Trust, and ten times those of the Guinness Trust.[2] Despite its wealth and considerable achievements since 1900, the William Sutton Trust remains relatively unknown.[3] This account is an attempt to give the Trust its proper proportion and to make its often puzzling conduct intelligible.

During William Sutton's lifetime, it appeared that 'Every enterprise this man embarked upon seemed literally to turn to gold.'[4] At his death, his generosity seemed to take on a regal quality and this 'merchant prince' was praised for the 'munificent sum' that he had left to the poor.[5] The commercial world, his family, government institutions and the world of philanthropy itself were shocked by benevolence on such a scale. For three decades after William Sutton's death, his Trust was subjected to efforts to limit its scope and constrain its activities. The William Sutton Trust became caught up in some fundamental social and political issues, in particular the role of central and local government in the provision of housing and the relief of poverty. At the same time, the Trust found itself at odds with the values of the philanthropic sector. The delivery of its benefits to recipients required a degree of organisation and management that seemed to go beyond any

sphere of kindness, and to require full-time professional commitment. As a substantial actor in housing provision on a national
scale, the Trust tested the ideological framework of both the
voluntary sector and of government at central and local level: this
was especially so in the period 1900 to 1939, but was also a
feature of the 1960s. Its wealth also raised fears that it could
monopolise housing for the poor, disrupting the social and the
spatial structure of local housing markets.

The work of the William Sutton Trust undoubtedly has considerable intrinsic interest, but the purpose of this study goes beyond
the analysis of one particular organisation. Its aim is to reevaluate
the place of philanthropic housing in England in the twentieth
century, based on a study of the conduct and impact of the
William Sutton Trust, one of the voluntary sector's largest and
most active members. It seeks to establish the Trust's specific place
geographically, socially, politically and organisationally. In
addition, it also examines the Trust's broader role – in the voluntary sector, in housing provision and in the apparatus of the state.

Understanding the operations of a housing organisation in the
voluntary sector invites consideration of several theoretical
approaches. Neither housing nor philanthropic organisations,
however, fit easily into commonly used economic and political
models. Consequently, there is a tendency to portray voluntary
sector housing in utopian terms.[6] Prochaska has suggested that
the history of philanthropy as a whole can best be thought of as
the history of kindness.[7] Useful as this may be as a general
insight, it is unlikely to provide a satisfactory explanation in
Sutton's case, at least in any direct sense, for the reasons that have
already been suggested. By contrast, other historians have viewed
philanthropy as a means of consolidating the power of the
wealthy while dividing the loyalties of the poor.[8] Both Marxists
and Whigs have agreed that philanthropy was bound to decline in
importance as a result of social and political changes in the
twentieth century and especially because of the growth in the role
of the state. In the 1900s, many voluntary bodies were remote
from government, receiving no financial support and subject to
very little official regulation. It has been argued that subsequently
they became increasingly harnessed to the expanding activities of
government – ceasing to be independent and self-directed and
becoming instead incorporated into government as agents or

clients. This process is sometimes regarded as having begun particularly early in housing with the provision of state subsidies to
local authorities *and* housing associations from 1919.

Many commentators, however, have had difficulty integrating
housing into their accounts of the changing role of the state and of
the voluntary sector. In twentieth century Britain, house-building
has occurred at the interface between the market and government.[9]
The market-state mix may take a variety of forms and philanthropic housing merely adds yet another, even less well-understood
dimension to the problem. Furthermore, the complexity of the
housing issue has tended to produce studies which are either very
general in scope, dealing with the 'rise' of council housing or the
expansion of owner-occupation, for example, or which are specific
to one town, often over a relatively short period.[10] What is needed
is an exploratory framework that enables the multidimensional
position occupied by agencies such as the William Sutton Trust to
be analysed, the interrelationship between the sectors in which
such a philanthropic housing agency was operating to be studied,
and the processes of providing 'not-for-profit' housing to be investigated. To these ends, a modified type of game theory has been
adopted in this study, and specifically a form of it described as
'nested game theory'. This approach helps to clarify the problems
that the William Sutton Trust has faced in discharging its obligations since 1900, what solutions were adopted and what organisational strategies were developed. In addition, through an analysis
of the Trust's tenants' records in the interwar period and through
interviews with tenants the human and social impact of the Trust's
activities is explored. The aim is to produce a better understanding
of the opportunities and limitations of the voluntary sector in
housing provision and of the significance of its relationship with
the state. What should also emerge is a more realistic theory of the
operation of nonprofit housing agencies and a clearer understanding of what it has meant to be a provider and a consumer of
philanthropic housing in the twentieth century.

WILLIAM SUTTON, BUSINESS AND CHARITY

This introductory chapter concludes by examining the context in
which William Sutton framed his charitable trust and in particular

it explores the relationship between business, housing and charity at the end of the nineteenth century. It is important to stress that in 1900 charity still constituted a significant element in English life. In the 1890s, a study showed that middle class households spent a larger share of their income on charity than on any item in their budget except food.[11] Indeed, Jose Harris has highlighted a situation where numerous social investigations at the time

> uncovered a vast, ramshackle mass of voluntary, self-governing, local, parochial and philanthropic provision that was attempting in a myriad of different ways to assist, elevate, reform or coerce the poor and other persons in need.[12]

Following Harris, historians now argue that in this context, the growth of the state was seen as dangerous.[13] Indeed Harrison has viewed nineteenth century philanthropy as the basis for Britain's 'peaceable kingdom', bringing together middle and working class based on shared values of decency, independence and animosity to the undeserving poor.[14] Previously, the prevailing view was that charity had been rejected as ultimately inadequate. Its failure in the face of the needs of industrial and urban society meant that state intervention was welcomed as both superior and inevitable.[15] Charitable giving has been attributed mainly to motives of self-interest – to assuage the 'deep and abiding sense of guilt' of the 'newly rich', to protect against threats of social disorder, to secure social control through reinforcing class positions or to exercise cultural 'hegemony' over society as a whole.[16] The nature of charitable giving, its character and its purpose have recently undergone a wide-ranging reevaluation, not least because of changes in current political philosophy about the 'third way'.[17]

Where should William Sutton be placed in the constellation of wealthy Victorian philanthropists? Most obviously, he was a 'newly rich' businessman with limited formal education who created his considerable wealth by exploiting opportunities in growing consumer industries, breaking new ground and undermining old rules.[18] He began his career in a small way in the 1850s operating as a carrier from the basement of the Fountain Inn in the City of London where his father had acted as barman. He used the railways to distribute the parcels he collected, making up all those destined for one place into a single package addressed to his agent. Sutton's profit came from the difference between his own charges for individual packets and those allowed by the railway companies for packages in bulk. The railway companies, however, regarded Sutton's profits as stolen from them. They imposed surcharges and even, at times, refused to carry his bulk packages.[19] Seven years' litigation followed on the 'packed parcels question' until finally the House of Lords found in Sutton's favour in 1868. This was a most important commercial case, opening up exploitation of the railway network to entrepreneurs like Sutton. Sutton continued to challenge attempts by railway companies to establish carrying monopolies.[20] In 1900, his carrying company had over 600 branches in major towns in Britain, the colonies and America. Drink, both alcoholic and nonalcoholic, was the second of William Sutton's major enterprises. He had shares in 11 brewing, bottling and distilling firms. He was director of a gin, whisky and brandy distillery, Sutton, Carden and Co., in Finsbury and of the New London Brewery Co. Ltd in Kennington. In furtherance of 'vertical integration' the brewery developed interests in hotels and inns, while William Sutton also promoted the development of parades of shops in suburban areas of London and elsewhere. He was also a major developer of offices and warehouses in Finsbury and the City of London, and an investor in railways, docks and mining enterprises worldwide.

There is no doubt that the fortune William Sutton had amassed on his death was the result of his own energy, hard work and enterprise. What debt did such a person owe to society and in particular what was the responsibility of the self-made rich towards the poor? In the United States, the mega-wealthy were divided in their views. In his 'gospel of wealth' pronounced in 1889, Andrew Carnegie expressed the belief that the people who had created wealth were naturally the best fitted to exercise care in society. Benevolence was therefore something to be conducted throughout life, while 'millionaire classes' should not leave anything to their own heirs since that would thwart the rise of the next generation of commercial and social leaders.[21] Carnegie's contemporary, the oil magnate John D. Rockefeller, was more traditional. He regarded his wealth not as a mark of personal superiority but as a gift from God. Though he complained in 1891 that his philanthropic activities were taking up as much time as his business, Rockefeller preferred 'not to give away everything to the

public and fail to give to my own family and friends'.[22] It seems
that 'no single other major (American) philanthropist of the early
twentieth century followed Carnegie's advice that heirs should
receive nothing'.[23] In England, as in the USA, such large scale
philanthropy was in any event rare. Wealthy industrialists and the
less well off supported mostly small-scale, local charities with
restricted budgets and limited objectives.[24] They saw philanthropic
action as a social duty derived from wealth and sought through
active participation in society to aid the development of civic
responsibility in both the donor and the recipient.

In terms of both lifestyle and inheritance, therefore, William
Sutton was a rarity. There is absolutely no evidence that during his
lifetime he was involved in any charitable or public activity of any
sort. Nor is there evidence of any religious affiliation. Though he had
an eye for good design, he was not a patron of the arts.[25] Active
participation in society through philanthropic action surrounded
him, not least in the City of London. Most directly, Sir Sydney
Waterlow, MP, a leading City figure who founded the Improved
Dwellings Company owned property next to Sutton's distillery in
Hill Street Finsbury.[26] Sutton, however, remained immersed in
business, forbidding even close associates to acknowledge him
outside his office.[27] His benevolence was wholly posthumous,
a strategy that had become most unusual by the end of the
nineteenth century. Furthermore, his benevolence to the poor
virtually disinherited family members. Twice married, he had no
children of his own, but his extended family was large, since both
his wives had brought children to the marriages. In 1895, William
Sutton made a series of changes to his last will. He provided
annual annuities of £5000 to his second wife and to his brother
Charles, but he revoked all other legacies previously included for
other family members. Only small sums to servants remained,
amounting to less than £350. Thomas Watson, a longtime
associate, inherited the carrying business but William Sutton left
the rest of his entire wealth to establish a trust charged with
building flats and houses for the poor to be called "The Sutton
Model Dwellings".[28] (See Appendix 2, The Last Will and Testament of William Richard Sutton)

As a Victorian philanthropist, William Sutton was clearly out of
sympathy with the prevailing norm of lifelong but small scale, ad
hoc involvement in the relief of social problems in a particular

community.[29] Passing such things by when alive, he was nevertheless prepared to virtually disinherit his family on his death in order to set up a trust. His goal was to help a broadly defined and widely dispersed class of people (the poor') by providing them with model dwellings and houses at low rents. If Sutton was an unusual philanthropist, the trust he set out to create was even more extraordinary. As a framework for analysing different types of voluntary action, Finlayson has identified four categories: individual, informal, commercial and statutory.[30] Only the first three are relevant to a discussion of activity at the end of the nineteenth century. 'Individual' philanthropy can be either 'selfregarding' or 'other-regarding'. The former found expression in mutual aid societies and the latter formed the basis for organised bodies of 'active citizens'. Neither of these variants can be applied to William Sutton's trust. Nor can the 'informal' type, characterised by mutual exchanges of help in time of need, which Prochaska has argued was so extensive and so significant an impulse in the nineteenth and twentieth centuries.[31] Commercial philanthropy, on the other hand, where charity was organised on business principles, certainly was an accepted part of voluntary housing in 1900. The model dwelling companies claimed that by making modest profits they were in fact serving the public interest. They argued that they were showing that working class housing did not have to be provided at a loss to investors.[32] Nevertheless, despite Sutton's request that the dwellings provided by his trust should be identified as 'model', he rejected the profit motive and sought only to have his bequest employed as a 'continuing' body, breaking even rather than showing any return. William Sutton's trust is indeed difficult to classify in terms of the prevailing examples.

There is another possibility to be considered, and that is the idea of 'scientific charity', which was gaining support on both sides of the Atlantic by 1900. This approach grew out of a distrust of much existing charity which was coming to be regarded as sentimental, reactionary and harmful. The answer was thought to lie in the disciplining of charitable impulses, with the machinery of philanthropy reconstructed according to scientific principles. In Britain, the primary example was the appropriately named Charity Organisation Society (COS). This body sought to bring discrimination to the distribution of charity through regulatory mechanisms and administrative refinements, based on reviews of individual needs. The work of the COS became highly regarded in the USA, especially during the Depression of the 1890s. Rockefeller took the idea further by proposing that the 'business of benevolence' could best be pursued through a properly managed trust.[33] In 1901, he urged 'men of worth and position' to 'erect a foundation, a trust, and engage directors who will make it a life work to manage, with our personal cooperation, this business of benevolence properly and effectively'. Such an organisation would not dispense charity – rather it would attack misery 'scientifically' at its source through the application of research.[34] In the next decade, Rockefeller, Carnegie and several other American philanthropists set up foundations whose aim was to advance knowledge rather than to relieve the needy. In Britain, in 1904, the Rowntree family set up three trusts. Two of them were committed to 'search out causes of poverty and distress, to promote debate about remedies and to influence public policy'.[35] In town planning, philanthropists including Carnegie and Thomas Horsfall provided funds to support international conferences where debates about directing social change and finding ways of dealing with urban problems took place.[36] Nevertheless, the desire to 'end' problems rather than to deal directly with their immediate manifestations, was restricted to a very small number of foundations. William Sutton himself, shared some but not all the aims of the emerging 'scientific' philanthropy. Whilst he wanted his trust to be run in a businesslike way, employing appropriate staff, he does not appear to have imagined that the organisation would involve itself in analysing social questions nor in seeking to influence local and central government in the decision-making process. (See Appendix 2, Section 5). He did believe that the housing problems of the poor could be prevented, and not just relieved, by his type of not-for-profit, wholesale philanthropy. His goals, however, remained specific – 'to provide proper and sufficient dwelling houses' for the poor. Unlike Rockefeller and Rowntree, he did not pursue general goals such as the understanding of poverty or the promotion of general welfare.

　　William Sutton's trust, therefore, was at the outset progressive, self-confident and business-like. It was also untried, since its founder had not applied himself to charitable actions during his lifetime. Its philosophical and operational foundations were consequently uncertain. The remit of the trustees was wide – they were to prevent poor people from becoming social casualties by providing good housing at rents within their means. Only the destitute and the 'broken down paupers' lay outside their remit.[37] What neither Sutton nor his trustees appear to have appreciated was the growing significance of local and central government in determining the public good. They did not recognise that tackling social problems required cooperation and tactical skill as well as boldness. Their optimism and self-confidence initially brought not progress but opposition and hostility. Both the legal and the public policy making process proved a great deal more complicated than they had realised.[38] Their experience of the Courts, the Government's legal officers, Ministries and local authorities was an object lesson in the diffuse nature of power within society. Though apparently the holders of unprecedented influence and resources, those entrusted with carrying out Sutton's will found themselves enmeshed in webs of authority that threatened to frustrate them.[39]

HOUSING, CHARITY AND PHILANTHROPY IN 1900

When William Sutton died in 1900, the categories of 'charity' and 'philanthropy' were not fixed but were widely contested. This was true not only in everyday usage, but also in a specifically legal sense.[40] It is not surprising, therefore, that certain disinherited parties challenged the legality of William Sutton's bequest. The essence of the action brought against William Sutton by his niece, Ellen Hillier Lewis, her husband, Thomas Christopher Lewis, and her brother, William Hillier Sutton, was that the will did not constitute a valid charitable purpose. Their opposition centred on the claim that the purchase of land was not a 'charitable purpose' in law so that 'no charitable uses (are) left'. That being the case, they argued, the (non-charitable) trust became subject to the 1890 Housing of the Working Classes Act which restricted the amount of land that could be given for such housing to five acres. It is interesting that Mr Justice Buckley himself, before whom the case was heard, declared that the provision of housing for the working class was not in itself to be regarded as charitable. The 1890 Act, he ruled is not an Act dealing with charitable matters, but is an Act providing for erecting dwellings for the working class. Now, the poor need not necessarily be poor of the class known as the working class, and many of the working class, as we know, are not poor.[41]

Throughout the nineteenth century a series of Mortmain and Charitable Uses Acts had sought to limit the extent to which charity could deprive a testator's family of their 'rightful due'. Since the sixteenth century, the trust had been established as the legal form most associated with institutional philanthropy and it ensured that the name of the donor could live on after death – a dynastic as well as a philanthropic device. The terms 'charitable' and 'charitable purpose' had evolved through a long process of legal decisions and differed in many respects from the popular meaning of the words. The result was that by 1900, the terms had 'taken on a somewhat eccentric life of their own'.[42] Nevertheless, the law had sought to distinguish and reconcile three contending entities in the practice of charity – namely family rights, the public weal and the potential beneficiaries of charitable trusts. The public interest came to be an increasingly important consideration during the nineteenth century, and in the 1880s and 1890s a series of Charitable Trusts' Acts established wide-ranging state supervision of charities.[43] Increasingly charities were required to be of 'public benefit' and not exclusively for the good of the potential benefici-aries. Since the potential beneficiaries were likely to be too poor or otherwise disadvantaged to defend their own legal interests, a 'guardian' of charitable trusts was established. In theory, this was the monarch, but in practice it was the Crown's principal legal agent, the Attorney General.

In the case of Lewis v Sutton, Counsel appeared for the plain-tiffs and for the defendants, who were the three nominated execu-tors, with William Sutton's widow (Eliza Anna Venus White) and his youngest sister (Mary Anne Sutton). The Attorney General also appeared in his role of guardian of the interests of the benefi-ciaries – 'the poor in London and other populous places'. The Attorney General took a prominent part in the case and argued that the plaintiffs were confounding 'means and purposes', in focusing on the land question. Land had been a particular concern for charity law, because of its fundamental significance for family inheritance. By the Mortmain and Charitable Uses Act of 1736, land could only be given if the recipient were a University, a college or a school.[44] If the plaintiffs could show that William Sutton's trust consisted 'simply in the purchase of land' then it followed that no 'charitable purpose' existed under Section 7 of the 1891 Mortmain and Charitable Uses Act. The Attorney General made the case that the acquisition of land was merely the machinery by which the trust would come into effect, and that the charitable purpose was clearly stated in section 7 of the will, namely

the devotion of the buildings when erected to the housing of people of small means at rents below the rack rental of the property[45]

Mr Justice Buckley determined that 'that is a good charitable trust' and rejected the plaintiffs' case.

By this judgement, it appeared that the rights of the beneficiaries had been held to outweigh those of the opposing family members. In principle this was indeed the case but some compensation was subsequently offered to the injured parties. By Order of the Court, several additional legacies were paid to all William Sutton's surviving nephews and nieces (whether or not they had been parties to the legal action), to his sister Mary Ann, to his widow and to his brother (in addition to their annuities). With two small legacies to non-family members, the total sum involved was £30,000.[46] Family rights and the interests of the beneficiaries had been reconciled, but the question of the public weal remained. The family had chosen to take its stand on the issue of land; for those concerned with the William Sutton Trust's effect on the public interest the issue was poverty and pauperism. These were fundamental public and political concerns at the beginning of the twentieth century. The immediate problem was to decide the means by which the administration of the William Sutton Trust could be supervised. How far could the wishes of the testator be overridden in the wider public interest? Who could exercise this power – the charity commissioners, the High Court or the Ministry responsible for housing matters, then the Local Government Board?[47] What was immediately clear was that some central supervision of the Trust was necessary and the High Court of

Chancery was the chosen instrument. How this supervision operated is discussed in subsequent chapters. What needs to be stressed here is its general significance for understanding the social and political position of the William Sutton Trust in 1900. Like other members of the voluntary sector, the William Sutton Trust did not occupy an independent sphere. It operated at a point where the legal/personal, charitable/commercial and government/public systems intersected.[48] Despite its unprecedented resources, the Trust's position was an ambiguous and contested one, and its conduct was likely to prove unpredictable and problematic.

THE STRUCTURE OF THE BOOK

The aim of this chapter has been to give a clear sense of the world in which William Sutton established his Trust. Subsequent chapters explore the conduct of the William Sutton Trust and its consequences for the development of housing policy and for the people who became Sutton tenants. The strategic uses to which tenants put their occupation of a Sutton dwelling are highlighted and also the contribution made by the people involved in the administration and delivery of the housing. The book is organised analytically and thematically within an overall chronological framework. Chapter 2 presents an overview of the output of the Trust in the one hundred years from its foundation in 1900. Chapter 3 discusses the links and interplay between the Trust and the voluntary sector in England as a whole, while Chapter 4 explores the value of game theory in understanding the behaviour of the Trust. It uses examples from the Trust's early legal and political encounters between 1900 and 1930. Chapters 5 and 6 shift the focus onto the Trust's contribution to poverty and the quality of life of its tenants before 1939, with special reference to income, rents and estate design. The final two chapters assess the Trust's performance from the end of World War Two in the context of changing housing policy systems, while Chapter 8 concludes with a review of the role of philanthropy and voluntary sector housing at the end of the twentieth century.

CHAPTER 2

The Performance of the William Sutton Trust 1900–2000

The purpose of this chapter is to provide a summary of what the William Sutton Trust has achieved in its first hundred years. It describes what housing the Trust has supplied, how it has managed its estates and what the characteristics of the tenants have been. This analysis sets the scene for the more detailed later chapters which seek to explain some of the most important aspects of the Trust's activities outlined here. After setting out the Trust's current (1999) position, the chapter reviews the Trust's output in three periods – 1900–1939, 1940–1974 and 1975 to the present.

The William Sutton Trust currently has 15,403 dwellings to let. It no longer ranks among the ten biggest housing associations in terms of size, but it is still one of the largest. (See Table 2.1) In contrast with some of those that now outrank it, it has built the vast majority of the stock it holds, rather than acquiring it from other agencies such as local authorities. The William Sutton Trust continues to be a national body with charitable status and a remit to provide accommodation in towns and cities across England. Its largest, and oldest, estates are in London. The majority of its estates are widely dispersed around the country, but recently the emphasis has again been on expansion in the south of England.[1] The Trust's Corporate Plan of 1994 set a target of 'At least 20,000 dwellings by 2004'. This figure represented a 39% increase on the existing stock of 14,400 and the Trust seems unlikely to achieve it without mergers or large scale acquisitions from other housing agencies.[2]

Two-thirds of the Trust's existing accommodation has two or more bedrooms and is suitable for families. Extensive demolitions and modernisation have taken place on some prewar flatted estates especially in London (St. Quintin Park, Chelsea and Old Street), but also in Salford and Newcastle (Benwell). New tenants

Table 2.1 The Largest Housing Associations in England 1980–1996

	1980		1986		1991		1996	
1	North	20,777	North	20,480	N British	28,800	N British	41,267
2	**Sutton**	**13,713**	N British	18,885	Anchor	28,072	Home	33,136
3	Anchor	12,640	Anchor	18,618	North	21,549	Anchor	30,134
4	Peabody	11,660	**Sutton**	**13,928**	MIH	16,465	L & Q	26,110
5	N British	9,654	Peabody	12,480	Sanctuary	16,357	Hyde	24,310
6	RBLHA	8,537	MIH	12,192	**Sutton**	**14,009**	Orbit	22,071
7	N Counties	7,998	RBLHA	11,686	Hanover	13,470	Sanctuary	21,557
8	L & Q	7,156	N Counties	9,828	N Counties	12,701	Riverside	21,165
9	MIH	6,541	Guinness	9,346	L & Q	12,397	N Counties	18,734
10	Guinness	6,877	L & Q	9,315	RBLHA	12,236	Guinness	15,575
							Sutton	**15,241**

Number of associations with:

	1980	1986	1991	1996
5,000 homes	12	18	36	63
10,000 homes	4	7	13	28

North is now Home; MIH is now Riverside; RBLHA is now Housing 21; L&Q is London and Quadrant. Figures shown are all group totals

have tended to be poorer and relatively more disadvantaged than those housed in the immediate past. The National Housing Federation's 'CORE' data for 1995–6 and 1996–7 shows that 80% of the William Sutton Trust's new tenants derived all or part of their income from state benefits. More than 50% were unemployed or not seeking work.[3] Almost one third of the new tenancies went to single adults, though 40% of all those housed were children and young people under 18. The overwhelming majority gaining accommodation were white (93%), with roughly 40% being nominated by local authorities, another 40% being direct applicants and 20% internal transfers. Despite the Trust's programme of expansion, almost all properties that become available for letting are from the existing stock – a stock that reflects location and design considerations often very different from today's. The rest of this chapter charts how the Trust's current holdings have been built up and what kind of resource they have represented to tenants over time. It also highlights some key management strategies, especially the role of estate staff, which have also proved very persistent.

ESTATE BUILDING 1900–1939

Despite the legal constraints imposed on it in Chancery, the William Sutton Trust initially received the Court's permission to begin its work in London. The Trust bought its first site in Bethnal Green in 1906, and in the following year acquired another in Finsbury at the junction of City Road and Old Street. By the outbreak of the First World War, two more sites in London had been developed – one alongside the docks in Rotherhithe and another very extensive one in Chelsea.[4] The Chelsea estate was considerably larger than any previously built by the four major housing trusts in London.[5] Two provincial estates were completed during the war. One was the Trust's first cottage estate designed along town planning lines in Alum Rock, Birmingham. The other comprised some bleak and unadorned blocks of flats in Barrack Road on the edge of Newcastle's Town Moor.

Until 1927, site acquisition was subject to Chancery approval and in London it seems some reliance was placed on LCC guidelines showing 'suitable neighbourhoods for the erection of dwellings'. Factors suggested for consideration were levels of poverty, adequacy of transport and overcrowding. The 1901 Census had identified areas where overcrowding exceeded 20% and in Bethnal Green the census showed almost 30% of the population living above the Registrar General's overcrowding standard. Chelsea was another area where overcrowding was intensifying as leases fell in and working class accommodation was cleared for other uses. The Medical Officer of Health logged the 'massive dehousing' that was taking place in the borough, with between 500 and 1200 people having to leave their accommodation every year through demolitions.[6] In the years before 1919, the William Sutton Trust's location strategy differed markedly from that of the other large trusts – it did not acquire sites cheaply from other philanthropic agencies or from local authorities nor did it abandon London's East End. Bethnal Green and Rotherhithe had already proved difficult for the Peabody Trust – residents seemed too poor and ill-disciplined, and tenant turnover too great to provide the financial returns that organisations like Peabody were looking for.[7] By 1900, the supply of cheap slum clearance sites in the East End had dried up, and the only way for other trusts to reconcile their financial requirements was to move out to the fringes of central London. Figure 2.1 shows an example of the westwood drift of philanthropic housing effort. The William Sutton Trust estates, by contrast, stood apart from the rest – larger, better equipped and located predominantly in areas others had abandoned for financial and management reasons. The Trust found its sites on the open market, and this was feasible because it was looking for a lower rate of return on capital outlay than comparable organisations like the Peabody and Guinness Trusts. (See Table 2.2., Sutton Model Dwellings Account 1924 and Appendix 4, The William Sutton Trust: Site Purchases 1900–1950)

By 1919, the Trust had constructed six estates, four of which were in London. It had provided 1,783 dwellings, all but 230 as flats. The houses on its estate in Birmingham were not initially let by the Trust, however, as they were requisitioned for war use in September 1915 and subsequently let to a subsidiary of Vickers. All the dwellings the Trust had provided were self-contained and none shared toilets or sculleries. Such sharing was still common in the 'associated tenements' being provided by local authorities and model dwelling companies at the time.[8] None of Sutton's flats had

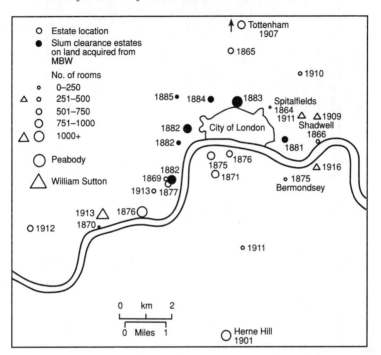

Figure 2.1.   Peabody and William Sutton Trust Estates in London 1862–1918

separate bathrooms, however, and not all the Birmingham houses were provided with a bathroom.[9] The price inflation that followed World War One, coupled with the continued control of the Court of Chancery and the Local Government Board, greatly restricted the building activities of the William Sutton Trust. The Birmingham estate gradually became available for letting by the Trust after 1922 and the Upper Street estate in Islington added 199 flats in 1926. Only two other estates were completed in the 1920s – Stoke (Trent Vale) opened in 1928 with 198 houses and Manchester (1929) with 340 houses. Nevertheless, the emphasis on building low density suburban housing estates outside London was becoming clear. (See Figure 2.2 Location of properties 1900-1939)

The 1930s saw the William Sutton Trust finally managing its own affairs with all the original assets realised and few legal

Table 2.2 Sutton Model Dwellings Account 1924

Number of Dwellings	Bethnal Green E. James St. 160	% of G.R.	Bethnal Green E. Coventry St. 15	% of G.R.	City Road E.C. 284	% of G.R.	Chelsea S.W. 674	% of G.R	Rotherhithe S.E. 194	% of G.R.	Newcastle 135	% of G.R.	Birmingham	% of G.R.	Total	% of G.R.
	£		£		£		£		£		£		£		£	
Gross Rent of Dwellings (G.R.)	3,394		464		6,217		13,691		4,719		2,875		7892		39,251	
Deposit Interest, etc.	13				12		22		10		15		26		98	
	3,406		464		6,229		13,713		4,729		2,890		7918		39,349	
Allowances to poorer Tenants	22	0.6			28	0.4	27	0.2					4		81	0.2
Empty Tenements and Sheds	6	0.1			9	0.1	8		5		2		10	0.1	39	0.0
Arrears of Rent, Bad & W/O							1				8	0.2			9	0.0
Staff Quarters and Wages	654	19.2	8	1.7	704	11.3	1,713	12.5	698	14.8	494	17.1	574	7.2	4,845	12.3
Rates (including water)	1,103	32.5	167	36.0	1,642	26.4	2,955	21.6	1,255	26.6	970	33.7	3110	39.4	11,201	28.7
Insurances	31	0.9	5	1.1	50	0.8	104	0.7	51	1.0	30	1.0	85	1.0	355	0.9
Gas	62	1.8	4	0.9	138	2.2	325	2.4	173	3.6	49	1.7	8	0.1	759	1.9
Sundries: Chimney Sweeping, Stationary, Hospital Subs., and Petty Expenses	116	3.4	8	1.6	114	1.8	273	2.0	107	2.3	63	2.1	103	1.3	785	1.9
Repairs (average as below)	288	8.5	45 Estimate	9.7	368	5.9	910	6.6	305	6.5	339	11.7	1000 Estimate	12.6	3,255	8.2
Total Debits	2,283	67.0	237	51.0	3,052	48.9	6,315	46.0	2,594	54.8	1,954	67.5	4893	61.7	21,329	54.1
Balance	1,124	33.0	227	49.0	3,177	51.1	7,397	54.0	2,134	45.2	936	32.5	3025	38.3	18,020	45.9
Add Shop Rents					1,227		1,641								2,868	
Profit	1,124		227		4,404		9,039		2,134		936		3025		20,888	
Profit equals percentage on Capital		2.3		2.5		2.5		3.3		2.7		1.3		3.1		2.7
Capital	£49,000		£7,030		£176,130		£275,400		£78,100		£67,500		£97,000		£750,160	
Interest thereon @ 2½ percent	1,225	2.5	176	2.5	4,403	2.5	6,885	2.5	1,952	2.5	1,688	2.5	2425	2.5	18,754	2.5
Average	288		Say 45		368		910		305		339		Say 1000		3,254	

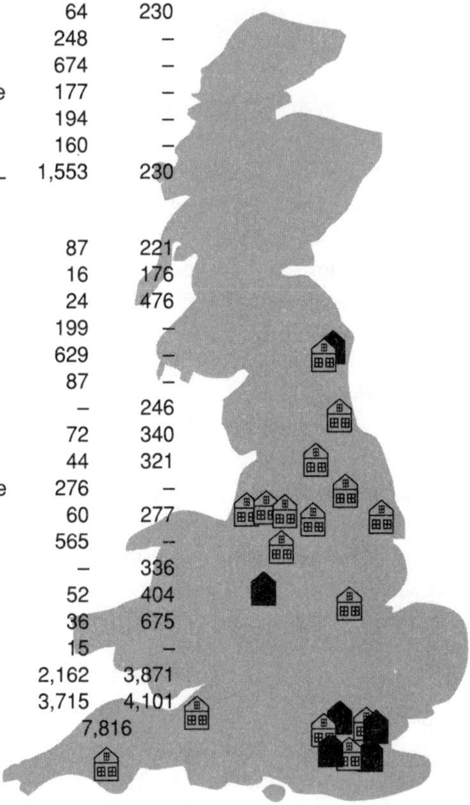

1900–1919 🏠	FLATS	HOUSES
Birmingham	64	230
Finsbury	248	–
Chelsea	674	–
Newcastle upon Tyne	177	–
Rotherhithe	194	–
Bethnal Green	160	–
SUB TOTAL	1,553	230
1920–1940 🏠		
Bradford	87	221
Bristol	16	176
Hull	24	476
Islington	199	–
Kensington	629	–
Leeds	87	–
Leicester	–	246
Manchester	72	340
Middlesborough	44	321
Newcastle upon Tyne	276	–
Plymouth	60	277
Salford	565	–
Sheffield	–	336
South Shields	52	404
Stoke-on-Trent	36	675
Bethnal Green	15	–
SUB TOTAL	2,162	3,871
OVERALL TOTAL	3,715	4,101
GRAND TOTAL		7,816

Figure 2.2 Location of Properties Built and Acquired by the William Sutton Trust 1900–31 December 1939.

constraints on its activities. With building costs falling, a very favourable financial position and a good deal of experience in dealing with officials in central and local government, the William Sutton Trust expanded rapidly – it built some 6000 dwellings in the 1930s. Apart from the St. Quintin Park Estate in North Kensington, the Trust built all its dwellings outside London. Houses exceeded flat construction by two to one in the 1930s and the estate layouts are marked by low densities, open space and communal facilities such as allotments, bowling greens, tennis courts and playgrounds. The Trust provided these facilities in a conscious spirit of 'self-help'.

> The management of these buildings and of the sports facilities has in most cases been handed over to Associations formed by the tenants on the various Estates. No rent is charged, but the Associations are expected to pay all ordinary outgoings, including maintenance charges. The recreational, social and cultural activities organised by the Associations and their helpful services to old people have done much to foster a spirit of community on the Estates.[10]

'The valuable work' done by 'Estate Superintendents and other members of their staff and their wives' [sic] in the activities of the Associations was readily acknowledged. The estate superintendent was indeed a key figure for tenants and Trustees alike. Housed on the estates, they were responsible for day to day management, collecting rents weekly, inspecting houses and grading housekeeping standards. For most tenants, they *were* the William Sutton Trust. One senior manager of the Trust in the 1930s described 'the ideal type'.

> The estate manager is usually an ex-regular sailor or soldier who has reached chief petty officer or similar rank, married and with adolescent children at the time of his appointment. His household is a model that his fellow-residents can respect. He and his wife know every resident, including children, on the estate. ... He is the man to go to both to pay the rent and to see when the window jams; the joint role has obvious advantages from the point of view of minimising arrears.[11]

It is emphasised, however, that 'the one thing that was not left to the estate manager is the selection of tenants'. In theory the system that was adopted protected the estate manager 'from even the suspicion of unfairness or worse'.[12] All applications for tenancies had to be addressed to the Trust's head office in London, where they were 'sifted' and 'those coming within the zone of consideration' were sent to the estate superintendent 'for investigation and report'.[13] Head office then made the final selection based on the superintendent's report, which often followed a home visit. It is difficult to avoid the view that the superintendent's role in selecting tenants was in practice a highly influential one.

CHARACTERISTICS OF WILLIAM SUTTON TRUST TENANTS 1909–1939

This section explores the impact of estate location, management practices and tenant selection on the Trust's aims up to 1939. In particular it is concerned with the question, did the Trust, in practice, by its own guidelines house 'the poor'? How did the Trust perform against other measures of poverty? How important were rules and measures of poverty for the actual outcomes?

The evidence used in exploring these questions is derived from fourteen Sutton Trust tenant registers that have survived for the period 1909–1939. The Trust's head office was responsible for compiling the entries in the registers. At the beginning of each tenancy, staff recorded information about the tenant and the household, including age, occupation, employer, wage of head of household, plus source and level of income for other members. Information was not routinely updated, but some additional information about changes in family circumstances, rent reductions, evictions, and destination on leaving are frequently found. Wages were checked with individual employers, and evictions followed if false information had been given by the tenant. The Sutton estate registers, therefore, provide a uniquely valuable record on incomes – one supplied by individuals, verified by their employers, and including not only the head of household's earnings, but that from wives, children, friends, charity, pensions and benefits. In total, records for 11,340 tenancies have survived – 4,556 provincial and 6,784 London tenancies.[14]

Details from all 11,340 tenancy records were analysed using SPSS (Statistical Package for the Social Sciences). Additional variables were calculated from the original data, including length of tenancy, occupational group, social class, and degree of poverty, based on various measures.[15] It is important to remember that entries in the registers represent particular moments in time – that of the granting of individual tenancies. In interpreting the findings from the registers, therefore, we can only characterise *tenancies*: we cannot describe *tenants* as a whole. The analysis presented here concentrates on applying a number of measures of poverty to the data. The aim is to assess the degree to which the William Sutton Trust housed 'the poor' before 1939. Conclusions are then drawn about what distinguished the poor among Sutton tenants, paying particular attention to factors such as sex, age, size of family, occupation and source of income.

Table 2.3   Poverty Measures 1900–1939

	1900–1919	1920–1929	1930–1939
The William Sutton Trust[1]	28/0d.	50/0d.	50/0d.
75%average semi-skilled wage[2]	20/0d.	36/0d.	39/0d.
Seebohm Rowntree[3]	21/8d.	–	43/6d.
	(27/2d)		(51/8d)
A L Bowley	–	39/0d	–
New Survey of London Life and Labour[3]			38 – 40/0d.
			(45/3d – 47/3d)
The Guinness Trust	25 – 28/0d.	–	–
The Peabody Trust	30/0d.	45/0d.	–

[1]Figures for the William Sutton Trust are taken from London Metropolitan Archives, Accession 2983/101/1-8. Those for Rowntree pre 1919 are based on his calculations of the sums necessary for 'physical efficiency' and for the 1930s on his revised calculations to allow for 'physical efficiency' plus clothing necessary for 'warmth and respectability'. The Guinness figures are based on income for a 2 roomed tenancy, which was raised from 25/- to 28/- in 1912 (Minutes 7/2/12). A L Bowley stresses that his income figure is based on total family income and specimen budgets. For the New Survey of London Life and Labour, Llewellyn Smith used methods based on Booth's - notional income levels and the opinion of school medical officers to establish a poverty line (1928) All the sums quoted are based on a family of 4 or 5 members

[2]The basis for this fugure is a table included in P. Johnson (ed), *Twentieth Century Britain Economic, Social and Cultural Change* (Longman, 1994) p.6 which is itself calculated from several statistical series on occupation and pay. (See Table 2.4. below).

[3]The figures in brackets include the average rent paid for a family of four in a William Sutton Trust dwelling.

Three main measures of poverty are used in the analysis. (See Table 2.3) The first is that drawn up by the Sutton Trustees themselves. Tenancy guidelines were agreed in 1909 before the first lettings at Bethnal Green, and were subsequently amended in 1920. They were based on earnings, with allowances for the number of children. The second measure, derived from the average wage of an adult male semiskilled manual worker, allows a scale of income to be calculated over the whole period.[16] In the following analysis, a benchmark of poverty based on low incomes is drawn using 75% of this average wage. (See Table 2.4) This arbitrary figure

Table 2.4   Wages and Poverty 1909–1939

Average earnings adult male semi-skilled manual worker

1913–14	26/8
1922–24	48/6
1935–35	51/6

'The Poverty Line' – 75% of average semi-skilled wage

pre-1919	20/-
1920–29	36/-
1930–39	39/-

proved to be the lowest of all the poverty measures employed. The third main point of comparison is the work of Seebohm Rowntree and his identification of 'primary and secondary poverty' set out in 1901 and revised in 1936.[17] Rowntree based his poverty line on necessary expenditure rather than on relative income. In 1901, Rowntree included rental payments in his calculations of necessary expenditure. However, these were based on average rents actually paid in York, amounting to 4/- [20p] per week. In 1936, he *excluded* payments for rent, on the grounds that these were varied and volatile but inescapable. Rowntree stressed that he regarded his limits for those in 'primary poverty' as an absolute minimum figure. Finally, for comparison, what is known about wage levels of tenants in other model dwellings, notably Peabody and Guinness are included together with others calculated by A. L. Bowley and the New Survey of London Life and Labour.[18] It should be noted that the amounts quoted for the Sutton Trust, Bowley and Rowntree guidelines, are those required for a 'moderate family' of parents and two or three children. For a 'moderate' family in a William Sutton Trust dwelling, rent would take between 7/6 [38p] and 9/- [45p] pre-1914, and between 6/- [30p] and 16/1 [80p] in 1939.[19] For the purpose of this analysis, an average rent for a family housed in Sutton dwellings has been calculated and added to the original Rowntree poverty line. When adjusted for Sutton rents, the Rowntree poverty line is only marginally below the William Sutton Trust guidelines before 1919 and is indeed slightly above it in the 1930s.

In the discussion that follows, tenants whose incomes exceeded the Trust's own limits are termed 'comfortable'; those who fell below the Trust guidelines are termed 'poor', while those who earned less than 75% of the average semiskilled wage are 'the very poor' or 'the poorest'.

The general picture can be briefly summarised. Taking every tenancy for which records survive for the period 1909–1939, the William Sutton Trust primarily housed small, young families.[20] Heads of household were overwhelmingly male, employed and in their early 30s. Almost half were semiskilled or unskilled manual workers, but over one-third worked in skilled manual or routine non-manual jobs. 20% earned less than three-quarters of the average semiskilled wage, taking them below this severely drawn poverty line. Household incomes were predominantly drawn from wages, but almost one in ten tenants relied chiefly on contributions from children. Very few depended on pensions or unemployment benefit. Many tenancies were of very short duration – 25% lasted less than two years and only 50% were still tenants after five years. Nevertheless, almost one-third of the total remained Sutton tenants, either moving on to another Sutton tenancy, or remaining in their original one until they died. Useful though these generalisations are as points of comparison, further analysis is necessary to understand the importance of poverty for Sutton tenants. As well as applying the various measures of poverty over time, the changing characteristics of new tenancies and the comparison between the London and provincial estates must be explored. The discussion will be structured around three periods – 1909–1919, 1920–1929, 1930–1939.

In the first period before 1919, 96% of all tenancies were in London – the Birmingham estate was requisitioned in 1915 before it had actually been completed and in 1919 the Barrack Road estate in Newcastle was still under construction. Of the 2,606 tenancies granted, 60% had incomes within the William Sutton Trust's own guidelines. With rental payments taken into account, almost as many fell below the limit set by Seebohm Rowntree as

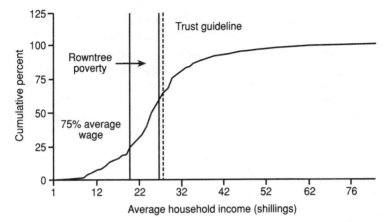

Figure 2.3   William Sutton Trust pre-1919 Tenancies

the minimum for physical efficiency. One-quarter of Sutton tenants had incomes below £1 per household per week. (See Figure 2.3) Furthermore it is clear from Figure 2.3 that 75% of Sutton tenancies were going to people below or hovering very close to the poverty lines set by the Trust and by Rowntree.

Surprisingly, what we have called the comfortable, poor and very poor Sutton tenants shared very similar profiles in most respects. They were all very similar in age, level and type of employment, size of family, and length of tenancy. The poor and the very poor, however, tended to occupy smaller flats (two rooms or less) where rents were lowest; they received less support from their children although twice as many of the poorest group were widowed compared with those who were better off. Indeed, it was gender that was the major distinguishing feature of the poorest group of tenants – over two-thirds of them were women, compared with 47% of the poor and 44% of the comfortable. Charing and domestic service were the commonest type of job among the lowest paid and the Chelsea estate had the largest number of very poor new tenants, followed by Bethnal Green. In terms of loyalty to Sutton, the very poor were marginally less likely to move on to another flat on the same estate than the other two groups. 25% of the poorest made this kind of internal move compared with 29% of the others.

In the 1920s, despite some expansion in the provinces, London was still the predominant source of lettings for the William Sutton Trust. The findings on incomes and tenant characteristics continue to reflect this distribution. Chelsea still produced the largest number of lettings in total, closely followed by Stoke (Trent Vale). Chelsea, however, had 50% more tenants in the 'poor' category and twice as many who were very poor than would have been expected on the number of tenancies alone. The new estates – Birmingham, Islington, Manchester and Stoke – had very few new tenants in the poorest category or indeed below the Trust's own guidelines. The trend to relatively higher incomes is shown in Figure 2.4. Almost 75% of new tenancies in the 1920s went to people earning above the Trust's revised guidelines and only one in ten fell into the poorest category.

Moreover, the profile of the poor and the very poor was beginning to diverge much more markedly from that of Sutton tenants as a whole. Whereas overall 70% of tenants were couples with children under 14, only 43% of the poor and 13% of the very poor were. Of the poorest, 42% were single; 12% were single parents and 14% were adult only households. Though Sutton's stock of houses increased, the poor and the poorest typically occupied one and two room flats. Twice as many of the poor and four times as many of the poorest were retired compared with the average. This is reflected in household sources of income . A much smaller number of the poor, especially the very poor, depended on

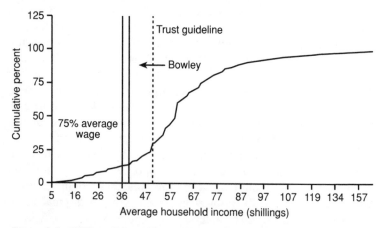

Figure 2.4   William Sutton Trust 1920–1929 Tenancies

wages and there was a corresponding reliance on pensions of various kinds. The level of dependency on children, however, did not change to compensate for dwindling incomes – indeed, the poor and the poorest received less help from this source than the better off. More than half the poorest were widows compared with one-third of the poor and 15% of tenants overall. Whereas the average age of all new tenants was 40, that of the poorest was 51. As before, the gender balance of tenants moved increasingly to the female as incomes dropped. In total, 79% of tenancies went to men, but among the poor this dropped to 54% and at the lowest income levels, 77% went to women. In the 1920s, poverty among the Trust's tenants was overwhelmingly a female, elderly, solitary, metropolitan condition.

The disparity of household incomes among the tenants was very wide. The mean income for all tenants was 61/- [£3.05] a sum 20% higher than the Sutton Trust's own guidelines and 69% higher than the poverty line based on average semiskilled wages. Those who fell below the Trust's guidelines had an average income of 36/- [£1.80] (exactly equal to the same 'poverty line') while the very poor received average incomes of only 24/- [£1.20]. Nevertheless, tenants in all categories of income showed the same propensity to leave – 25% left within three years and 50% within seven years. The poorest, however, were less likely to move on to another Sutton tenancy, compared with their better paid neighbours – it was more often death that ended their tenancy.

As far as the 1930s are concerned, registers for eight of the sixteen provincial estates have survived, together with the six in London. It is on the records from these fourteen estates that conclusions about this decade are drawn. In all, for this later period, there are records for 6036 tenancies, split almost equally between London and the provinces. Analysis of the impact of the Trust's move out of London highlights differences in the character of poverty in the provinces compared with that in the capital.

In this later period, fractionally under 40% of all tenancies went to households below the Trust's own revised guidelines. Almost 45% were below Seebohm Rowntree's poverty line recalculated in the mid 1930s. Provincial estates were over represented in the poor and very poor categories, and Chelsea no longer stands out as the poorest. Salford, South Shields, and Stoke (Abbey Hulton) each housed the same proportion of poor and very poor tenants as

Chelsea. Estates such as Islington and St. Quintin Park, on the other hand, consistently 'under performed' in housing the poor. Average incomes for all tenants were only marginally above the Trust's own guidelines, and were almost exactly equal to Rowntree's revised poverty line (adjusted for rents). Average incomes for the poorest were 30/- [£1.50], 40% below the limit set by Rowntree. (See Figure 2.5.). The degree of poverty among Sutton's new tenants in the 1930s had clearly become more severe than had been the case in the 1920s. Tenant poverty was not as pervasive, however, as it had been before 1919.

This low level of income is not to be explained by an increase in the numbers of small poor households where the Trust looked for lower incomes among prospective tenants. On the contrary, during the 1930s the Trust continued primarily to house families with young children. Although there was still a sizeable minority of the poor living alone (between 20 and 25%), the majority were young families. Among the poorest, 40% were retired or unemployed, compared with 24% of the poor and 12% of tenants as a whole. Compared with previous decades, what stands out is the unprecedented significance of unemployment for the poverty of the Trust's tenants and its prevalence among young families. Of the total number of tenants, 82% earned wages, but only 68% of the poor and 50% of the poorest did. Five times as many of the poorest tenants were reliant on unemployment benefit as tenants

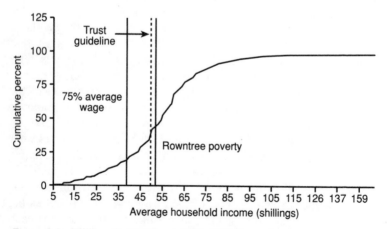

Figure 2.5   William Sutton Trust 1930–1939 Tenancies

in general and three times as many depended on some kind of pension. Children's contributions appear less frequently as tenants' incomes dwindle – 16% of all tenants received some income from their children, but only 9% of the poor and the very poor. This may reflect the different stage in the life cycle where Sutton tenants were experiencing poverty. It was no longer the condition of an aged (female) parent, and the younger families now being affected may well have found children unwilling or unable to help. Certainly the predominance of poor women granted tenancies ended after 1930. Over 70% of poor tenancies went to men and 59% of the poorest.

How far did London remain distinct in terms of tenant characteristics? In particular, how far did metropolitan poverty differ from that encountered by the William Sutton Trust in the provinces? As for income levels, poverty among London and provincial tenants was surprisingly similar – mean incomes of the poor were between 36/- [£1.80] and 38/- [£1.90] and those of the poorest between 28/- [£1.40] and 32/- [£1.60]. New tenants in London, however, were very much less likely to be unemployed than their provincial counterparts. Only 5% of London tenancies went to people who were unemployed compared with 27% of provincial tenancies. Where income was derived from wages, the metropolitan jobs with the lowest pay cited most frequently were porters, messengers and domestic servants of various sorts, together with dressmaking and charing. In the provinces, it was unskilled labouring and coal hewing that appeared most often among the low paid. Among the poorest tenants, there is a marked contrast between the London scene where single person households predominated and the provinces where the majority were households with young children. (See Figures 2.6 and 2.7) This situation is reflected in age and gender differences. Provincial tenancies were granted to people in their late 30s, five to ten years younger on average than those in London. At the same time, 41% of London's poor tenancies went to women and 61% of its poorest. In the provinces the corresponding figures for women were only 18% and 27%. A Sutton tenancy appeared less as a haven to the provincial poor, of whom only one in five moved within the estate compared with one in three Londoners. They were also the tenancies with the fastest turnover. 25% of poor provincial tenancies were over within a year and 50% within three

The Conduct of Philanthropy

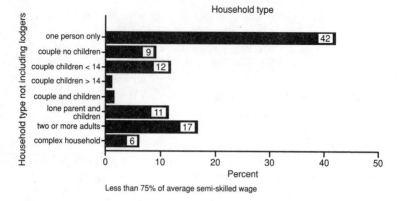

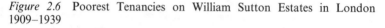

Figure 2.6 Poorest Tenancies on William Sutton Estates in London 1909–1939

years. In London, poor tenancies lasted longer, with 25% lasting up to two years, and 50% surviving for four or more years.

There seems no doubt that over the period 1909-1939, the William Sutton Trust went further towards housing the low paid in separate, self-contained dwellings than any of the other housing trusts.[21] Its wage limits for prospective tenants were set to meet the requirements of the Court of Chancery that it must aim for a 2.5 per cent return on capital. Initially, this put the Trust's guidelines for tenants' earnings 40% higher than the benchmark of

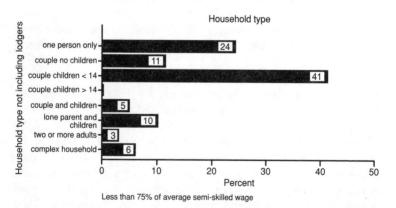

Figure 2.7 Poorest Tenancies on William Sutton Trust Estates in the Provinces 1909–1939

three-quarters of the average semiskilled wage. This ratio was maintained in the 1920s, but in the 1930s the Trust's guidelines were only 28% above this benchmark. Both Rowntree and Bowley would have regarded such an income as below subsistence level. Figures 2.3., 2.4. and 2.5 show that although the Trust consistently housed people above its own guidelines, most of those who exceeded them were only narrowly above the limit. It also housed extremely poor people, on incomes that Rowntree's analysis suggests would not have born the expense of moving and settling in. Not surprisingly, most of the tenancies were short-lived and the length of tenancy inversely related to income. Nevertheless, a number were of surprisingly long duration, not least among the low paid domestic servants who took tenancies on the Chelsea estate. True to the instructions of the founder, some rent was always paid, but rebates were also granted, in a few cases up to the point where the family entered the workhouse. Paupers were not excluded short of a total inability to pay anything. Failure to pay rent, however, even for very short periods, resulted in eviction.

The Trust continued to operate with a very small central office staff based in London.[22] Sites that the Trust might develop were identified primarily by local authorities, often acting on the advice of local architects or surveyors. The Trust worked in a reactive rather than a proactive way and it was much more closely allied to elected agencies than for example Peabody or Guinness. One of its senior managers at the time, moreover, detected a feeling that

> the Trust could not continue to be run as a wealthy family trust might be in the back rooms of a solicitor's office, but should take its place as a significant provider of low-rented housing working in cooperation with local authorities.[23]

For the time being, the Trust continued to proceed intuitively and opportunistically. Despite some modernisation of its record-keeping, there were no means of anticipating or reviewing the impact of its housing activities, except in a strict budgetary sense. By 1940, it was the only one of the 'big four' housing trusts with significant investment funds still available. (See Table 2.5 Performance of the Principal Housing Trusts). Only a few local authorities had exceeded the Trust's output and its impact on the poor was unparalleled. Operating without social or intellectual analysis,

Table 2.5 Performance of the Principal Housing Trusts

Year of Commencement	Trust	Capital and Contingency Accounts		Investment Funds Available		Surplus for Year		Number of Dwellings	Population
		1940 £	1932 £	1940 £	1932 £	1940 £	1932 £	1940 £	1940 £
1902 Approximate value of Sutton Estate = £2,000,000	**Sutton Dwellings Trust**	4,158,130	3,376,294	249,141	981,091	80,190	94,750	7829 4681 (1932)	32,102 22,293 (1932)
1862 1862-73 Mr Peabody donated £500,000 Late Henry Fox bequested £27,887.74 and Anonymous donations of £22,065 Total - £549,952	**Peabody Donation**	3,205,015	2,697,555	12,500	9,863	70,982	56,777	8074 7355 (1932)	23,705 25,409 (1932)
1909 1931 S Lewis borrowed up to £100,000 on mortgage from Alliance Insurance to erect dwellings in Hackney	**Samuel Lewis Trust**	1,218,698	1,056,918	-	-	15,212	35,665	2137 2355 (1932)	8080 7947 (1932)
1889	**Guinness Trust**	1,148,973	781,775	-	59,304	38,494	28,641	3682 3123 (1932)	10,085 10,063 (1932)

Source: London Metropolitan Archives, Acc. 2983/231 (Accounts 1931)

the William Sutton Trust avoided the pitfalls of subdividing the poor, and in practice aggregated them across its estates. Its dwellings provided an extra option for a wide range of poor people: their design was an advance on anything previously provided. Over time certain estates developed their own particular character, and became identified with certain types of poor tenant. This was less the result of policy, however, than the necessity of managing specific types of dwelling such as the one and two room tenements of Chelsea.

ESTATES AND ACQUISITIONS 1940–1974

The Second World War brought an end to the William Sutton Trust's building programme. Initially, it continued to find sites in the hope that the Trustees would 'be in a position to commence building work soon after the termination of the war'. In 1940, thirty acres were bought in Hartlepool and 36 acres in Sunderland, and plans for houses and flats were drawn up.[24] The War, however, changed not only the Trust's resource position but also the political climate surrounding housing provision. One sign of the changed environment is the fact that the site acquired at Hartlepool was subsequently sold to the local authority for housing purposes. In common with the other major trusts, the William Sutton Trust needed to redefine its role.

> The steady growth of housing as a public service and the ever increasing part in it played by the local authorities have displaced the old charitable housing trusts, of which Sutton is the biggest, from the leading role which they once held in this sphere.[25]

It sought another purpose partly by reinventing itself as a 'specialist' housing organisation, especially in relation to the elderly. It also accepted government invitations to experiment with new schemes designed to diversify types of rented housing. In addition, though its building programme was small in this period, it found alternative ways to grow. Primarily, this occurred through the acquisition of stock from other housing agencies whose own position had become untenable in the new climate. (See Figure 2.8. William Sutton Trust Activity 1945–74)

The physical impact of the Second World War was less severe on the Trust's stock than it was on that of other comparable agencies. This was in large part because of its geographical spread. Nevertheless, four of Sutton's London estates suffered 'severe damage', while several provincial estates suffered 'light damage'. In all 53 flats and 17 houses were damaged, but by 1949 only 10 City Road flats had not been rebuilt. By contrast, the Guinness Trust lost 479 dwellings, 13% of its prewar stock.[26] The major problem for the Sutton Trust was not physical, but financial. In 1949, the Trustees reported that for the first time they faced 'a standstill' on income. This was not due to arrears, which in 1950 stood at £38 – just 0.02% of the annual rent roll. The problem was steeply increasing costs and continuing rent controls that brought the annual rate of return down to 0.19% in 1949–50. William Sutton Trustees sought a little comfort in the knowledge that they were surviving because they had not borrowed to finance their previous expansion.

> The Trustees cannot but view with misgiving a position in which some £4,000,000 laid out in useful housing work over the past half century should now bring in an insignificant annual net return with the prospect of annual losses in the future, unless costs fall substantially or the Trust is put in a position to increase rents to cover necessary repairs.[27]

The Trust actually returned a deficit in 1955 but other trusts that were carrying overdrafts found themselves in an even more serious position.[28]

Small infilling schemes and extensions on existing estates seemed the only feasible strategy immediately after the war. A frequent feature of such schemes was accommodation reserved for the elderly. Both the LCC and the Ministry of Health were indicating that financial support might be available for those housing associations that provided housing for the elderly.[29] The Trust's annual reports of the late 1940s and early 1950s stressed their concern for old people, which they claimed had been a feature of Sutton estates from the very beginning.

> *Old people* – since 1909, when the trustees built their first flats at Bethnal Green, London, it has been their practice to provide,

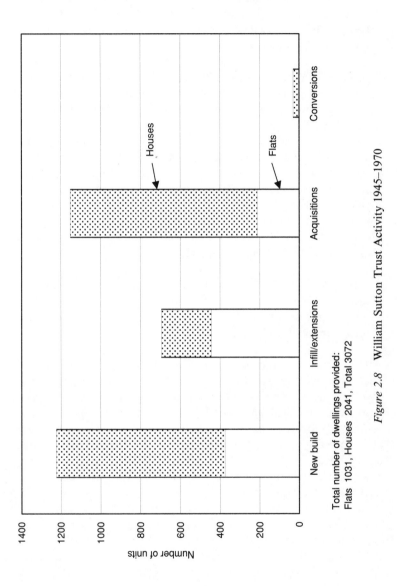

Total number of dwellings provided:
Flats 1031, Houses 2041, Total 3072

Figure 2.8   William Sutton Trust Activity 1945–1970

wherever possible, special accommodation for old people. In all, 495 one-room flats and 76 two-room flats have been so provided and a good proportion of the other 1,150 other two-room flats not specifically reserved for old people are in fact occupied by elderly couples.[30]

Given the general structure of its existing stock and its repeated emphasis on family housing, this re-creation of the Trust as a 'specialist' housing organisation reflects more than anything the need to identify a new role for voluntary housing agencies.

The William Sutton Trust's approach, however, was imaginative and astute. Not for it the 'homes for poor ladies' or 'elderly people's hostels' such as those undertaken by Guinness – Sutton's flagship project was the Miles Mitchell Village at Crownhill in Plymouth.[31] This was presented as the 'creation of an old people's community' based on a careful assessment of their needs, both physical and psychological. Plans were drawn up by Louis de Soissons, architect of Welwyn Garden City.

> The special features of the (semi-rural) site, and the requirements of the scheme as a home for old people have been woven into an informal pattern of village character, which is practical, interesting and a pleasant setting for those who live in it.[32]

Attractive as the Miles Mitchell Village was, the initial plans had been even more ambitious. It was intended that the village would involve a network of voluntary and statutory agencies, providing a range of medical and social facilities. These plans, however, foundered and the village was restricted to 'old people who are able bodied or who can at least manage for themselves in a one storey house'. This was a 'great disappointment' to the Trustees, who were attempting to bring together the kind of 'partnership' that was quite exceptional for the time. Nevertheless, the Trust's reputation was enhanced and it was to the William Sutton Trust that the Parker Morris Committee on housing standards turned for guidance about housing for the elderly.[33] Furthermore, on an extension to the existing Salford estate, the Trust pioneered the use of a high rise block exclusively for elderly people with club room, residents' lounge and shops.

Rising standards for space, design and amenities in postwar

housing were challenges for the Trust, given the age of its stock and the rising cost of building work. In 1949, the Trustees acknowledged that 75% of their stock was more than 25 years old and that until now, they had carried out repairs on a reactive rather than a planned basis. Repair costs had risen to more than twice 1938 levels.[34] The Trust, however, was again in a better position than the other large trusts since its stock was newer and had been built to higher specifications originally. The Guinness Trust, for example, was burdened with its old estates of associated tenements. Despite being 60 years old, the dwellings had not received any systematic improvement. The Peabody Trust was in a similar position. The character or their old stock not only made improvement more costly and more difficult, it cut these trusts off from the Government grants. The 1949 Housing Act initiated improvement grants but they were only available for dwellings which already had exclusive use of bathroom and WC facilities.[35] The William Sutton Trust could report in 1954 that 1765 dwellings in total had been improved with the installation of modern fireplaces and back boilers. All its estates had electricity by this time, something that the Guinness Trust achieved only in 1961.

The rent situation eased when the 1954 Housing Repairs and Rent Act allowed increases to recoup expenditure on maintenance, but the William Sutton Trust continued to look for alternative activities to low rent, family accommodation. Its opportunities came in the early 1960s because of approaches from central government. As with housing for the elderly, the William Sutton Trust appears to have been seen as a body that was willing and able to experiment with new ideas. In 1962, the Trust's new chairman, Major-General G. N. Russell, was asked by Dame Evelyn Sharpe, Permanent Secretary to the Ministry of Housing and Local Government, to help promote cost rent housing.[36] This was part of the government's strategy, begun with the 1961 Housing Act, to revive the private rented sector. The experiment was designed to promote the construction of 'essentially middle-class' accommodation at rents that covered costs using Treasury funds and loan guarantees.[37] The William Sutton Trust's chari-table status excluded it from the terms of the subsidy, so an independent organisation was formed with the Trustees as members. This was the Hastoe Housing Society Limited which went on to build over 300 flats by 1964.[38] It also went on to promote another housing society – the Swanston Housing Society Ltd – to promote co-ownership schemes. Housing societies involved in co-ownership schemes were eligible for funding from the Housing Corporation, newly established by the 1964 Housing Act. These early experiments took the William Sutton Trust and its staff into new spheres. They also led to concerns about the effect on the Trust's traditional activities and in 1968 these led to a decision to stop the management and promotion of other housing societies.

The changing fortunes of existing housing societies and associations could not be altogether ignored, however, and here again the William Sutton Trust was looked to as a stable but flexible organisation that could help to solve problems. Small associations like the Plymouth Housing Improvement Society dating from the early 1930s had lost their initial backers and become a burden on whoever was formally left in charge. The Trust bought the Plymouth Society's 21 flats in 1966. Moreover, there were considerably larger stocks of dwellings in the hands of housing associations set up by industrial companies to house their own workforce. Often more recently built, these estates were nevertheless also becoming a problem for management. They lost their value as mergers redefined company priorities and the better paid workforce opted for individual owner-occupation rather than a corporate let. The Kingsway Housing Association was owned by the General Electric-English Electric Group and managed ten estates with nearly 1500 houses and flats. The William Sutton Trust was probably the only organisation with the resources to buy and absorb such a large and widely dispersed stock.[39] Acquiring most of the Kingsway stock brought the biggest ever single annual increase in Sutton's holdings. Indeed, in total, acquisitions almost matched building on new estates in contributions to the William Sutton Trust's stock during the period 1940–1974. (See Figure 2.8). The acquisition policy of the Trust contrasted with other bodies like Guinness who were themselves disinvesting – in the late 1960s, Guinness sold or leased three of its estates to other agencies. In the 1970s, Guinness even considered merging with another association to escape from its 'somewhat Dickensian reputation'.[40]

The William Sutton Trust's acquisition of the Kingsway properties inevitably greatly affected the mix of tenants housed. Although the turnover in the Kingsway houses was generally high, it took a considerable time for assimilation to take place. Indeed, some oral evidence suggests that these estates are still not entirely recognised as part of the William Sutton Trust.[41] In the rest of the stock, the evidence suggests that demand remained high, with few vacancies and substantial waiting lists.[42] It was, however, recognised, first in London but later in provincial estates also, that tenants were 'substantially' better off than they would have been in earlier years.[43] Moreover, rents remained controlled while the size of households diminished sharply. Many estates saw reductions of 25% in their total populations between 1954 and 1974. The traditional population housed by the William Sutton Trust was shrinking in absolute terms because of changing social patterns. Furthermore, the admixture of tenants from acquisitions and experiments was creating a more diverse tenant body. Nevertheless, the accustomed commitment to resident estate staff continued, with their round of annual inspections 'to ensure that the tenants themselves occupied their dwellings in a manner worthy of the buildings'.[44]

From the mid 1960s, the William Sutton Trust was expanding rapidly through new build and acquisition and its modernisation programme was accelerating, particularly outside London, albeit with some loss of accommodation. The Trust borrowed to finance these activities from a number of sources, including central and local government. A degree of central control over building standards was accepted, while after the introduction of 'fair rents' by the 1972 Housing Finance Act, clearly the Trustees' freedom to assess rents had 'virtually disappeared'.[45] The system of providing housing was changing rapidly and the decision was taken to set up regional offices in the northeast, northwest, the midlands and London. At the same time, the Trust changed its name to the Sutton Housing Trust, dropping the word 'dwellings' that had featured in its title since 1927 since it gave 'a false impression … of the form of activities of the Trust'.[46]

ESTATES AND SUSTAINABILITY 1975–2000

Despite the return of a Labour government in 1974, the new emphasis on housing associations as providers of rented housing begun by the Conservatives was endorsed. The 1973 White Paper had shown the role envisaged for housing associations – to counteract the municipalisation of rented housing by acquiring and managing property in the stress areas of the inner city (the 'Housing Action Areas') and by offering a wide range of choice in rented accommodation. Labour's 1974 Housing Act was substantially the same as the one introduced before the election by the Conservatives. In return for registering with the reformed Housing Corporation, and submitting to supervision and monitoring by this central government agency, housing associations entered a 'copper-bottomed' source of funding – Housing Association Grant. This grant – not a loan – supplied housing associations with funds to cover *the whole cost* of houses provided apart from what would be recouped from a 'fair rent'. Any increased expenditure incurred during development was met by adjustments in the original allocation and if there were any unforeseen difficulty the revenue deficit grant was available to make good the deficiency. Despite fluctuations and uncertainties in Housing Corporation funds, these arrangements led to 'explosive growth' in the voluntary sector in the 1970s.[47] Nevertheless, since the focus of attention was on giving security to 'penniless "stress area" associations', it is not surprising that initially there were 'growing pains' for new and established housing associations alike.

Whereas the Guinness Trustees received an optimistic account of the new regime, the Chairman of the William Sutton Trust presented it as a process that sought to 'reconcile the unreconcilable' – the needs of prospective tenants, local authorities, government priorities and Housing Corporation standards and procedures.[48] He likened the complexities of the new system to the life pattern of a salmon

which has to surmount incredible difficulties to reach the spawning pool in which it was born in order to renew life, thereby ensuring that only the strong, healthy and purposeful succeed.[49]

While the principle of providing the means for housing associations 'to reach their potential' was welcomed, the complexities and compromises that were necessary in practice proved frustrating and difficult for the William Sutton Trust. In the years immediately following the 1974 Housing Act, the William Sutton Trust redefined its priorities. It cancelled the acquisition of green field sites and replanned its development programme to focus on 'stress areas' and the modernisation of its oldest flatted estates. By 1978, it could report 'a record year' both for capital spent and additions to the stock.[50] Two large schemes at Derby and Hemel Hempstead had been commenced with Housing Corporation funding. Its modernisation programme, however, failed to keep pace and in 1981, 4400 dwellings built before 1940 still remained unmodernised.[51] This record contrasts with that of the Guinness Trust. Guinness reacted to the new regime with a 'scatter-gun approach' to development almost anywhere, doubling its stock between 1973 and 1979 and reducing the number of unimproved associated tenements to 132 by 1980. It has been claimed that the 1970s were 'the most important decade for the (Guinness) Trust since the 1890s'. This was certainly not true for the William Sutton Trust.[52]

In important respects, changes in national housing policy and economic crises were taking the Trust further from its 'birth-pool'. Hastoe, the cost rent organisation and its associated companies, had to be taken back into management in 1975 because they could not contain their losses.[53] Sutton rents, set at fair rent levels by the Rent Officer, were no longer a matter that Trustees could control. They were no longer 'low', certainly not in comparison with local authority rents. Theirs were set on a 'reasonable' basis, and the widening gap meant rents several pounds below those prevailing on Sutton estates. This was a particular problem because the Trust offered 50% and sometimes 100% of all new lettings to the local authority. Nominees reportedly objected to a rent '£3 to £5 above that of the local authority'. Such a situation not only created 'an unhappy basis for our relations with our tenants' but raised the possibility of 'empties where there is no housing shortage'.[54] Management concerns were also expressed about the effect of the Housing Corporation's 'cost yardstick' controls on development. At a time of very rapid inflation, these yardsticks continually fell behind prevailing prices depressing housing standards and the visual appearance of estates. The Trust resigned itself to the fact that 'We now live in an era of changed circumstances'.

One result so far as the Trustees are concerned is that they will not in future be able to build houses to the same extremely high standards as those they built in the past by making use of tolerances above yardstick cost limitations.

Trustees, after much soul searching, have therefore decided to build as far as possible within yardstick limitations and to rely on basic good management and maintenance to make life pleasant for their new tenants in their new homes.[55]

Having, as they saw it, lost control over important features of their operations, it is interesting that the Trust presented its management system as its defining feature in the 1970s. The Trustees renewed their commitment to local resident management.[56]

Each new estate or group of 50 houses or more coming into the Trust's ownership or management will have a small local office within a half mile radius of each tenant's house.

In 1981, the Trust's management was praised by Anne Power, consultant to the Department of the Environment, who was studying 'hard-to-let' estates. She visited the Trust's Islington, Rotherhithe and St. Quintin Park estates and commented publicly that she thought the Sutton estates were 'the best managed high density estates she had seen'.[57]

The William Sutton Trust does seem to have been viewed as an organisation with something to offer in the development of housing policy generally. Nominations to the body of Trustees provided an opportunity for governments of both political persuasions to get younger people active in housing reform onto the William Sutton Trust. Harold Campbell, General Secretary of the Cooperative Party, was nominated by Richard Crossman and Richard Best, supporter of Shelter, was nominated by Peter Walker. Both of them also held important posts in the national housing arena. Harold Campbell was Deputy Director of the Housing Corporation and Richard Best was Director of the National Federation of Housing Associations. These political connections kept the Trust in touch with policy developments and underlined its reputation as an organisation that 'could make things happen'.[58]

The priorities of the Conservative government elected in 1979, however, made it an unlikely ally for the William Sutton Trust. The emphasis on cutting public expenditure and promoting private ownership reduced the scope for housing associations. Cuts of 50% in Housing Corporation funds in 1980, followed by a moratorium, left associations in a serious financial situation. The grants they had received under the 1974 Act were effectively converted into loans through the introduction of the Grant Redemption Fund – proving right those Sutton Trustees who could never believe the terms on which the money was originally given and who had predicted that one day the government would 'want its money back'. For the William Sutton Trust this meant that the £17 million received in grants in the 1970s became a debt to be serviced from surpluses.

The 1980 Housing Act allowed the sale of houses built by charitable housing trusts like Sutton, but the Trustees decided against this radical step. Only a concerted effort in the House of Lords, however, prevented sales from being made compulsory in 1983. The Trust also challenged the Housing Corporation's emphasis on shared ownership and 'special needs' in its development programme, arguing that

> The plight of people on low incomes seeking accommodation in some cities could become worse than any period since before the first world war.[59]

Lengthy waiting lists were reported in the midlands and the south and 'only in the north is it possible for low income families to obtain a Sutton tenancy without a long wait'.[60] Its own lettings continued to provide overwhelmingly for families, though about 25% went to the elderly. Making a virtue of necessity, the Trustees also agreed to experiment with letting some of their unimproved property. Where progress with improvement had been halted due to funding cuts, tenancies were granted to students and other 'special' groups like refugees from Vietnam. The new climate also provided the opportunity to 'float off' once more the Sutton (Hastoe) Housing Association. Hastoe and its associated organisations sought 'to be in the forefront with other housing associations involved in the new housing initiatives in the 1980s'.

For what the Trust regarded as its mainstream business, however, the 1980s brought only 'a series of blows'. Return on the insured value of estates fell to 0.25%, and completions stayed below 100 dwellings for several years. In 1985 it was calculated that £75 million pounds worth of modernisation work remained. The Trustees recognised that 'public funds have been almost withdrawn from housing associations for new building, except in inner city areas'. Consequently, they agreed for the first time since 1970 to go on with the development of estates using the Trust's own resources and loans from building societies and banks'.[61] It was expected that such building would produce only 50 dwellings per annum. The Trust found little room to manoeuvre in a situation that put large organisations at a disadvantage. It suffered because of the Housing Corporation's emphasis on small, local specialist associations, and because its old estates still needed modernising when local authority funding was no longer available.

The Trust's local management, however, continued to be seen as a model. After it was suggested that its methods might usefully be extended to 'moribund' local authority estates, the Trustees approached several local authorities. The only outcome, however, was the acquisition of a group of flats in Hull originally developed by the Society for the Improvement of the Labouring Classes. Nevertheless, the Trust gave evidence to the National Federation of Housing Associations Inquiry into British Housing emphasising the value of 'managing estates with resident staff despite the increasing difficulties of recruiting them'.[62] In other ways, the Trust's management methods were having to alter. In 1981, it set out its allocations' policy and for the first time it was evident that waiting lists operated on a date order basis, with a separate list for each estate. In 1982, and not without some signs of irritation, it was reported that

> For 75 years, the Trust has let all its dwellings on weekly tenancies without written tenancy agreements.

Now, however, because of the complexity of landlord-tenant legislation, the Trust had to introduce a tenancy agreement.[63]

At the end of the 1980s, the Government radically redefined the roles of housing providers again. It put housing associations 'centre stage' in an attempt to remove local authorities from the provision or management of housing. At the same time, it system-atically cut the amount of public funding available for developing and improving the housing stock. Local authorities became 'enablers', determining local plans and strategies while housing associations, more than ever reliant on private funding, became 'part of a modern business sector' 'forced to keep as much of an eye on interest rates in the City as on the needs of tenants'.[64] The 1988 Housing Act made private funding for housing a prerequisite of public funding. Housing associations had to bid competitively for shrinking levels of Housing Corporation grant, supporting the extra funding needed by raising loans on the security of existing estates. The Act also decontrolled rents on mixed funding estates to make up some of the shortfall arising from the cutbacks in 'bricks and mortar' subsidies. Rents rose faster than average earnings, and housing benefit to tenants rather than housing grants to their landlords 'took the strain'. Housing associations responded to the promise of growth, providing three times as many dwellings in 1996 as they had done in 1974. They also worried about rent levels and their consequences for employment, 'benefit dependency' and 'poverty ghettoes' on their estates. While larger associations were better able to raise private finance than smaller ones, the prospect of 'pawning the family silver' and eroding future financial strength was disconcerting.

The William Sutton Trust might have been expected to take its place in the 'super league' that the new arrangements seemed likely to produce. In fact, it seemed to falter.[65] There was a period of external scrutiny and self-examination. At some time in the early 1990s, the Housing Corporation made the William Sutton Trust 'a supervision case'. This status was not formally notified to the Trust but its effect was to prevent it from receiving any subsidy from public funds. A major concern appears to have been the Trust's operating procedures, including equal opportunities. Without reference to the 'supervision case' status, the Trust's new Chief Executive was appointed in 1992 with three objectives – to ensure the Trust 'punched its weight' on development, to improve the Trust's key external relationships, and to establish the struc-ture and organisation necessary to achieve the first two objectives. The Housing Corporation removed the Trust's supervision status in 1994, and the Trust was then able to address opportunities offered by the new funding regime. Fundamental organisational changes ensued. There was greater devolution of decision making and budgeting to enlarged regional offices, explicit corporate planning and a greater emphasis on tenants' groups and community development. Trustees were directly exposed to residents in workshops, discussions and presentations. Staff turnover not surprisingly accelerated, with half being replaced in the six years up to 1998. In the same period, private finance totalling £140 million had been negotiated with major lenders including building societies and banks to finance development and modernisation programmes.[66] The William Sutton Trust has reestablished itself in a position where its traditional independence of thought and its almost one hundred years of experience could be brought to bear on its own strategy, and on that of a sector still unsure of its current and future role.

CHAPTER 3

Philanthropy and Housing in England since 1900

The William Sutton Trust is one of only a few Victorian housing associations that are still operating at the end of the twentieth century. Over the last one hundred years, the composition and fortune of the voluntary housing sector has fluctuated widely. This chapter reviews the role of housing associations during this period, and offers a critique of previous accounts of their history. Many historians have believed that in 1900, when William Sutton died, the voluntary sector had already failed and local authorities were beginning to launch their own council housing programmes.

> The importance of the model dwellings in the history of working class housing is limited. ... Their failures, however, were in themselves important. The fact that these patently admirable, financially respectable, able and determined businessmen, working on the best commercial principles should fail, had great influence on the future development of government housing policy. The development of social theory running parallel with the unfolding experience of the model dwellings associations led to a growing belief that state help must be essential. ... The conviction grew that housing should not be left to charitable enterprise but should become a state responsibility.[1]

Gauldie's view that the voluntary sector was a failure from which state action necessarily arose has been widely shared. Owen, for example, said that a major theme of his study of English philanthropy 'was its ultimate inadequacy when measured against the requirements of industrial-urban society'.[2] Even more directly, Tarn described his version of philanthropic housing as 'an account of how council housing was born'.[3] The growing involvement of the state, both through direct provision of housing for rent and through fiscal and legal support for owner occupation, stands as a major theme in twentieth century housing history.[4] Equally, it is agreed that the deterioration of the private rented sector – which provided about 90% of all housing before 1919 – went on steadily. The causes of the decline are still debated but it seems that the sector's structural problems were compounded by political and social factors. Private renting was beset with rent control and by images of grasping landlords on the one hand and struggling widowed landladies on the other.[5] The role of the voluntary sector has not been subjected to the same long term scrutiny. A review of the evidence for the whole of the twentieth century, however, suggests that the voluntary housing sector did not enter an inevitable decline after 1900. This revised assessment gains particular force in the light of the experience of the William Sutton Trust. The questions addressed in this chapter reassess the relationship between the public, private and voluntary sectors. What position did the voluntary sector hold as the housing situation changed through the twentieth century? What role did other agencies want the voluntary sector to play, if any? Was it to be a 'third arm' operating between the public and private sectors? Was it to be a substitute for the declining private rented sector? Was it to be an adjunct to local authorities, fulfilling functions that local government was unwilling or unable to carry out? Was it to be a forcing ground for new housing experiments, preparing the way for others to follow?

In other European countries with similar housing problems, the voluntary sector has played the major role. Here, voluntary agencies have provided most of the rented housing in the twentieth century, supported by state funding and subject to state regulation.[6] In Britain too, it has retained powerful advocates in government and in public life generally as a sensitive and independent housing agency. As certain characteristics of council housing and owner occupation became matters for concern, the voluntary sector was periodically looked to for supplying distinct kinds of housing provision and management. Nevertheless, in Britain, philanthropic housing seems to have occupied a marginal position throughout most of the twentieth century. Its various elements remained fragmented, separated by divergent aims, legal status, effectiveness, resources and values. The William Sutton Trust, in particular, frequently stood apart from other housing trusts and societies. It was unique, distinguished by the scale of its endowment, its legal situation, the character of its trustees, and its unique relationship with central government and local authorities. How did this situation come about? This chapter attempts to answer this question by reexamining the nature of 'the housing problem' as it was defined from the end of the nineteenth century. In the light of changing definitions of the 'problem', the ability of the voluntary sector to respond appropriately is reassessed. We need first to review the voluntary housing sector as it had developed by 1900.

THE 'HEYDAY' OF PHILANTHROPIC HOUSING

In the nineteenth century, voluntary action to address social problems is said to have been one of Britain's defining characteristics.[7] 'No country on earth' claims a recent historian of the subject, 'can lay claim to a greater philanthropic tradition than Britain'.[8] Prochaska's definition encompasses all acts of benevolence whether these occur in a formal or informal setting, and whether they involve the exchange of money or goods or not. While housing philanthropy cannot encompass as wide a range of 'kindness' as that envisaged by Prochaska, several different types can be distinguished. By 1900, distinctions can be seen between those philanthropic housing activities where a transfer of goods (here, accommodation) took place; those where reform of the recipients' and/or landlords' lifestyle was stressed; those with a religious purpose and those where private benefit to philanthropists themselves was looked for (notably in gaining near market returns on charitable gifts and/or improved social standing). In this latter group can be included those enlightened employers like Salt, Cadbury, Rowntree and Lever who built model villages for a conveniently located and healthy workforce. Applying even these few definitions produces a complex typology of voluntary housing agencies, which at least helps us to distinguish some of the contradictory elements within the sector. It also enables us to identify the position of William Sutton's housing trust at its inception in 1900 compared with the rest of the voluntary arena.

Housing philanthropy expanded from the 1840s as a response to the insanitary, overcrowded and decaying living conditions prevailing in the poorer parts of British cities, and above all in London. Usually, though to varying degrees, the aim was to do more than simply supply better quality, more sanitary houses for the working class. In Britain, 'they [the philanthropists] sought to reform the family through a moral and physical cleaning of the nation's homes', Prochaska has written.[9] Physical and moral evils were thought to reside together in urban slums,[10] so that provision of better housing was 'a means to an end, not the end in itself'.[11] The goal of many early housing reformers was to improve standards of morality, as well as of mortality and morbidity. Dr Southwood Smith, public health reformer and founder of the Metropolitan Association for Improving the Dwellings of the Industrious Classes, claimed in 1854 that 'The intemperate have become sober, and the disorderly well-conducted since taking up their abode in these healthful and peaceful dwellings'.[12] Later in the century, the trustees of the Peabody dwellings stressed their intention to improve the 'intellectual, moral and social welfare' of the beneficiaries.[13] A most striking aspect of William Sutton's bequest, however, was its emphasis on the provision of 'sufficient and suitable' accommodation and its silence on modifying the behaviour or lifestyle of those to be housed. This brought major problems for the early Trustees who were accused of undermining the accepted distinction between the 'deserving' and the 'undeserving' poor thereby bringing the prospect of extensive and destabilising pauperization.

For some philanthropic housing agencies, their broader social aims were civil and secular. The better housed were expected to attain 'a higher tone of moral feeling'.[14] Many held that alcohol was the root social problem, undermining health, wealth and morals. The Artisans, Labourers and General Dwellings Company took steps to reduce consumption of alcohol among its residents. The Company banned beershops from its new estates and attempted to block applications to sell alcohol even in the neighbourhoods around.[15] The Samuel Lewis Trust estate in Chelsea had a Temperance Society Hall built right alongside it. In striking contrast, flats built at the same time on the William Sutton Estate opposite actually shared some of their party walls with a pub – the 'Marlborough Arms'. At Bethnal Green, the Sutton Trust's first estate, a similar situation prevailed. (See Plates 3 and 28). For other agencies, though again not for the

William Sutton Trust, there was a distinct religious goal. The rise of evangelical Christianity stressed both personal sacrifice on the part of the philanthropist and piety in the recipient. The Earl of Shaftesbury was one such housing reformer driven by social concern and religious conviction.[16] The Society for Improving the Condition of the Labouring Classes specifically sought to maximise religious observance among its tenants, having concluded that 'keep their physical condition low and you almost effectually bar the door against entrance of every evangelist effort'.[17] Some societies were even more specific. The Four Per Cent Industrial Dwellings Company was set up in 1885 to house the Jewish poor, though in practice it housed others as well. The Peabody Trust and the William Sutton Trust, by contrast, explicitly emphasised their non-sectarian character.[18]

Some housing societies sought to provide for their tenants' general welfare and not just for their physical and moral standards. The Society for Improving the Condition of the Labouring Classes, for example, offered allotments and loan funds, while the Artisans, Labourers and General Dwellings Company planned schools, libraries, swimming baths and a gymnasium.[19] The William Sutton Trust also initially envisaged these kinds of features for its estates, but cost and political pressure caused it to reconsider.[20] Other trusts rejected this approach because though a 'model' in one sense, it was less than ideal in another. Such lavish provision would have undermined an aim that many of them shared – to demonstrate to other landlords and potential philanthropists that housing for the working class could be sanitary, affordable *and* profitable. Sidney (later Sir Sidney) Waterlow, printer and stationer and Lord Mayor of London, set up his Improved Industrial Dwellings Company to show that poor housing could be improved, while still making a reasonable profit. The return that he and others looked for was between four and five per cent, a rate that compared favourably with the prevailing government consul rate. This 'five per cent philanthropy' sector was very important. Its 'semi-philanthropy' or commercial philanthropy included bodies such as the Artisans, Labourers and General Dwellings Company, the Metropolitan Association for Improving the Dwellings of the Industrious Classes, the Society for Improving the Condition of the Labouring Classes and also the Improved Industrial Dwellings Company.

Commercial philanthropy provided by far the greatest number of improved dwellings for the working class up to 1900. Data recently compiled by Morris shows that in London in 1915, these 'commercial philanthropists' provided over two-thirds of the dwellings in the voluntary sector.[21] By contrast, endowed charitable trusts like Peabody and Guinness did not depend on continuing investment, nor indeed on private philanthropic giving. They operated on a 'break-even' basis, with a notional return of less than three per cent. George Peabody wanted his trust to be simply 'reproductive and perpetual', while Guinness initially set no specific rate of return. The Guinness trustees set themselves a target of 3.5%, but in practice, the Guinness Trust Annual Accounts show returns of three per cent.[22] William Sutton stipulated merely that his trust should be a 'continuing one', but formally 2.5% came to be looked for following political pressures.

The voluntary housing sector of 1900, therefore, was both more varied and more commercial than the title 'philanthropic' might suggest. It was also still growing – Sutton's bequest in 1900 was followed by the establishment of the Samuel Lewis Trust in 1906. The various organisations had a range of aims, some of which were complementary and some contradictory. Each organisation's operation might include some or all the following – provision of new purpose built and sanitary dwellings; provision of community facilities; rehabilitation of existing dwellings to improved standards; supply of property and tenant management services and furnishing of propaganda or promotion services, with for many a healthy if modest return on capital. Octavia Hill, granddaughter of Southwood Smith, stands out as the proponent of one very personal and individual type of housing philanthropy. She combined a strategy of personal finance through individual gifts and subscriptions, voluntary labour, and acquisition and rehabilitation of slum properties with reform of existing tenants *and* landlords. She rejected the environmental argument, claiming that it was not the houses that were the problem but the tenants, whose destructive behaviour was reinforced by bad landlords. While in numerical terms her achievements were small, her influence was substantial. Her voluntary rent-collectors were models for women's early involvement with social work and her methods of management influenced many later housing trusts and some local authorities.[23] Some of London's largest landlords offered their properties to her to be managed beginning in 1884 with the Ecclesiastical Commissioners. She was widely consulted about housing problems, helping to draft the 1875 Artisans' and Labourers' Dwellings Improvement Act (the Cross Act) and giving evidence to the Royal Commission on the Housing of the Working Classes in 1884. Soon after William Sutton died, his trustees wrote to Octavia Hill seeking her advice on management organisation.

By 1900, however, a considerable gulf lay between Octavia Hill and the rest of the voluntary sector. The contrast was especially strong between her and the large housing charities like Peabody and Sutton, with their emphasis on large scale building, preselection of tenants, and resident, paid, male estate caretakers or superintendents. Further conflicts of interest within the philanthropic sector emerged as the scale and resources of the large charitable trusts brought 'unfair' competition to bear on the commercial philanthropy of the four and five per cent housing companies. These organisations claimed that the charitable trusts could outbid them for housing sites especially in London, thus undermining their own activities and in particular frightening off investors. George Peabody was said to be 'usurping the functions of commerce' with his munificence that threatened to destroy 'not only tumbledown dwellings, but also well-meaning Dwellings' Associations at the same time.'[24] It has been estimated that by 1900, the nine principal housing trusts had housed 120,000 people in some 24,000 dwellings.[25] Almost all these were in London, where local authorities together had built only 13,048 dwellings by 1914.[26] More detailed research by Morris suggests that figures such as these underestimate the continuing contribution of the voluntary sector as a whole. In London alone, her calculations show over 35,864 dwellings provided by all types of voluntary organisations by 1914. Of this total, just over 10,000 dwellings had been provided by the four charitable trusts – Peabody, Guinness, Samuel Lewis and Sutton.Voluntary sector housing as a whole, therefore, represented over four per cent of the total number of working class dwellings in the county of London in 1911 and between eleven and sixteen percent of new working class housing built between 1856 and 1914. In the same period, the sector had contributed two and a half times the number of dwellings built by the London County Council, (LCC), the metropolitan boroughs and the City Corporation combined.[27] The ability of the voluntary sector to continue to make a contribution on this scale depended on its ability to secure mutually satisfactory strategies between its various constituent members. It also had to negotiate agreements with both local authorities and, increasingly, with central government.

The proper relationship between philanthropic housing agencies and government, however, was a growing area of dispute. Octavia Hill's view was clear. She opposed all state involvement in housing on the basis that it was indiscriminate and open to abuse.[28] Lord Shafestbury joined the Liberty and Property Defence League to oppose state intervention in the name of liberty. By 1900, however, housing was established as a matter of political concern and many philanthropic housing agencies had become closely involved with government through assistance with finance and site acquisition. Under the 1875 Cross Act, local authorities had the power to acquire and clear 'unhealthy areas', but rebuilding had to be carried out by other agencies, including philanthropic housing bodies, who bought the cleared sites. This mechanism brought hidden subsidies to philanthropic housing – first through loans from the Public Works Loan Board at 3.5–4.25%,[29] and secondly from cheap sites that had previously been acquired at near market prices by the Metropolitan Board of Works (MBW), the forerunner of the LCC. These subsidies were substantial – by 1914, the Public Works Loan Board had lent nearly £2.5 million pounds to housing societies in England.[30] The MBW losses on its slum clearance sites amounted to £1,076,470. Receipt of government subsidies laid the voluntary housing sector open to a number of criticisms. Some said its independence and integrity were threatened by reliance on state funding. Others criticised the 'commercial philanthropists' in particular because they diverted public funds to reward private investors rather than using them to reduce rents for tenants.

The voluntary sector, it seemed, was not answerable to those who funded it, whether these were individual charitable givers or elected authorities. The MBW and subsequently the LCC did attempt to exercise control over the dwellings that the semi-commercial and charitable housing bodies built on these slum clearance sites. Housing organisations found their efforts 'clogged with conditions' as central and local government tried to vary the rents, design, size and building materials of dwellings.[31] The authorities had little success, however, since too stringent conditions meant no purchasers at all could be found. Even Peabody and Guinness argued that high densities and reduced standards were inescapable if their modest financial needs were to be met. The Guinness Trust warned that it could only go on with building if it remained 'largely free handed'.[32] Despite considerable misgivings about the height, layout and sanitary arrangements proposed by the Guinness Trustees for a site in Cable Street, Shadwell, the LCC was forced to withdraw almost all its objections when its financial officer, the Valuer, advised them that there was no possibility of finding another developer for the site in question.[33] On both sides, it seems, there was hostility and irritation between government and the voluntary housing sector. In London, the LCC's attempt to impose general conditions through a series of local acts was opposed by a consortium of voluntary housing organisations.[34] Circumstances were such that government and the voluntary housing sector needed each other, but their relationship was at best one of suspicion and at worst one of fundamental rejection. For local authorities, the politicisation of the housing question after 1890 brought something near contempt for the voluntary sector. This was especially so in London, where the empty sites the LCC inherited from the MBW were regarded as a scandal. The winning coalition of Liberals and Progressive at the first LCC election in 1888 advocated the direct involvement of local authorities in the building and management of working class housing. The Housing of the Working Classes Act of 1890 gave local authorities power to build on their own account, although they were not expected to remain owners and managers of housing in the long term. Kirkman Gray detected the development of a new metropolitan consciousness and proclaimed the end of philanthropy as an agent of progress

> the ad hoc body is doomed because of the stronger homo-geneity of administration obtained when one local authority replaces several overlapping independent authorities. ... The day of the little society, proud of its subscription list and annual report, is passing.[35]

The strong political commitment of local authorities like the LCC was altering the environment in which philanthropic housing agencies operated.[36] Furthermore, robust architects' departments like the LCC's were ready to challenge narrow financial perspectives. Political and professional principles heightened the conflict of authority between the voluntary and public sectors over the provision of rented property for urban areas. How philanthropic housing agencies were to function in relation to central and local government, private property owners, their tenants and fellow members of the voluntary sector were key issues as the twentieth century began.

The housing question continued to be a major concern even during critical events such as the First World War. Housing conditions in many areas remained unhealthy, ugly and uncivilised. Attempting to remedy the situation on the scale that was necessary, while building to better standards and at reasonable cost, was daunting. In many respects, the problem was simply too difficult, straining the bounds of what was acceptable politically and feasible financially and administratively. *All* housing agencies – public, commercial and voluntary – struggled to address these problems. Moreover, whereas in 1900 housing reformers had to deal primarily with the vested interests of landlords, by 1939 local authorities were also key actors. They had made large investments in urban property and had interests of their own to defend. On several occasions, government sought to contain the housing problem rather than to solve it – to tackle fragments of the housing situation rather than deal with it as a whole. The role allocated to the voluntary housing sector derived from government's need to legitimise its own formulation of the housing problem, rather than from any intrinsic characteristics of the sector or of the housing situation. The 'Homes for Heroes' campaign after the First World War and the redevelopment of urban centres in the 1930s are two examples that will be discussed – in both cases the role to be played by the voluntary housing sector was a matter for explicit debate.

MODEL HOUSING 1900–1918

In 1914, despite the significant housing programmes that had been carried out by the voluntary sector and by local authorities, the scale of the housing problem had not diminished. The continued growth of urban populations, demolitions in city centres and the famine of private sector house-building meant that in purely numerical terms, the acute shortage of housing remained.[37] Furthermore, rising expectations about urban and house design fuelled by the garden city and town planning movement meant that even recently built housing which met the requirements of building bylaws was becoming unacceptable. In this respect, many estates built by the trusts and semi-philanthropic companies could now be seen as part of the problem, rather than part of the solution. A new element in the voluntary sector emerged, however, that sought to meet the new design criteria and utopian social ideals.

These were the public utility societies, registered under the Industrial and Provident Societies Act, 1893, most of which were copartnership housing trusts.[38] Though ignored in many accounts of early twentieth century housing, Martin Daunton has called them 'extremely influential' and a 'key element' in Edwardian housing policy. Skilleter has claimed that between 1900 and 1914 copartnership housing was at least as important as that of the much better documented forms: limited dividend societies and trusts, employer villages and council housing.[39] Copartnership societies combined cooperative and business principles and had close links with the garden city movement.[40] They raised their capital from shareholders including tenants with dividends limited to 5%.[41] Rents were set at market levels, but profits were credited against the value of the houses so that tenants might ultimately become owner-occupiers. The idea of public utility society housing was promoted through the Cooperative Tenant Housing Council whose executive committee included leading housing reformers and advocates of garden cities – Ebenezer Howard, Raymond Unwin, W. H. Lever, George Cadbury and Henry Vivian. In 1907, Copartnership Tenants Ltd. was set up to act as a development agency for local societies, providing expert advice, capital, and economies of scale through bulk orders of building materials. Public utility societies were heavily involved in the development of Hampstead Garden Suburb and Raymond Unwin designed almost all the copartnership estates up to 1914. By 1916 their total contribution nationally was put at 7,767 houses[42] and in 1914, Skilleter asserts that there were at least 40 copartnerships, with another 10 established before the end of the war. Although these societies attracted support from across the political spectrum, it was unlikely that they could help people on low incomes, especially if they were casually or insecurely employed. Nevertheless, particularly outside London, copartnership estates achieved a wide social mix. They sought 'cooperation and mutual helpfulness amongst the members' with clubs and societies, recreational facilities and annual festivals.[43]

The 1909 Housing and Town Planning Act had given larger local authorities the power to make town planning schemes for their developing suburbs, though not yet for their built up areas. This meant that suburban house builders could expect to face further controls on the design and layout of their estates and especially requirements to keep densities low. Such regulations could increase building costs and reduce rental income. By 1916, both Peabody and the Sutton Trust had developed suburban estates along town planning lines, but they were the exception among the established housing societies. Design was increasingly seen as a major element in solutions to the housing problem and here, apart from the public utility societies, government rather than the voluntary sector held the initiative. From 1910, the Local Government Board was offering advice to local authorities on house design for 'the poorer classes' and by 1913 it had devised five basic house types. Using subsidies from the rates, local authorities could point to new working class dwellings that were cheaper and better designed than the voluntary sector equivalent. Furthermore, after 1909, they were no longer required to dispose of the houses they built to other landlords.

In the historiography of British housing history, the First World War has often been represented as the watershed when local authority building swept aside all others in the provision of working class homes. Local authorities have been represented as the only providers of housing that were capable of meeting the need for housing. They alone could build at the numerical and geographical scale required and with due attention to design criteria and authorised rent levels. Such historical inevitability, however, is no longer accepted and the establishment of local authorities as a permanent and dominant feature in the pre-1939 housing scene is now represented as a problematic process.[44] The role of the voluntary sector, however, has not up to now been reexamined from this more critical perspective. Had they, in fact,

'left the field' in 1919? How was their response to the postwar
housing programme determined? The evidence suggests that it was
not defeat or admission of failure that undermined the voluntary
sector at the end of World War One. Rather it was the outcome
of specific objectives of government housing policy that required
high profile local authority building on the one hand and token
patching and Octavia Hill style management of slum property on
the other.

The 'defeat' of the voluntary housing sector has been attributed
to its small scale, its inability to raise capital, its lack of geographic
coverage, its failure to cooperate with government agencies and its
conservatism in philosophy and design. Such 'intrinsic' failings are
difficult to prove, although some of them certainly do apply to
particular elements within the sector. Nevertheless, it is important
to note that by 1917, the voluntary sector had provided twice as
many dwellings in England and Wales as local authorities.[45] While
the charitable and semi-commercial sectors were not expanding in
numbers, the public utility companies continued to grow and to
expand geographically. There was a suspicion, however, that they
might succeed only in 'high rent' towns.[46] Bryce Leicester, a
leading figure in copartnership housing, claimed the number of
cooperative housing and public utility societies had reached 106 in
1915, an increase of 50% since 1912. (See Table 3.1.) This finding
compares with Johnston Birchall's recent count of fewer than 50
of these bodies, though their wide geographical spread probably
explains at least some of the undercounting.[47] Bryce Leicester
valued the copartnership housing sector's assets at over £3 million
pounds in 1916, some one and a half times greater than their value
just four years previously in 1912. The charges about lack of size,
capital and geographic spread are challenged by these calculations
and even more by the experience of the William Sutton Trust.
After all, here was a body with assets estimated at £2,500,000 in
1918.[48] The Trust was not restricted to London, and had already
built or acquired land in Newcastle, Birmingham, Manchester and
Bristol. It was a 'model' agency in its acceptance of town planning
principles, community facilities and cooperation with local authorities and central government. Such an agency provides a kind of
historical 'counter-factual' since in so many ways it possessed the
features that the voluntary sector has been deemed to lack. Can
we conclude that if all the independent housing agencies had been

Table 3.1 The Growth of Co-operative Housing and Public Utility Societies

	1903	1902	1912	1915	1916
No. of Societies	2	19	69	106	103
	£	£	£	£	£
Rents from property	9,930	34,400	78,192	154,058	176,689
Management expenses	1,047	15,550	17,694	23,049	24,454
Profit for disposal	280	6,964	13,966	7,500	10,730
Liabilities					
To Share-holders	7,457	96,050	240,481	334,004	341,064
To depositors			17,637	365	422
To creditors for loans	36,207	544,860	1,291,820	2,455,195	2,608,277
Other liabilities			43,372	65,112	65,376
Total liabilities	43,664	640,910	1,593,310	2,854,676	3,015,139
Assets					
Value of freehold land & buildings			990,147	1,313,016	1,399,871
Value of leasehold land & buildings			548,371	1,422,658	1,503,011
Total value of land & buildings		625,705	1,538,518	2,755,674	2,902,882
Other investments		23,217	62,894	46,510	66,533
Other assets				53,316	83,617
Total assets	46,856	648,922	1,601,412	2,855,500	3,053,032

Source: Report on Public Utility Societies by Bryce Leicester, Secretary of Co-Partnership Tenants Ltd. PRO Ministry of Reconstruction

like the William Sutton Trust, this sector would have left the field victorious in 1919? The experience of the Sutton Trust suggests the opposite – the Local Government Board's tactics were to disarm and contain it while steering local authorities to enter the fray as the primary combatants.[49]

Central government took a close interest in the William Sutton Trust from the beginning. The evidence of the Trust's early development suggests that the charges of lack of resources, conservatism and poor relations with local authorities made against the traditional voluntary housing sector need to be modified. Apparently Peabody and the other London trusts continued to generate substantial annual profits well into World War One. Central government, however, regarded the potential of the best endowed trust of all not as an asset but as a threat. The aggressive response of the Local Government Board to the William Sutton Trust suggests that from at least 1910, local authorities were being prepared to take the lead in housing provision for the low paid at the expense of independent housing associations. Local authorities were preferred because they were regulated through Parliament and legitimised through the electoral process. Furthermore, local authorities could be trusted to protect local property values since they depended on them to support their rateable income. This last point was vital for successive governments who still looked to the private sector to provide for most housing need. Local authorities did not threaten to undermine the existing urban social and property structure, unlike the voluntary sector, and especially its largest and wealthiest member, the William Sutton Trust.

The particular circumstances of the war underlined the importance of these mutually reinforcing mechanisms in housing provision. The introduction of rent controls in 1915 and steeply rising land and building prices meant that house building was clearly going to be a loss making enterprise after the war. Landlords were under pressure and it was unlikely that private investors would enter the housing field in these circumstances. To appallingly unhealthy conditions in existing housing was added intense housing demand as the end of the war approached. Some level of Government subsidy seemed essential if housing was to be provided in the emergency conditions thought likely to prevail; the issue was who should receive it, at what level and on what conditions? The local authority and private landlord sides of these questions have been extensively debated, but the experience of the voluntary sector has not.[50] It seems that during the war, some elements of the voluntary housing sector did indeed choose to 'leave the field'. Others declared themselves ready to be in the vanguard, only to be allocated instead a role on the sidelines. Again it was the public utility societies that the government viewed most positively. As late as 1918, the Housing (Financial Assistance) Committee argued that it was 'essential' to involve them in building immediately after the war, using government subsidy and 'the highest degree of encouragement'.[51] The government's appraisal of the voluntary housing sector during the war helps to illuminate its stance as the acute financial and political circumstances of 1918 developed.

In so far as the large charitable trusts were concerned, they mostly ruled themselves out of post war housing provision, even if government subsidy were available, preferring to wait until a normal market in land and house building prevailed.[52] Peabody and Samuel Lewis were not prepared to consider taking subsidies of any kind. Guinness would only contemplate them if they were available 'without undue restrictions being imposed as a condition of such help'. Rowntree did not rule out accepting subsidy but warned 'much will depend on circumstances'. Initially overlooked by the Committee in its enquiries, the William Sutton Trust took the initiative and submitted a closely argued case. William Balmain, Secretary to the William Sutton Trustees, noted that the current estimated costs for its Manchester estate were running at 75% above prewar levels. He pointed out that the increased costs were reducing the funds in hand and 'adversely affecting the accumulation of surplus rents'. Such a situation was bound to lead to delay or interruption of further house-building since 'it is bad policy to spend if there is a reasonable chance of better value being obtained at a later time.'[51] Nothing short of a subsidy that immediately made good 'the diminution of spending power suffered by the funds' would induce a trust like Sutton's to build in the prevailing circumstances. The Trust therefore said that what was required was 'a grant of 75% of the difference between prewar costs and present day prices'. It had no qualms about conditions that might accompany the grant since the policy of the Trust is so much on the lines laid down by the Local Government Board and the objectives of the Trust have so much in common with present progressive ideas as to housing displayed by local authorities, that the control suggested would not be such as to interfere with the present working of the Trust.

The Trust appealed for a place in the front line of postwar housing provision on the grounds that it was indistinguishable from a local authority in its approach. This argument, however, was not sufficient to convince the Committee. It does, however, show how far from the other charitable trusts William Sutton had moved by 1918.

The case of the public utility societies further demonstrates how they, favoured elements in the voluntary sector, were also denied the support they needed to extend their work in the aftermath of the war. Initially, the Housing (Financial Assistance) Committee endorsed public utility societies. It saw them as organisations that leant themselves 'most easily to state assistance and supervision' while keeping good, accessible accounts and offering opportunities for tenant involvement.[54] Their lack of geographical spread, it was felt, could be overcome through support for the Federation of British Industry's (FBI) idea of setting up an organisation to promote 'public utility societies in all districts where housing was needed'. The Committee concluded, however, that the contribution of the public utility societies would only be achieved if public funds supplied 'the whole abnormal loss', since the societies had no access to other income from investments or rates. Political argument surfaced at this point with some members of the Committee contending that the societies were 'bodies of private capitalists' housing the superior artisan. Local authorities, in contrast, represented the community and housed primarily its poorer sections.[55] The prospect of private bodies being left ultimately with large capital sums after state loans had been repaid offended the constitutional sensitivities of a minority of the Committee's members. In the event, the 1919 Housing and Town Planning Act did bring both housing trusts and public utility societies within the new state subsidy system, but the effective rate was very low – only 30% of loan charges on money borrowed from the Public Works Loan Board.[56] Employers' housing was excluded and the FBI withdrew its support for expanding the sector. No central organisation, therefore, appeared and instead the societies became 'a minute and partial responsibility' of the Ministry of Health (successor to the Local Government Board). Public utility societies entered the 1920s 'with neither an adequate position within the state machinery for housing provision nor the ability to attract substantial amounts of private capital'.[57]

Whereas the supporters of public utility societies wanted to be of 'real service' in solving the acute housing problems of 1918,[58] they found this role denied them. Captain Reiss, a leading housing reformer, set out his strategy for the 'one really effective way' to deploy public utility societies. That was, he advised, to use them 'as an adjunct of local authorities' supported both by government subsidy and local contributions from the rates. 'Why' he asked, 'in view of the admitted advantages of the Public Utility Societies should not they be admitted into the partnership already proposed between the State and the Local Authority?'[59] Such language, familiar though it sounds today, was unacceptable in 1918. The public utility societies were effectively sidelined by the financial provisions of the 1919 Housing and Town Planning Act. The divisions between different elements of the sector became increasingly bitter. Members accused each other of falsely using the 'garden city' tag simply to attract investment, of undermining the interests and democratic control of small investors, and of turning cooperative institutions into capitalist ones.[60] The societies' coordinating and promotional body, Copartnership Tenants Ltd., came in for particularly sharp criticism.[61]

Where did these developments leave the voluntary housing sector in 1919? The evidence presented so far suggests that the sector as a whole had certainly not deserted the housing field. Many of the established charitable trusts had clearly signalled their unwillingness to embroil themselves in the state subsidies that they needed to continue building. The largest and most active of them, though, the William Sutton Trust, saw no problem in working closely with government at central and local level. After an initial suspension of building post war, the Trust went on to embark on its most active period of building using both state subsidy and rate contributions. The penalty the Trust paid was that its output and its rents were subject to the vagaries of government policy.[62] By contrast, the 'near capitalist' housing societies which aimed to pay 5% dividends were simply squeezed out by the financial situation. Employers' organisations did continue building for their own workforce despite the situation simply because 'they must have the houses'.[63] The subsidy offered to public utility societies relegated them to a minor role in the postwar 'Homes for Heroes' campaign and instead of the platform for growth and recognition that had been expected, there was fragmentation and resignation.[64] Nevertheless, the public utility societies lived to fight another day as did the Octavia Hill style management agencies. What was needed, however, to deliver a house building programme on the 'heroic' scale that the wartime cabinet thought was necessary were the local authorities. It was they who had been increasingly groomed for the role both before and during the war and over whom government could exercise financial and constitutional control. The developing nexus between local and central government and the involvement of the William Sutton Trust is discussed further in Chapter 4.

SLUMS – VOLUNTARY HOUSING SOCIETIES IN THE FRONT LINE
1919–1939

There was one aspect of the housing problem that neither central nor local government was ready to tackle in 1919 and that was the existing slum. The 'Homes for Heroes' campaign was designed to deliver high-quality houses in estates created on garden city lines and occupied by the regularly employed and better-off working class. Direct action to remedy slum conditions was ruled out, specifically because the scale of the problem was so immense that to open a 'second front' here would have been to invite utter defeat. Yet the situation could not be ignored, and some token response was considered necessary not least because the 'housing famine' was driving better off families to share overcrowded accommodation in the 'unhealthy areas'. Local authorities were unwilling to get directly involved for financial and political reasons. They did not relish the idea of holding and managing 'atrocious' slum property, especially as the state assistance on offer was sufficient only for basic 'patching' of a few hundred dwellings in each major urban centre.[65] This was the 'gap' in housing provision where new housing societies offering Octavia Hill style management found their major role in the interwar period. Reviewing the 'front line' in the battle against the slums in 1930, T. Speake emphasised that for most housing societies, their efforts were being directed in one of two ways,

> either (a) to purchase houses of a size suitable for occupation by two or more families, to improve the housing conditions by reconditioning them, to let them and manage the same on the Octavia Hill system; or (b) to clear and carry out reconstruction of small slums, which the local authorities are not prepared to deal with.[66]

There are said to have been fourteen of these 'front line' societies in London by 1934, the best known being the St. Pancras House Improvement Society Ltd. and the Kensington Housing Trust. Other towns saw the creation of similar societies. In a 1930 survey, fifty-three recently founded housing societies were listed including Liverpool Improved Housing, Newcastle Housing Improvement Society and COPEC in Birmingham. (See Figure 3.1) Christian congregations and COPEC – Christian Organisations for Politics, Economics and Citizenship – were very active in promoting new housing trusts in the 1920s. Indeed support was widely drawn, and sponsors included a range of church denominations, political parties, women's groups, chambers of commerce, Masonic lodges and councils of social service.[67]

Except for the William Sutton Trust, it was reconditioning rather than building that was the voluntary sector's major field of operations in the 1920s.[68] Speake clearly describes how societies had been effectively 'frozen out' from house building by local authority financial manipulations.[69] Marian Bowley estimated that some 300,000 houses were reconditioned annually between 1919 and 1930, while as few as 17,000 slum dwellers were actually rehoused.[70] Table 3.2. shows that between 1919 and 1928, only 10,255 dwellings had been built by voluntary housing agencies in England and Wales using available subsidies. The William Sutton Trust was uniquely active, building 1,972 dwellings in the same period. This was almost twenty per cent of the whole voluntary sector new housing total.

Throughout the 1920s, local authorities could command the sphere of house building largely as their own. Housing societies

Table 3.2   Post war housing in England and Wales 1919–1928

Analysis of returns showing the number of houses which have actually been completed since 1st January 1919
Houses completed with state assistance at 1st March 1928

Addison Scheme:

Housing, town planning, etc. Act 1919	174,593
Housing (Additional Powers) Act 1919	37,186
	213,779

Chamberlain Scheme:
Housing etc. Act 1923

(a) By local authorities	63,012
(b) By private enterprise	252,824
(c) By Public Utility Societies etc.	9,829
	325,665

Wheatley Scheme:
Housing (Financial Provisions) Act 1924

(a) By Local Authorities	174,256
(b) By Private Enterprise	2,563
(c) By Public Utility Societies etc.	426
	177,245

Total number of houses completed with state assistance at 1st March 1928:	716,689

Housing completed by Private Enterprise without State Assistance

Estimated number completed between 1st January 1919 and 30th September 1927:	348,518
Grand total	1,065,207

Source: Frederick W. Platt. 'A Brief Review of the Present Condition of National Housing', JRSI (49) 1928–29, p. 168.

Name of Society	Date founded	Initiator	Source of Capital			
			D¹	S²	L³	L.A⁴
ALTRINCHAM AND DISTRICT C.O.P.E.C. HOUSING SOCIETY, LTD.	1927	COPEC	✓	✓	✓	
THE AYLESBURY HOUSING IMPROVEMENT TRUST, LTD.	1927	Sanitary Inspector	✓			✓
BARNSTAPLE	1930	Local Committee	✓		✓	
BANGOR COPEC HOUSING SOCIETY, LTD.	1927	COPEC	✓	✓	✓	
BATH TENEMENT VENTURE	1923	Not specified	✓	✓	✓	
THE BETHNAL GREEN HOUSING ASSOCIATION, LTD.	1926	Settlement Houses	✓	✓	✓	
BIRMINGHAM COPEC HOUSE IMPROVEMENT SOCIETY.	1924	COPEC	✓			✓
BOSTON HOUSING SOCIETY LTD.	1928	Local Committee	✓	✓	✓	
BRISTOL CHURCHES TENEMENT ASSOCIATION.	1926	British Council of Christian Churches	✓	✓	✓	✓
CAMBRIDGE HOUSING SOCIETY, LTD.	1927	United Council of Christian Witness	✓		✓	
CARLISLE HOUSING IMPROVEMENT SOCIETY, LTD.	1930	National Council of Women/Carlisle Council of Social Service		✓		✓
CHELSEA HOUSING IMPROVEMENT SOCIETY.	1926	Local Committee	✓		✓	
CHURCH ARMY HOUSING, LTD.	1924	Church Army	✓	✓	✓	
THE COVENTRY HOUSE IMPROVEMENT SOCIETY, LTD.	1929	Local Committee	✓	✓	✓	
THE CREDITON HOUSING ASSOCIATION, LTD.	1929	Local Committee	✓	✓	✓	
EDINBURGH WELFARE HOUSING TRUST, LTD.	1928	Local Committee	✓		✓	
EXETER WORKMENS DWELLINGS COMPANY, LTD.	1926	Local Committee				
FULHAM HOUSING IMPROVEMENT SOCIETY, LTD.	1927	Bishop of London	✓	✓	✓	
GRANTHAM VOLUNTARY HOUSING COMMITTEE.	1929	Major of Grantham	✓		✓	✓
HAMPSTEAD HOUSING ASSOCIATIONS, LTD.	1928	Not specified		✓		
THE HENLEY AND DISTRICT HOUSING TRUST.	1929	Local Committee	✓			✓
THE HOYLAKE AND WEST KIRBY HOUSING SOCIETY, LTD.	1929	Local Committee	✓	✓	✓	
ST HELENS HOUSING, LTD.	1929	United Council of Christian Witness	✓	✓	✓	
THE IMPROVED TENEMENTS ASSOCIATION, LTD.	1900	Captain R.P.P Rowe	✓	✓	✓	
THE SOCIETY FOR IMPROVING THE CONDITION OF THE LABOURING CLASSES.	1830	Labourers' Friend Society	✓	✓		
KENDAL AND DISTRICT HOUSING SOCIETY, LTD.	1925	Local Committee	✓	✓	✓	✓
THE KENSINGTON HOUSING TRUST, LTD,	1927	Local Committee	✓		✓	✓

KEY
1. Donations;   2. Shares (limited interest);   3. Loans (limited interest);
4. Local authority assistance eg. guarantor for bonds: provision of land/dwellings at reduced cost: subsides from rates: use of council officers.

Figure 3.1   Directory of Housing Societies 1930

Name of Society	Date founded	Initiator	D[1]	S[2]	L[3]	L.A[4]
			Source of Capital			
LAMBETH HOUSING, LTD.	1928	Christian Social Council of Lambeth	✓	✓	✓	
LIVERPOOL IMPROVED HOUSES, LTD.	1928	*see below	✓	✓	✓	
LINCOLN VOLUNTARY SLUM CLEARANCE COMMITTEE	1928	Citizens Meeting	✓			✓
THE LONDON HOUSING SOCIETY, LTD.	192?	Not specified		✓	✓	
LEAMINGTON SLUM CLEARANCE, LTD.	1926	Not specified	✓			✓
THE LEICESTER VOLUNTARY HOUSING ASSOCIATION LTD.	192?	Advisory Council, including Lord Mayor and Church Leaders	✓			y
MARKET DRAYTON HOUSING SOCIETY, LTD.	1926	Anonymous supporter of voluntary Housing of the Poor Crusade	✓			
MANCHESTER HOUSING , 1926, LTD.	1926	** see below	✓	✓	✓	
ST MARYLEBONE HOUSING ASSOCIATION.	1926	Local women	✓	✓	✓	
NESTON AND PARKGATE HOUSING SOCIETY, LTD.	1928	Neston and District Council of Social Service		✓	✓	✓
NEWCASTLE-UPON-TYNE HOUSING IMPROVEMENT TRUST, LTD.	1929	Not specified	✓	✓	✓	
NOTTINGHAM HOUSING IMPROVEMENT ASSOCIATION, LTD.	1928	Not specified	✓	✓	✓	
OSWESTRY HOUSING TRUST.	192?	Not specified	✓	✓	✓	✓
THE ST. PANCRAS HOUSE IMPROVEMENT SOCIETY, LTD.	192?	Magdalen College Mission		✓	✓	
PRESBYTERIAN HOUSING, LTD.	1925	Presbyterian Church of England			✓	✓
RIPON HOUSING IMPROVEMENT TRUST, LTD.	1930	Rotary Club		✓	✓	
SALISBURY COURTS, LTD.	1926	Not specified		✓	✓	
SHREWSBURY HOUSING TRUST.	1927	Local councillor	✓			✓
THE SQUARE BUILDING TRUST, LTD., NORTH SHIELDS.	1929	Presbyterian Church Bible Class	✓	✓	✓	✓
STEPNEY HOUSING TRUST, LTD.	1929	# see below	✓	✓	✓	
THE TRING HOUSING IMPROVEMENT ASSOCIATION.	1929	Chairman, Tring Urban District Council	✓	✓		✓
THE THISTLE PROPERTY TRUST, (STIRLING).	1926	National Council of Women (Stirling Biarch)	✓	✓	✓	
THE UNITED WOMENS HOMES ASSOCIATION	1925	Copartnership members		✓	✓	
WILLESDEN HOUSING SOCIETY, LTD.	1926	Local Anglican Church	✓	✓	✓	
WIMBLEDON PUBLIC UTILITY SOCIETY LTD.	1929	Wimbledon Guild of Social Welfare	✓	✓		
WORCESTER HOUSE IMPROVEMENT SOCIETY.	1928	Worcester Christian Social Service Union	✓	✓	✓	
THE WELSH TOWN PLANNING AND HOUSING TRUST, LTD.	192?	Great Western Railway Company		`	✓	
THE YORK HOUSE IMPROVEMENT SOCIETY LTD.	1927	National Council of Women (York Branch)				

*   Liverpool Personal Service Society and a Group of the Women Citizens' Association
**   Manchester-Salford and District Council of Christian Congregations
#   St Paul's School Union for Social Work

Figure 3.1   Continued

generally filled 'the gaps' while lobbying the public and their elected representatives to support their 'crusade' against the slums. The 'Homes for Heroes' campaign was short-lived, but subsequently housing policy remained focused on new suburban building rather than on slum clearance. By 1928, the private sector was deemed capable of meeting general housing demand through building for owner occupation, and the issue of slum conditions reappeared on the political agenda. From 1930 onwards, new ways had to be found of approaching the problem and a further reassessment of the respective roles of local authorities and the voluntary housing sector took place. In the early 1930s, it was even argued that the voluntary housing sector should supplant elected authorities at both central and local level in most kinds of low cost housing provision. By 1939, however, local authorities had emerged with their power reinforced, deemed the only agencies to whom urban reconstruction, including slum clearance and rebuilding, could be entrusted.[71]

The reevaluation of the role of the voluntary sector took place alongside a debate about the scale and complexity of the problem of unfit housing. The three elements of a solution – clearance, rehabilitation and rebuilding – raised distinct issues and posed questions about the desirability and legitimacy of action by public and voluntary bodies. In 1930, there were some areas of agreement. Despite the political differences between Labour and Conservative Parties about the state's total role, both agreed that slum clearance and rehousing were matters for local authorities. They also shared the view that the 'voluntary housing movement, except in one or two notable instances, is in a state of suspension'.[72] The revival of the voluntary sector came about because of the initial unwillingness of local authorities to exchange the 'model' world of suburban tenants for that of the grossly overcrowded, impoverished slum dwellers. The Housing Acts of 1930 and 1933 abolished subsidies for general local authority building and reserved them for slum clearance. Nevertheless, local authorities were reluctant to expose themselves to an activity that 'bristled with difficulties', not least the provision and management of accommodation suitable for the people involved.[73] Their caution was reinforced with the onset of the Great Depression. Reassigning the problem to the voluntary sector which had extensive experience of remodelling both unfit houses and their tenants seemed worth considering. In March 1933 the Minister of Health set up a departmental committee under Lord Moyne (Chairman of the Guinness Trust) to consider 'the proper path for voluntary effort in this new crusade'.[74]

Slum clearance itself was outside the terms of reference of the Moyne Committee, and the suggestion was that in future the 'housing policy of the country would rest securely on a tripod'.[75] Private enterprise would meet the normal need for new houses, local authorities would demolish the slums, building and managing replacement dwellings helped by public utility societies and housing trusts, and the voluntary sector would primarily concentrate on the reconditioning and management of the poorest houses 'outside the technical slum'.[76] The Committee argued that the 'fruitful field' of reconditioning would greatly expand the scale of operations of the housing societies. Indeed, the Report was said to amount to the 'glorification of the public utility societies'.[77]

To ensure adequate, independent financial support for the expanded role of housing societies the Moyne Committee proposed new supervisory and funding agencies responsible to the Ministry of Health. Rehabilitation schemes endorsed by a Central Public Utility Council, appointed by the Ministry of Health, would be forwarded directly to the Minister for his approval of capital advances. The aim was to separate housing society funding completely from local authorities. What was being proposed was 'central finance, with proper safeguards' combined with 'local administration by independent societies'.[78]

Two minority reports from the Moyne Committee went even further – Sir Raymond Unwin stressed the role of housing societies in building new houses 'at rentals within the means of poorer workers'. Another even more radical set of proposals from two Liberal MPs aimed to take housing largely out of the political sphere, replacing both local and central government with a National Housing Corporation and independent housing societies. The voluntary sector's reputation for 'wise, efficient and economical management' meant that these radical schemes were widely regarded as plausible and desirable. They foundered, however, on the opposition of local authorities 'jealous of their powers'[79] who pointed to their own accumulated experience of municipal housing since 1919. The Minister of Health himself rejected the idea of 'setting up a rival to local authorities' that 'could not be contem-

plated'. He concluded that housing societies were 'totally inadequate' to replace 'the powerful organisation of local housing
authorities'.[80] Here, as in 1919, it seems local authorities were
propelled into the front line by the Ministry of Health. Before the
First World War, local authorities were groomed to take on new
house building for the working class; before the Second World
War, they were being urged to take on urban reconstruction on a
grand scale. In both cases, the Ministry wanted to ensure that the
revolutionary role envisaged for local authorities was not upset by
the intervention of independent housing societies.[81]

After 1935, the municipalisation of housing was consolidated
especially with the growing power of the Labour party in many
major cities. Housing societies were steadily excluded from any
significant role, retreating to lobbying, advisory and propaganda
activities. The exception was the William Sutton Trust for whom
the 1930s was the era of maximum expansion – the Trust built
4,000 dwellings during this period, 1,500 of them after 1935.
Nevertheless, most of the Moyne Committee's recommendations
remained 'a dead letter'.[82] Instead of the strong supervisory
Central Public Utility Council advocated by Moyne, the 1935
Housing Act set up the Central Housing Advisory Council
(CHAC). Purely an advisory body, CHAC had power only to
make recommendations to the Minister on matters of mutual
concern.[83] Some voluntary bodies responded by setting up their
own National Federation of Housing Societies but it was not
widely supported. Its initial membership of 75 included only
public utility societies and garden suburb development societies.
None of the commercial philanthropic societies joined and of the
charitable trusts only Guinness was a member by 1940.[84] The
voluntary sector, it seemed, was accepting that it could not
supplant the mutually reinforcing power of central and local
government in housing and redevelopment. Unlike many other
welfare services at the time, there was no place in housing for the
voluntary sector as either provider or partner.

RETREAT AND REGROUP – THE MANOEUVRES OF THE VOLUNTARY
SECTOR SINCE 1945

In the 'Brave New World' ushered in by the postwar Labour
government, local authorities held the key and housing societies

remained largely excluded. Subjected to rent controls and denied public sector finance, they retreated to mend their damaged property and manage their existing estates. As happened after World War One, some employers continued to provide substantial numbers of houses for their workers, notably the Coal Board, British Airways Employees' Housing Society and English Electric.[85] A few 'gaps' were again found where societies could operate, notably in housing the elderly, but effectively they had been written out of housing provision. When the Conservatives returned to power in 1951, it appears that the position of housing associations (as members of the sector were increasingly called) was extensively reviewed, but no change to the situation was proposed.[86] Instead, the priority of the new government shifted to the revival of the private sector, both for rental and owner occupation. By 1960, local authorities had built over 2 million houses since 1945, and private builders 1.3 million, but housing associations (excluding employers) had only achieved 46,000.[87] Most of the associations were very small, with an average holding of about thirty-five houses each. Clearly at this point, housing policy was resting on a distinctly uneven tripod.

Before leaving office in 1964, the Conservatives tried to use specially constituted housing associations to improve the range of the private rented sector. Cost-rent associations were encouraged to provide for the middle market, and especially to promote self-build cooperative schemes.[88] The middle market, however, voted with its feet, choosing instead to enter the subsidised council sector or the expanding owner occupied sector. The incoming Labour Government revived the concept through the funding of coownership societies. The Housing Corporation was set up to control the flow of public funds to the new associations. This experiment was much more successful both in numerical terms and in establishing the links and mechanisms for expanding and subsidising the sector in subsequent decades. The William Sutton Trust returned to new building after 1955, with a particular emphasis on its 'old people's village' at Crown Hill in Plymouth.[89] In all the Trust built 1,223 dwellings between 1945 and 1974. Almost as important was its programme of acquisitions from other voluntary providers, notably from English Electric (Kingsway Housing Association) and from the Plymouth Housing Improvement Society, totalling together 1,138 properties. The voluntary sector was clearly commencing some fundamental restructuring, both because of government initiatives and from within.

From the early 1960s, housing associations were singled out to tackle an aspect of the housing problem somewhat reminiscent of the 1930s. These were the 'twilight areas' or 'stress areas' suffering a combination of environmental and social problems, untouched by postwar slum clearance schemes. No less than in the 1930s such areas 'bristled with problems'. Their large houses were suffering the degradations of multiple occupation, intimidation and neglect by landlords for whom 'Rachman' became the emblem. Preventing further deterioration in these areas and rehousing their tenants were not projects that local authorities themselves welcomed. Not least of their concerns was the fact that in London and other large cities, immigrants occupied many of these houses. Housing associations were commended for their ability to deal with

> the misfit who is not acceptable to the council; the large poor family who cannot afford council rents; the immigrant. ... By accepting these types of tenants, the Society helps to release council tenancies for the rather better off families who wish to progress from a tenement to a new flat.[90]

Again, the role played by the voluntary sector was being set by distinctions devised by government about the deserving and the undeserving, the fit and the 'misfit', with the emphasis on protecting the interests of local authority housing departments. Between 1968 and 1988, half of all housing association investment went on acquiring and rehabilitating street properties.[91]

There was cross party agreement about encouraging housing associations. The 1974 Housing Act, which expanded the role of the Housing Corporation and the funds it distributed to the voluntary sector, was prepared by the outgoing Conservative administration and passed by the incoming Labour one. To gain access to Housing Corporation funds, housing associations were required to register with the new quango. The lure of public funding attracted a wide range of existing societies, from almshouses to industrial housing associations. The William Sutton Trust 'applied for and received registration, necessarily accepting some loss of freedom in consequence'.[92] The 1974 Act certainly changed the profile of the voluntary sector. Many cost-rent and coownership societies converted into more conventional providers and registered with the new regime. North British, Sanctuary and Orbit Housing Associations took this route. New associations specialising in rehabilitation were established, many of them, as in the 1930s, associated with church groups. The Notting Hill Housing Trust, Paddington Churches Housing Association, Bristol Churches Housing Association and the Catholic Housing Aid Society engaged both in rehabilitation of property and promotion of more societies like themselves. Most of the largest housing societies that exist today were founded in this recent period of expansion.

By 1976, the Housing Corporation had given approval for building or modernising 50,000 houses in England and Wales. The financial system (HAG) met all the expenditure incurred by housing associations except that covered by the controlled (fair) rents. This meant that the voluntary sector enjoyed more generous state support even than local authorities in the 1919 'Homes for Heroes' campaign. Like the local authorities of that earlier period, housing associations were promoted as model providers but the parameters of their activity were strictly set by central government. In 1974 as in 1919, the chosen instrument of policy was the one that could defuse rather than solve fundamental social and also housing problems. In 1919, the problem was the supposed revolutionary mood of returning soldiers; in the 1970s, it was the fear and hostility created in areas of high immigration. In 1919, local authorities identified with the solution that was required, but in 1974 (as in 1935) their primary goal was to protect their existing property interests and those of their tenants.

After 1974, registered housing associations became a major element in providing housing. It is, however, misleading to characterise them as 'centre-stage' or 'mainstream' since it was individual owner occupied housing that held this position. More accurately, it might be said that housing associations increasingly supplanted local authorities as providers of what was becoming a residual and contracting rental sector. They quickly learned the truth of the remark that 'they have harnessed themselves to the coach of state and must obey the reins'.[93] When the Conservatives returned to power in 1979, massive changes for the voluntary sector followed, driven by the government's radical ideology, political goals and financial strategy. Though it was local authorities who initially found themselves 'in the front line' of government cuts, housing associations soon followed. A moratorium on Housing Corporation spending occurred in 1980 and there was increasing pressure to extend owner occupation, even on charitable associations like William Sutton. Though these immediate threats subsided, the output of associations diminished, unaffected even by the urban riots of 1981 and 1985.

It has been said that during the 1980s and 1990s, the character of housing associations was transformed from the 'charitable' to the 'commercial'.[94] Primarily this was because the government fundamentally altered the funding regime, introducing fixed (and steadily reducing) grant levels and reliance on private borrowing. Associations, therefore, became subject to the discipline of the money markets. They responded by resorting to competition between one another, deals with local authorities over nomination agreements and compromises over building standards. Central government increasingly used them to 'tweak' policy in other sectors – whether it was to reduce the glut of private dwellings through a purchasing package in 1982–3, or to receive housing estates transferred out of the local authority sector. The previous work in 'stress areas' had to be curtailed because it was not feasible under the new funding regime. At the same time, rents rose to near market levels and, supported by Treasury contributions to housing benefit, housing association estates threatened to become 'ghettos' of very poor and vulnerable tenants.[95] With the return of a Labour Government in 1997, uncertainty about the role of the voluntary sector was reinforced. 'Strategic rethinks' were the order of the day; for a sector 'pulled apart' by changes since 1988, there could be no common approach. Competition had replaced shared purposes, and increasingly disparate views were expressed about the most appropriate way forward.[96] There was a particular divide between the largest, well-resourced organisations, of which the William Sutton Trust was one, and the small to medium size organisations who felt vulnerable in the increasingly competitive environment. The 'commercial philanthropists' of the late twentieth century seem poised to dominate the voluntary sector while other traditional segments, unless they can transform themselves, are likely to be forced from the field.[97]

It would appear likely that for a survivor such as the William Sutton Trust, the changing role of the voluntary sector in the

	Pre 1914	1920s	1930s	1970s	1990s
Charitable Trusts and Not for Profit Housing Providers	⇐	⇒	⇒	⇐	⇐
William Sutton Trust	⇐	⇐	⇐	⇔	⇐
Commercial Philanthropy	⇒	⇒	⇒	⇒	⇐
Employer	⇐	⇐	⇐	⇐	0
Housing Management — Private Sector	⇔	⇐	⇐	⇐	⇒
Housing Management — Public Sector	0	trace	trace	0	⇐
Coownership/cooperatives	⇐	⇒	⇒	⇒	⇒

Key   ⇐ expanding   ⇔ steady: ⇒ declining   0 absent

Figure 3.2 Voluntary Housing Agencies in Britain 1900–2000

twentieth century has had a significant impact on its conduct and performance. Yet, as has been shown, the evidence suggests that conditions in the voluntary sector did not affect the Trust in predictable ways. At several points, the Trust acted against expectations, not least in the period between 1919 and 1939. This implies that it is a mistake to 'read off' the role of philanthropic housing from government policy statements and housing legislation alone. The situation is more complex as Figure 3.2. illustrates. Housing associations have not simply 'shadowed' the state, at least not before the 1990s.[98] Until the 1960s, it was the Government's need to contain the visibility of the extent of the housing problem that set local authorities in the forefront of housing policy. Local authorities, rather than voluntary housing agencies, were more readily disciplined and organised in pursuit of central government's specific housing objectives. This did not mean that voluntary organisations were less competent or less capable, but rather that Government strategy required them to be presented as such. The recurrent conflicts over the definition of housing need and housing priorities were used to identify the Government's preferred 'high ground', where tasks were allocated to the local authorities. The voluntary sector, by definition, was 'relegated' to the 'lower levels' where in fact the provision and management of property were often more difficult and more urgent. After 1970, as the general housing situation eased, local authorities were no longer required to sustain a central role in housing policy. Housing associations, now increasingly reliant on private funds, became the mechanism for transferring local authority housing into the voluntary and commercial sectors. It is the *political salience* of the housing issue, rather than the relative effectiveness of local authorities and housing associations that has decided the role of the voluntary sector in England during the twentieth century. It is to capture something of the complexity that has attended the conduct of housing philanthropy that we next consider the potential of game theory as an analytical tool.

CHAPTER 4

Game Theory, Nested Games and Voluntary Housing Organisations

The conduct of English housing associations during this century is in many respects surprising. The associations have played a remarkably small role here compared with many other European countries. Even the largest and best endowed have had less impact than their resources might lead us to expect. I have argued in the previous chapter that the apparently suboptimal contribution of the voluntary housing sector cannot be explained either by its own inherent weakness or by the innate superiority of state provision. My aim in this chapter is to consider how game theory might help in explaining some apparent anomalies in voluntary housing provision. I shall first give a brief account of the ideas involved in game theory and of the kinds of situations to which they have been applied most frequently. I then go on to assess some questions that the theory raises for the conduct of institutions like voluntary housing agencies. Using nested game theory, I explore the dynamics of the sector and the explanations that are suggested for the pathways followed after 1900. In this chapter, I shall primarily use evidence from the early experience of the William Sutton Trust. Concentrating on the Trust's development up to 1930, I show how the Trust formulated and implemented basic strategies, especially building location, rent levels and the selection of tenants. The cases of Liverpool and St. Quintin Park in London are then explored in some detail. These episodes throw particular light on the interlocking arenas in which the William Sutton Trust was engaged during this period.

CONCEPTS OF GAME THEORY

Game theory has attracted adherents from many disciplines, primarily economics, but increasingly from across the social

sciences.[1] The theory posits situations (ie games) where a number
of 'players', whether individuals or groups, seek to maximise their
own 'payoff' (perhaps money, prestige or satisfaction). In doing
so, they use strategies and procedures that are set by the 'rules of
the game'. Games may involve cooperation between players or
may be noncooperative. Players may each have an 'uncondition-
ally best' strategy available or their optimal solutions may depend
on what each of the other players chooses to do.[2] They may have
full, partial or no knowledge about what their fellow players will
do based on information or experience.

Two examples of the kind of game on which the theory is based
will perhaps help to clarify some of these ideas. The most
frequently cited game is the prisoners' dilemma.[3] This is a two-
person game, where each player achieves an optimum payoff by
choosing a particular strategy no matter what the other player
does. Its second feature is that despite this, the outcome is not the
absolute best. If both players had chosen to cooperate, they could
have achieved a better outcome for each of them. The prisoners'
dilemma may be recounted in the following way – two prisoners,
convicted of a serious crime, are held separately in jail. Each is
offered a deal under which, if one of them confesses and the other
prisoner does not, the person making the confession goes free. The
other receives a maximum sentence. If each confesses, they will
both be released with a moderate sentence. If neither confesses,
the sentence will be smaller than if both confess. In isolation,
defecting – choosing the strategy offering the surest individual
outcome – in this case, confessing, offers the best 'pay-off.' In this
context, distrust is mutually reinforcing and confessing is likely to
be established as a persistent (ie *dominant)* strategy. But if the
prisoners had been able to cooperate, an agreement that neither
would confess would have brought the lightest sentence for them
both. This game has been used in many settings from international
relations to collective action and markets. It hinges on *rational*
behaviour by participants and posits the possibility of a game
either reaching *equilibrium* or experiencing *instability*. These are
important ideas to which we will return when discussing the games
that housing institutions may play.

Games that have collective as well as individual consequences
have generated their own scenarios. The 'tragedy of the commons'
suggests that any one user who controls her exploitation of

common land, does so in the knowledge that other people's use cannot be controlled. Her personal loss will be the others' gain.[4] Yet continued overgrazing will destroy the common asset on which all depend. In a similar way, a collective good such as clean air or improved housing can benefit everyone, no matter whether they have contributed to the better conditions. The prevalence of such 'free riders' means that powerful disincentives prevail in providing for the public good, and everyone suffers because too little is provided. Where it is decaying housing that threatens the collective good, tensions between private and public interests are exacerbated. Landlords of poor property calculate that they will maximise their individual returns through a strategy of overcrowding coupled with minimum investment in their property. Their response, however, accelerates the decline in living conditions. Such a strategy was certainly the rational one for many inner city landlords at the turn of the last century given the inability of tenants to pay higher rents.

Game theory, indeed, predicts that *defection* will be the best individual strategy no matter what the other participants do. Nevertheless, social action to promote collective good can arise through voluntary cooperation, state coercion or the regulation and enforcement of modified *rules of the game*. Trust may be built over time through the *iteration* of encounters involving payoffs that have *salience* for the learning of the agents involved. It has been argued that in achieving these conditions for building mutual trust, formal institutions are crucial in overcoming the problems of 'free-riding' and defection.[5] How and why formal institutions take such a role and how they operate are questions that have recently exercised social and political scientists taking game theory as their starting point.[6]

Game theory has been used to analyse behaviour at the individual, societal and international level.[7] This analysis should help us to frame questions about the strategies of voluntary housing agencies in the twentieth century. The serious study of institutions using game theory, however, is only just beginning.[8] Institutions pose obvious difficulties because of their organisational complexity, their long life, their often extensive operational networks and their varying norms and goals. Institutions that operate in the housing sphere pose additional problems because of the nature of housing itself. Housing has a private and a collective dimension. In practice participants provide dwellings that form a private good for occupants and also a general good for society. Deciding what 'game(s)' a voluntary housing agency is playing at any particular time and place is not easy, but at the very least posing the question prompts us to identify the options that have structured the activities of these agencies. Game theory suggests key questions, until now unexplored, in relation to social housing bodies like the William Sutton Trust. Specifically, what are the goals of such organisations? What is optimal behaviour for such an organisation in pursuit of these goals? Who, from the point of view of such organisations, are the other players in their game? What kind of game is being played – is there a mutual interest in coordinating so that everyone can be a winner, or is the contest a "zero-sum game" where one player's gain is another player's loss?

These questions will be explored through a study of key events in the development of the William Sutton Trust up to 1930. Before moving on to that, it is important to be clear about some of the terminology already referred to. The central ideas are *rational choice, equilibrium, instability, rules of the game, iteration* and *salience for learning*. These elements have particular significance when the players under investigation are institutions.

Rational choice is a fundamental concept of game theory. It is, however, based on assumptions that are seldom applicable to institutions. Not only are players assumed to deploy strong rationality in making initial decisions (however stressful the circumstances), but they are also reckoned to apply it subsequently in updating and assessing outcomes in relation to objectives. Such assumptions are unrealistic in relation to institutions, where rationality is often unattainable even if it is wanted. They may be unattainable because the rules under which players are operating are insufficiently clear, making rational choice inapplicable. It is clear from Chapter 3 that at a number of points during the twentieth century, the rules and assumptions underlying housing provision were fluid. It will be argued in this and subsequent chapters that during these episodes the William Sutton Trust showed 'low rationality' in its behaviour. Furthermore, rational choice lacks a historical dimension – it can neither describe dynamics nor account for the paths actors took in reaching an optimal strategy. For our purposes, the concept must be modified to allow 'bounded rationality' where rationality is not the whole, but a subset of human behaviour.[9]

'Using these more prudent assumptions', Bengsston asserts, 'game theory is a useful tool in analysing real life interaction'. Actors can be assumed to 'try their best' to maximise utility within the constraints of limited information and imperfect cognitive capacity.[10]

Equilibrium represents a state of play where all the players have reached a strategy combination from which no-one has any incentive to deviate so long as no-one else does.[11] Game theory suggests that such convergence will be reached quickest where decision-making is most frequent, and where the *'salience for learning'* in each encounter is high. In other words, learning to cooperate in the mutually best strategy will result where numerous encounters occur. The encounters will be more powerful if they repeatedly have consequences that are fundamental to the primary objectives of the parties concerned. As the basic game is repeated, the *iterative* encounters generate correlated tactics, and knowledge derived from previous experience can help players develop optimal strategies. Where there is one strong player in an iterative game, less powerful ones may cooperate by acknowledging the power of the dominant party and their own dependent status.[12] No matter how a particular equilibrium is arrived at, threats may be needed to deter any deviation. More generally, 'rules of the game' need to be generated to increase the predictability of encounters and reinforce the status quo. The legal and political response to the establishment of the William Sutton Trust in 1900 is a good example of such a response. A detailed analysis of this situation follows. In summary, the Trust's wide aims, the scale of its assets and its acceptance of a minimal rate of return meant that at the outset it was thought capable of disrupting both local property markets and established principles for dealing with the poor. This was indeed a new and powerful actor in the game. Its fate, however, was to be largely 'taken out' of the situation through lengthy court proceedings. In the meantime, new rules of the game based on state supported council housing and a revived private market were established.

Rules of the game are vital for the application of game theory to real life situations, especially in the political and policy sphere. The rules of the game apply to basic issues such as who can become a player? What set of moves is permissible? What order of moves is permissible? In settling these rules, institutions themselves are very important. They help to define clear boundaries and to provide mechanisms for resolving conflict. By their nature, they increase the stability of the game, generating predictable encounters and outcomes that build the trust necessary for mutual confidence.[13] The maturing of central–local relations after 1900 between White-hall and town hall framed the rules of the game for voluntary housing agencies. Clearly, however, change also occurs. One player may be powerful enough to break out of the available choices and to redefine the rules of the entire game, generating a new set of options. The William Sutton Trust had the potential to achieve this in 1900, especially since the reinforcing power of central and local government in the field of housing had not yet been established. The Trust's failure to modify the way the housing game was being played is due to the fact that political agents themselves intervened to restrict the Trust's power. At the same time, they regulated the housing sphere and set their own rules of engagement.[14] The ability to redefine the rules of the entire game and to enlarge the successful actor's strategy space by adding previously unavailable options has been termed *institutional design*.[15]

The example of responses to the setting up of the William Sutton Trust brings us to an important group of concepts developed from game theory which are key to our study. These are the concepts of *sub-games* and *nested games*. Figure 4.1 represents a situation where the interaction in a sub-game between two players is modified by the impact of a third party on their payoffs. Central

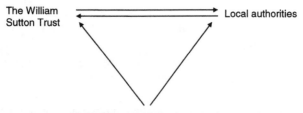

Figure 4.1 Graphic Representation of Nested Game where Outcomes Depend on Outside Conditions. Adapted from G. Tsebelis, *Nested Games* (1990) p 59)

government intervention in the relations between the William Sutton Trust and local authorities in Liverpool and London in the decade before 1919 is a good example of such third party influence. It will be discussed further below. From this type of interaction, the idea of *nested games* is introduced where the payoffs of players in one arena vary according to the situation prevailing in other arenas or by the moves made in other arenas. The idea of nested games has been used to account for puzzles and anomalies in behaviour and to show the systematic impact of contextual and institutional actors.[16] The arenas in which the activities of housing agencies are nested are illustrated in Figure 4.2. Housing organisations like Sutton are to be regarded as operating not in one but in three arenas – organisational, market and political.[17] These arenas are not self-contained but are interrelated or "nested". Operations and choices in any one arena therefore have payoffs in the others. The resulting payoffs may be important enough to carry over and determine the rules of subsequent games. Understanding an organisation's goals and explaining its strategy requires the study of the network of games in which the organisation is involved. The investigation of such a dynamic process over time is largely untried, but this study of the William Sutton Trust attempts the necessary 'process tracing'.[18]

Bengtsson has suggested that the leaders of housing organisations, interacting with other actors, have to mobilise members of the organisational arena, make favourable economic transactions in the market arena and influence housing policies in the political arena.[19] Housing provision has been presented as 'an ongoing strategic interplay between politicians, bureaucracies, firms and

Figure 4.2   Nested Games in Housing – Strategic Arenas

individual households'.[20] Figure 4.3 shows some of the components of the three arenas for organisations like the William Sutton
Trust. The Trust's interactions lie within the voluntary (housing)
sector, between the voluntary (housing) sector and national/local
government, between Trustees and property owners, and between
staff and tenants. From the Trust's point of view, the crucial
games in the twentieth century have been about tenure in the
policy arena. The structuring of the arrangements through which
possession of housing is organised and the political and financial
institutions established to regulate and support them have been
critical in determining conditions both in the market and the
organisational arenas. This conclusion is clear from the review of
the voluntary housing sector in Chapter 3, and will be explored
further in relation to rents in Chapter 5. The discussion will be
developed here in the detailed study of the early experience of the
conduct of the William Sutton Trust that now follows. The period
1900–1930 is divided into two sections – 1900–1918 and 1919–
1930. In each period, the focus is on the political and organisational arenas. The role played by the Local Government Board is
highlighted especially in building equilibrium among the players
engaged in housing provision. In each period, one major decision
taken by the William Sutton Trust is explored as an example of
'non-rational' behaviour. These are the decision not to build in
Liverpool in 1916 and the decision to develop an eight-acre site in
St. Quintin Park, North Kensington in 1928.[21]

SETTING UP THE WILLIAM SUTTON TRUST 1900–1918

Following the precepts of game theory, it is assumed that the
rational path for the William Sutton Trust was to maximise the
satisfaction of its objectives. Initially, the essence of William
Sutton's intent was given in the final version of his will made in
1894:

> 1. Upon trust to purchase or acquire from time to time freehold
> or copyhold land in London or any other populous place or
> town in England as sites for the erection of model dwellings
> and houses ... and to pay all monies for the purposes aforesaid
> out of the trust premises.

Political arena

- National   ideological

                                 financial

- Local   legal

Market arena

- Supply   capital

                                 land

                                 building materials

                                 structure of land ownership

- Demand   rents

                                 empties

                                 overcrowding

                                 alternative tenures

Organisational arena

- Internal organisation: staff

                                 tenants

- Voluntary sector: general

                                 housing

Figure 4.3   Players, Arenas and Housing Agencies

7. ... to create a continuing Trust for the purpose of supplying
the poor in London and other populous places or Towns in
England with proper and sufficient dwelling houses or lodgings
at such rents (however low) as my Trustees shall in each case in
their absolute discretion consider the tenants can afford to pay
or see fit to charge them (but I wish that some rent however
small in each case be reserved and paid and that no person or
persons shall be allowed to live in the said dwelling houses or
lodgings rent free) but so nevertheless that my Trustees are to
be left in complete control of the said trust and to have the
amplest and fullest powers and discretions as to the methods by
which the same shall be carried into effect....[22]

The executors of the will, who were also the original Trustees,
believed that they had a firm grasp of Sutton's aims. All three had
been closely involved with him in both his business and personal
life. They were Charles Sutton (William's brother and business
partner), Charles Lamb (his solicitor) and Thomas Watson
(manager and inheritor of Sutton's carrying company). All three
Trustees asserted that

We know the Testator's wishes on the subject and are ready as
we promised him to give our personal time and attention to
carrying out his scheme...

They felt that by his will, William Sutton had reposed in them a
very particular 'personal trust' and they were anxious to set to
work.[23] In practice, the three found themselves considerably
frustrated in carrying out the terms of William Sutton's trust.[24]

Their problems were certainly not financial. Although there
was initially some uncertainty about the size of the bequest, it
rapidly became clear that the sum was substantial. At probate,
William Sutton's estate was provisionally declared at £8,673
(apparently the sum in his current account).[25] A business
colleague, James Collin, thought it likely that Sutton himself did
not know how much wealth he possessed. After duties and individual legacies had been settled, the amount identified for Sutton's
charitable purpose was £2,059,795. At 1997 prices, this sum represents about £77 million.[26] *The City Press* commented at the time
that

A more princely legacy has never been left by any merchant prince in London or any other commercial centre in the country.[27]

Housing charity on this scale was indeed unprecedented – the Sutton Dwellings Trust was ten times larger than Guinness, five times larger than Samuel Lewis and four times larger than Peabody measured by their original endowments.

In pursuing Sutton's simply stated remit, the strategy with the best 'payoff' would have been to find cheap sites in appropriate urban centres, to build 'model dwellings' at a minimal rate of return and to allocate them to tenants who, though poor, could pay at least a token rent. These key strategic elements of the location, construction and allocation of the 'Sutton Model Dwellings' moved the Trust very clearly into the three operational arenas already identified – the political, market and organisational. The interrelated nature of these arenas and the primary influence of the political dimension is shown by the manoeuverings that followed immediately once the challenge to William Sutton's will by some family members and their associates had been settled in 1901.[28] It seems that the freedom which William Sutton intended to bestow on the Trustees to give effect to his 'one great idea' and to build healthy homes for the poor was repeatedly challenged. The Trust was opposed because it did not accord with prevailing rules of charity and its organisation, with the orthodox role of markets, hierarchies and networks in the housing sphere, and with current attitudes to poverty itself. Game theory suggests that the William Sutton Trust did not simply join an existing game as an additional player. It provoked a reconsideration of the rules of the game relating to housing provision as a whole.

There was persistent uncertainty about the operation of the Trust, and in particular its consequences for the 'public benefit' and for those who were housed. Counsel for the family members who challenged the legality of William Sutton's will stressed the unprecedented and boundless scope of the proposed Trust. He warned that 'it was impossible to say what it would amount to' if the will were not thrown out or severely restricted. *The City Press* drew comparisons with Peabody whose bequest had doubled its initial endowment in 30 years 'by means of accumulation'. With Sutton, it went on the trust represents four times the original Peabody bequest, and the possibilities of accumulation are unlimited, especially having regard to the fact that the trustees are given authority to nurse the estate as they think fit, and are not called upon to realize anything in a specified period.[29]

After the initial hearing, and on the recommendation of the Attorney General, the administration of the estate and the Trust was made subject to the Court of Chancery. The purpose of this was to determine 'the principles applicable to the fund'.[30] The Court maintained control both of the initial funds and of any surpluses generated. The prospect of a fully funded, professionally staffed, broadly directed and ever expanding 'Sutton Model Dwellings Trust' highlighted the need to regulate this unexpectedly bountiful housing agency. This prince among housing trusts was said to present 'elements of considerable difficulty in settling a scheme for its administration'.[31] Matters remained unresolved in the Court of Chancery for 25 years while the Trustees struggled to maintain their independence. In 1906, a stay of 'say two years' was proposed before any scheme could be drafted. During this time, the Court intended to have consultations with the Local Government Board and 'any other body of persons whose views may be valuable as to the mode in which such a charity as this can best be administered and also to inquire into the method of administration of similar charities such as the Peabody Trust'.[32] The Trustees opposed 'most strongly' the suggestion that the Local Government Board should be consulted before the scheme was drawn up.[33] They themselves had 'entered into communication with the governing bodies of the Peabody Donation Fund and the Guinness Trust and we have received help from both' but they went on

> We object most strongly to this charity being mixed up with any other or in any way made dependent on any other scheme or being brought under the authority of any borough or district or of the Local Government Board.[34]

The Assistant Secretary to the Local Government Board set out precise conditions for getting Ministerial support in the making of a management scheme for the William Sutton Trust. They involved fundamental changes in the original intent of the Trust in relation to location, construction and allocation of dwellings. In particular, he advised that to safeguard 'the reasonable interests of neighbouring property' only 'the accommodation essential for decent and healthy conditions' should be supplied. Furthermore the rents should be 'not far below ordinary commercial rates, though provision might be made for special reductions in exceptional cases'.[35] Clearly the Court of Chancery was being employed to keep the William Sutton Trust within the established bounds of housing charity and subject to the tutelage of local and central government. Between 1900 and 1914, a series of encounters between the Court of Chancery, the Local Government Board and town councils reinforced the constraints on the new housing player. The experience forced the Trust to defer to the choices of senior civil servants and local councillors. Simultaneously, new rules of engagement were forged between local authorities, the Local Government Board, the voluntary sector and the William Sutton Trust in particular. The effect was to restructure relationships between the private, voluntary and public sectors in providing housing for the poor.[36] The episode may usefully be understood as a type of nested game where the contest centres on the generation of new rules of the game. In such a game, the aim is to increase the predictability of encounters between the participants and thereby establish and reinforce stability. What was at stake was *institutional design*, where one player – the Local Government Board – employed both coercion and the promise of financial reward to foster the equilibrium that was wanted.

The consequences for the Sutton Dwellings Trust of its time in Chancery were profound. By 1914, rules had been set relating to its internal structure that affected its mode of operation. At the same time, external rules set terms of engagement with central and local government, property owners, local employers, potential tenants and the wider body of the poor. The Sutton Trustees were not in a strong position to counter these moves – unlike the Peabody, Guinness and Rowntree Trusts there were no well-known or titled people among them. Indeed, Charles Booth, Austen Chamberlain, the Bishop of London, and Alfred Lyttleton all refused invitations to become Sutton Trustees because they considered the duties too onerous for volunteers.[37] The Trustees were denied the power to retain a consultant architect to investigate housing sites on the grounds that this too was inappropriate for a charity. The Attorney General refused to sanction payment of the Trustees and in 1913, the Court of Chancery approved the establishment of an Advisory Committee to oversee their work. When the Advisory Committee was being set up, Sir Noel Kershaw Assistant Secretary to the Local Government Board urged, 'It seems to me to be important that the Board should be kept in close touch with this trust. Its operations will be on a sufficiently large scale to affect housing conditions in various areas considerably'. He went on 'the matter is of sufficient importance to justify the nomination of the Comptroller of Housing and Town Planning' (J. A. E. Dickinson). The Advisory Committee was therefore made up of senior members of the Local Government Board and representatives nominated by the London County Council (LCC) and the Mayors of Birmingham, Manchester and Liverpool.[38] The original Trustees expressly objected to the inclusion of a representative of the LCC on the grounds that they did not intend to develop any further estates in London. They were overruled.[39] The Advisory Committee's functions were specifically set out in an affidavit in June 1913. Its role was to advise on locations for development, on the selection of sites and the price to be paid, on building costs, the character of dwellings, the scale of rents, the selection and payment of architects, and the management of estates. They could also recommend the powers to be included in a 'Permanent Scheme when the same comes to be bought forward for the approval of the Court'.[40] Express provisions in William Sutton's will were suspended *because* they would have put his Trust on the independent footing he wanted. In November 1914, fourteen years after William Sutton's death, and with a stock of over 1200 dwellings, the Treasury Solicitor was still telling the Trustees that they had insufficient experience to be granted a permanent scheme of administration.[41] Internal organisational matters were deferred until external rules of engagement had been settled – where, how, for whom and at what cost was the housing to be provided? Such questions related above all to the distinction between poverty and pauperism and the potential that the Trust was perceived to have for dissolving accepted distinctions between the two.

Officials at the Local Government Board initially believed that there was nothing 'to suggest that the provision to be made (by

Sutton) is likely to extend to paupers'. The Treasury Solicitor, on the other hand, warned that the undifferentiated terms of the will would cause serious problems 'unless carefully fenced about by restriction of those eligible'.[42] Not only was it felt that large scale provision of good quality houses at low rents would attract 'undesirable people', it was also argued that a broad spectrum of poor people would be pauperised by the downward pressure on wages of large supplies of dwellings let at below market rents.[43] At the same time, the LCC expressed concerns about the effect of the Trust's unfettered activities on the income of local authorities and of ratepayers, particularly landlords of similar property.

> With regard to the effect upon the neighbourhood of the erection of dwellings … it appears … the erection of a large number of cottages or block dwellings in any district to be let at low rents would have the effect of lowering assessable value of that district and consequently raising the rates.[44]

The basis for calculating rents of 'Sutton Model Dwellings' was the first principle to be tackled. Whereas William Sutton's will required the Trustees simply to manage a 'continuing' trust with no specific return on capital, the Court in 1906 laid down a return of 2.5%. The Solicitor for the Treasury insisted on this, declaring that 'he would not have the people pauperised'.[45] Before the Trust's first block at Bethnal Green was occupied, the Court approved rents, occupancy levels and wage limits for applicants. Rents were undoubtedly higher than they would otherwise have been given the need to show a 2.5% return. In 1914, for example, rents on the William Sutton Trust's Birmingham Scheme had to be raised to comply with the 2.5% requirement fixed by the Court.[46] Preventing pauperism required maintenance of the prevailing equilibrium – underpinned by property and labour markets and bolstered by the financial and electoral interests of government, especially local authorities.

Settling the location of the William Sutton Trust's housing for the poor was equally crucial. William Sutton had simply specified that provision be made in London and other 'towns and populous places' in England. Such a geographically broad remit significantly extended the scope of voluntary housing. The prospect of an agency four times the size of Peabody (itself limited to London)

descending on some undefined 'populous' place was distinctly
destabilising. Fears increased with evidence that from the beginning small places were clamouring to collaborate with the Trust.
In March 1906, the Trustees produced thirty-five letters before the
Court of Chancery. They were from Town Clerks urgently
'requesting the charitable trust to be carried out'.[47] The three
original Trustees were convinced that William Sutton had wanted
to help the poor in smaller towns like Norwich as much as in
London or major industrial centres. They argued that the town
population limit of 200,000 which the Local Government Board
was advocating would virtually exclude the south of England.
They stressed that 'it was never intended by the testator that the
north of England should benefit at the expense of the south'. Size,
they said, had appeared irrelevant to William Sutton since 'it
might be considered appropriate to erect dwellings in a town of
say 50,000 if there is proper accommodation for 40,000 people
only'.[48] Officials at the Local Government Board viewed with
alarm efforts such as those of 'a committee at Plymouth....to
induce the Board to intervene so as to get the benefit of the Trust
for that town'.[49] They drew attention to preliminary returns from
the 1911 Census showing 43 towns in England with a population
over 100,000, 22 over 150,000 but only 17 over 200,000. They
advised the President of the Board that both 'attraction of
undesirables' and 'depreciation of adjoining property' would be
felt less in towns of 200,000. Their recommendation was that the
Trust's activities be restricted to this group.[50] The Court indeed
went even further, naming just eight provincial towns and three
areas of London as suitable for the operations of the Trust. They
were Birmingham, Manchester, Liverpool, Newcastle upon Tyne,
Kingston upon Hull, Sheffield, Leeds, and Bristol, plus (in
London) Bermondsey, the south east (including Rotherhithe) and
'a district in North London'. Without doubt, the 'personal trust'
of William Sutton had been reshaped. The limitations imposed
were designed to prevent it from damaging the interests of private
property owners and the stability of rates' conscious local authorities. Furthermore, they were meant to ensure that the William
Sutton Trust did not undermine the standing of the Local Government Board nor that of the very people 'whom the Trustees
desired to benefit'.[51] The 'rules of the game' that were to prevail in
providing houses for the poor had been reaffirmed.

THE PUZZLE OF CHARITABLE HOUSING DURING THE FIRST WORLD
WAR

The relationship between central and local government over
housing provision during and after World War One has been
much debated by historians.[52] The purpose and timing of the
Government's introduction of state subsidies for housing in 1919
have been variously interpreted. They have been seen as an ideological response to a perceived revolutionary threat from 'heroes'
returning from the Great War, as a reaction to the immediate or
longer term collapse of the private housing sector, or as a con-
comitant policy to deal with the consequences of the Government's
own action in maintaining the rent controls initially introduced in
1915. Though the theories offered vary, the problem to be
explained is clear – why did the Government, apparently so
unwilling to introduce subsidies before 1919, nevertheless decide
to do so? And why, having taken that decision, were the chosen
instruments local authorities rather than housing associations?
The failure of the housing association sector to develop in Britain
after World War One has been described as 'one of the more
puzzling features of the British housing system'.[53] Some of the
general reasons for this outcome have already been discussed. The
specific experience of the William Sutton Trust in seeking to
develop estates during World War One provides new and important evidence. In particular, the history of the Trust's involvement
in Liverpool shows that as early as 1916 the Local Government
Board was using the prospect of government subsidies to deter
Liverpool Corporation from cooperating with the William Sutton
Trust. It was also hinting strongly that publicly provided assets
ought to remain within the public sphere. They should not be
made available to, or shared with, other bodies, even charitable
ones.

Although in 1913 the Advisory Committee had agreed the list
of cities deemed appropriate for the Trust's activities, it went on
to closely regulate the Trust's relationship with the local authorities concerned. The Corporations of Manchester, Birmingham and
Liverpool jointly nominated one representative to the Advisory
Committee. Their first representative was Colonel Kyffin-Taylor,
Chairman of Liverpool's Housing Committee and an advocate of
the 'magnificent work that the Sutton Trustees were doing'.[54] He

acknowledged Liverpool's own achievements in 'rehousing the actual people turned out of insanitary dwellings' but said 'They could not have too much competition in work of this kind'. As early as 1909, the Trustees had been reported looking for sites in the city for 'model cottages'. In September 1913 they visited Liverpool at the invitation of the Mayor.[55] Civic leaders entertained them to lunch and then took them on a tour of Liverpool's own housing work. They went on to inspect sites in the hope that the Trust would build. Charles Sutton Junior, nephew of William Sutton, expressed the hope that the dwellings would be 'an ornament and a credit' to the city. He spoke vividly of his uncle's 'one great idea' of providing healthy housing for the poor.[56]

In Liverpool, however, the Sutton Trustees faced both sectarian politics and desperately poor slum dwellers. Housing in the city seems to have aroused frequent sectarian feuds. In 1909, for example, a meeting of the City Council heard claims that Protestant families had been intimidated and forced out of their homes in proposed clearance areas while their places had been taken by Catholic families. It was said that 'it was not possible for Protestants at present unhoused to live in Corporation dwellings'. Colonel Kyffin-Taylor defended the Housing Committee and firmly denied any suggestion that they were 'working along sectarian lines'.[57] Kyffin-Taylor's 'tolerance and courtesy' during his 12 years as Chairman of Liverpool's Housing Committee was later said to have brought the city 'for a whole generation ..an almost unbroken sectarian peace'.[58]

Despite the moderation of sectarian divisions in Liverpool housing and repeated attempts by both the Corporation and the William Sutton Trustees to identify a suitable site, negotiations foundered.[59] In 1914, Liverpool Corporation offered 'a site free in consideration of the Trustees building thereon' in an attempt to overcome the reluctance of the Trustees.[60] Both Kyffin-Taylor and Bernard Marshall, the LCC representative, recommended that the Trustees and the Advisory Committee should accept the offer.[61] Liverpool claimed to be acting under the Liverpool Corporation (General Powers Act) 1905. Legal advice on Liverpool's interpretation of the Act proving unclear, the Local Government Board intervened directly to prevent the gift going ahead. J. A. E. Dickinson, the Board's Comptroller of Housing and Town Planning and a member of the Advisory Committee to the Sutton

Trustees, warned that the plan was 'altogether premature'.[62] He advised Liverpool's Town Clerk 'that a strong case would have to be made out for *giving* land.' Furthermore, he reminded him that the Corporation remained legally committed to an "unhealthy area" scheme should the deal with the Sutton Trustees fall through.[63] The Local Government Board had already learned that the Trust Secretary, William Balmain, had been seeking to capitalise on Liverpool's offer of a free site. He had been suggesting to other local authorities that they should do the same.[64] Dickinson urged Liverpool not to sacrifice prospective financial reward and central government support. He told the Liverpool Town Clerk and City Treasurer that '*I was not impressed with the proposal to give the land away*'. (Original emphasis)

> The argument was that by giving the land and getting the Trust to build they (Liverpool Corporation) would save £5,200 a year for the 60 year term. On the other hand they would be giving the land away and would have *nothing* to show for their expenditure on the land. If the Corporation retained the land and built on it they would own property at the end of 60 years, bringing in good rental and at the end of 80 years would own free of debt the land having (probably) appreciated in value[65]

Finally, Dickinson recommended Liverpool not to jeopardise future relationships with the Local Government Board 'without very strong grounds'. He advised them 'to be noncommittal at present in case something in the nature of Government assistance to housing should be forthcoming'. This firm hint was made in June 1916 although central government subsidy was not in fact available until 1919. Nonetheless, the Sutton Trust never did build in Liverpool. This is a puzzling outcome which neither local circumstances nor factors related to the William Sutton Trust can satisfactorily explain. Indeed, one of William Sutton's closest surviving relatives had earlier chosen a visit to Liverpool to make a most explicit statement about the aims of the Trust. William Sutton, he said, simply had

> one great idea, and that was to crystallise the old proverb that prevention was better than cure. He believed that healthy homes and pure air and sanitation were better than all the hospitals that could be built.[66]

For its part, Liverpool was prepared to go as far as donating a housing site rather than see the Trust 'give up Liverpool as a building place'.[67] What the Liverpool episode shows is that during World War One the key housing game was being played in the national policy arena. The outcome was that the largest charitable trust in the land could not counter the alliance that was being built between local and central government in relation to housing.

In general, opposition to the Trust during its first quarter century focused on its undifferentiated interest in 'the poor' in 'London and other populous places'. The Trust posed problems through its unprecedented scale, unbounded scope, and lack of intellectual or political grounding. As a result, the Trust was placed in Chancery. During its time there, it was subjected to the tutelage of the Local Government Board and the Board's allies in the LCC and large municipal authorities. It was confined, regulated and even threatened with dismemberment if it attempted to follow its original aims rather than those that the Board considered necessary. The Treasury Solicitor warned the Trustees that if they spread their provision too widely, they might find any permanent scheme of management requiring 'separate and entirely distinct sets of trustees for London and each of the provincial Dwellings'. That would mean 'withdrawing the provincial Dwellings altogether from the jurisdiction of the Trustees in London'.[68] The effect was to subdue the William Sutton Trust, to isolate it and undermine independent relationships with local authorities. In practice, the Trust found itself excluded from both the voluntary and public spheres. We have seen that the Ministry of Reconstruction initially overlooked the William Sutton Trust when it asked the Housing (Financial Assistance) Committee to explore the contribution that similar bodies might make to the postwar housing effort.[69] The neglect of the Sutton Trust may seem surprising because a 'back of the envelope' calculation within the Ministry underlined its dominance in the voluntary housing sector. Its estimated £2,500,000 worth of assets available for housing was set against Rowntree (£11,500 and £11,000 per annum), Samuel Lewis (c£275,000) and Peabody (£200,000).[70] Nevertheless, an understanding of the games being played by the Local Government Board in the High Court of Chancery to negate the impact of the William Sutton Trust and to groom local authorities for a state financed housing role helps to clarify the puzzle. It suggests that the Local Government Board was indeed pursuing a long-term strategy of state funded housing provision via local authorities.[71] Furthermore, the actions of the William Sutton Trust cast doubt on the conclusion that the emergence of local authorities as primary providers of housing in 1919 was due to the 'lack of interest' by the voluntary sector.

'SEPARATE SPHERES' – GOVERNMENT, THE VOLUNTARY SECTOR
AND THE WILLIAM SUTTON TRUST 1919–1930

The 1919 Housing Act and even more the 1923 and 1924 Acts fixed the central government/local authority nexus as the rule in building working class housing for rent. The relative contribution of the voluntary sector declined after 1919 – it provided 4,500 of the 170,000 dwellings built under the 'Homes for Heroes' campaign and only 10,255 during the whole period 1919–1928. (See Table 3.2) Furthermore, housing associations and local authorities operated for the most part in separate spheres. Local authorities concentrated on new suburban building while the voluntary sector pursued reconditioning of property and the management of tenants in decaying urban areas. Housing associations also occasionally took on the clearance of 'small slums' where the local authority was unwilling to act. During the 1920s, however, the William Sutton Trust developed a profile unique among contemporary housing associations. In outlook and behaviour, the William Sutton Trust was more in tune with local authorities than with other housing charities and trusts. In 1927, the Trust finally emerged from Chancery with its own scheme of management as a housing charity though direct links with William Sutton were by now few. The following section describes the final stages of the Local Government Board's game of *institutional design* that enabled the William Sutton Trust to be released from Court with confidence. It also discusses one price paid by the William Sutton Trust for its freedom. The penalty was the construction of a further 540 flats in London against the Trust's own expressed intentions.[72] Such highly salient encounters, it will be argued, reinforced the prevailing rules of the game. They built the confidence of the Local Government Board that the William

Sutton Trust had 'outgrown its origins' and would in future predictably pursue its allotted role. Any tendency to deviate would be prevented by the continued surveillance of trustees (the majority now drawn from central and local government) and the barely susceptible discipline of the Charity Commissioners.

Some previous significant encounters between the William Sutton Trust and the Local Government Board during the First World War, especially the Liverpool episode, have already been discussed. Their effect can be seen when the Trust based its argument for a place in the postwar housing programme on the grounds that its housing activities were indistinguishable from those of a local authority.[73] In internal organisational terms, there had been a parallel erosion of the original administrative framework and its replacement with another associated with private business and with government. Charles Sutton had died in 1911. He was William's brother and one of the original three executors. On many occasions, Charles had expressed a clear and direct commitment to the original purpose of the Trust. He was succeeded as a Trustee by his son, also Charles, but on his death in 1915, a similar replacement was impossible. After discussion with the Advisory Committee, the Court agreed to the appointment of Henry Storey and Henry Wakefield. Storey had been William Sutton's co-developer in the St. Luke's area of Finsbury, while Wakefield had strong links to the carrying business through his company, Globe Express Ltd. These two now joined James Collin (Sutton and Co. Carriers) and members of the Advisory Committee who were J. A. E. Dickinson (Local Government Board), Bernard Holland (LCC) and Gerald Kyffin-Taylor (Birmingham, Manchester and Liverpool). The Trustees' original close association with William Sutton's charitable intent had been almost totally lost. The management and direction of the Trust lay in the hands of nominees appointed either by the Court or by central and local government.

The question of releasing the William Sutton Trust from Chancery was reopened in 1920. The atmosphere had clearly changed from prewar. In 1914, Kyffin-Taylor's suggestion that 'the time had now arrived when the question of a scheme could be considered' had been rejected by the Treasury Solicitor on behalf of the Attorney General. He recommended that a scheme should be delayed 'until experience was gained of the working of Model

Dwellings in the provinces'.[74] After the War, the response was distinctly more positive. This is somewhat surprising since the Draft Scheme for the Trust drawn up in 1920 tried to restore some of the original features that had been eroded during the long sojourn in Chancery.[75] (See Appendix 3). The proposed scheme was initially prepared by the solicitors Lamb and Prance, who had played a central part in drawing up William Sutton's will and in the early years of the Trust. The first clause of the 1920 Scheme stated that the Trust 'shall be governed and managed in accordance with the trust of the Will of William Richard Sutton ... as explained by this Scheme'. It went on to confirm that the Trust was to operate 'in or in the neighbourhood of any populous place in England'. While acknowledging that 'up to the present' such places had been defined as those over 200,000, the Draft Scheme did not propose that this should necessarily continue. It acknowledged that a return of 2.5% return on capital outlay should be 'borne in mind'. The Trustees were left free 'in particular cases of poverty or misfortune to charge any rent however small to meet the circumstances of the case'. The Draft Scheme sought to deflect criticism that such a charity would attract 'undesirables', requiring tenants to be 'of good character' with preference given to 'married men with families' for the larger dwellings. Furthermore, despite the expanding role of local and central government in social affairs, the Draft Scheme repeated the intention of the Trustees to provide allotments, infant nurseries, reading rooms and 'any provision tending in the opinion of the Trustees to promote the health and moral welfare of the occupants'. The Draft Scheme also returned to the controversial question of management, recommending the appointment of paid officers, including an architect, and the payment of fees as well as expenses to Trustees. In many respects, the 1920 Scheme closely resembled previous ones that had been put forward in 1906 and in 1914: the earlier ones, however, had been rejected as 'very slight and sketchy', premature and damaging to the social and political framework.[76]

The 1920 Draft Scheme was, however, studied carefully within the Local Government Board and by the Charity Commissioners. The conclusion was that although 'some questions might be raised' few objections were likely to be sustained.[77] While this outcome owed something to the deft drafting of the Scheme, it had more to do with the confidence that the Local Government

Board felt in the moves that the William Sutton Trust was likely to make in practice. Edward Forber, Principal Secretary at the Ministry of Health who had taken primary responsibility for the William Sutton Trust following the early retirement of J. A. E. Dickinson, responded with equanimity to the proposed Scheme. Waiving the need for any definition of 'poor' and 'populous', he commented that as the Trust was now operating in places with a population greater than 200,000 and was seeking a 2.5% return '...these points may now be passed over'.[78] Despite his retirement in 1920, Dickinson continued to serve on the Advisory Committee to the Trustees until August 1923. In his final note to Forber he commended the Trustees and their Secretary, commenting that they 'are more competent than the Advisory Committee and do their work well'. The Advisory Committee, he reported, had involved work 'so slight as to be almost negligible' and its meetings had dwindled to one a year after 1919.[79] Forber took Dickinson's place on the Advisory Committee, since it was nevertheless felt that, despite this, the position should be filled by someone 'in a position to speak with authority'.[80]

Other members of the Advisory Committee expressed similar confidence. Cecil Levita, now the LCC representative, expressed the view that the proposed Scheme seemed 'reasonable and wide enough to cover changes of time'. Levita was Chairman of the LCC Housing Committee and, like Forber, he was sanguine about the need for precision on the Trust's scope and purpose. 'When definition is not essential, I favour its omission', he wrote. Kyffin-Taylor supported the widest possible powers for the Trustees under the proposed Scheme. He thought they should

> have the power of selecting land, in the neighbourhood of, or related for residential purposes to, any populous place in England, for consideration, would themselves obtain a Valuation or Valuations of land thought to be desirable, and also reports on a proposed housing scheme, and would themselves decide whether they would proceed with it, and I think that the Trustees should now have these powers...[81]

Commenting on Kyffin-Taylor's stance, a Ministry of Health official advised Forber that while 'this is an unusually wide power' (of acquiring and developing land) 'The whole Trust is ... an unusual one and so is the composition of the body of Trustees. I think the power should stand'.

The Draft Scheme was passed to the Charity Commissioners for their consideration early in 1926 and was subsequently approved by the Court of Chancery, largely unaltered. The first meeting of the new Trust took place on 12 January 1927, with the three previous Trustees, and the existing members of the Advisory Committee. An additional member was William Carden, business partner of William Sutton in his distillery company. Future Trustees were to be nominated by the carriers, Sutton and Co. (one member), the Ministry of Health (four members), the LCC (one) and the Association of Municipal Councils (one). The first General Manager and Secretary of the Trust was William Balmain who had been the Secretary to the Trustees since 1901. It was decided to omit the word 'model' from the title of the Trust because the Minister of Health himself commented that the term now had 'a somewhat unpleasant flavour in connection with housing'.[82] Despite being a body regulated by the Charity Commissioners, the new Trust was subjected only to 'certain minimum safeguards'. Indeed, the Scheme left the Trustees 'remarkably free' to exercise their discretion and run their affairs as they thought best.[83]

The William Sutton Trust emerged from Chancery following a period when it had achieved little by developing new estates. Indeed, in March 1924 a member of the Charity Commission had commented that 'It struck him as surprising that so little had been done in 20 years'.[84] Progress since the war had been particularly difficult, and plans to develop sites acquired at Islington, Bristol, Manchester and Sheffield had been shelved 'owing to the general dislocation of industry, restriction on building and other factors connected therewith'.[85] At the beginning of 1923, however, matters were reopened following a fall in the cost of building and the prospect of financial assistance under the 1923 Housing Act. In 1924, the Trustees' account of their activities to date, showed six completed estates of 1,756 dwellings. (See Table 2.2) They began negotiations to acquire further sites in Leicester and Leeds and paid exploratory visits to Hull, Stoke on Trent, Salford, and Hither Green in London.[86] These initiatives, it was hoped, would bring about a considerable expansion of activity. The emphasis was on developing provincial estates where Trustees had been told they needed to prove their competence. The appearance of St. Quintin Park, North Kensington, on the Trust's list of probable developments in 1926 is therefore unexpected. Its emergence and implementation are examples of the way that government agencies continued to shape the William Sutton Trust. Their aim was to ensure the Trust's compliance with prevailing patterns of behaviour once it was free of the tutelage of the Court. Not all the consequences, however, were the ones intended, especially regarding the balance of the Trust's activities between London and the provinces.

In the late 1920s, North Kensington was a particularly complex housing arena. Its problems were severe, mainly because of multiple occupation and overcrowding by very poor families in large houses and basements.[87] Few clear sites remained to be developed, except in the St. Quintin area in the north, and most of the rehousing had been undertaken by local housing trusts.[88] In the public sector, the LCC and Kensington Borough Council shared responsibility. The Borough Council had acquired a section of St. Quintin in 1919 and had developed the 'Balfour of Burleigh Estate' with 202 cottages and flats.[89] The LCC had not built in the borough. Both the LCC and the borough preferred indirect tactics in North Kensington. They selectively allocated tenants to estates outside the borough and they manipulated 'chains of relief' based on a series of carefully arranged moves within local areas. Kensington Housing Association provides an example of the way these processes worked. This Association received subsidy from the borough council and in return it accepted the Council's nominees from clearance and improvement areas. This was said to allow housing associations to deal with 'rather difficult cases', while 'more desirable tenants' were offered a place on the Council's estate. Where appropriate, the landlords of property from which tenants had been moved were also visited and asked to relet only to 'suitable' local families.[90]

South Kensington was active in providing assistance to its poor northern neighbours, and the links between the voluntary sector and the borough council were frequent and close, not least in housing. The primary aims of local housing policy were to manage 'careless' tenants, to prevent deterioration of property, to use rehousing opportunities to reward good conduct and to prepare tenants for further moves up the housing ladder. Rents were kept 'on the lowest possible scale' to assist local tenants. To prevent 'influx from outside'[91] tenancies were allocated as far as possible to people from Kensington.[92] The result was close regulation of tenants using the 'Octavia Hill' system of management in both borough and housing association property and an exceptional degree of integration between public and voluntary sector housing.[93] These were all serious disincentives to the William Sutton Trust which aimed to provide new 'model' dwellings for tenants selected according to its own criteria and procedures. Their decision to develop first eight and then a further one acre of St. Quintin land involved compromises over building standards and tenant selection that were unprecedented for the Trust. The decision to develop was the result of pressure from the LCC's representative on the Advisory Committee, Cecil Levita, who as well as being chairman of the LCC Housing Committee was councillor for North Kensington.

Poised as it was in the mid 1920s to receive an independent scheme of management, the William Sutton Trust was vulnerable to government pressure. It needed to demonstrate both its building capability and its willingness to compromise its own principles to cooperate with other housing agencies. The sole remaining undeveloped site in North Kensington was clearly a prestigious opportunity. It was the LCC that first investigated purchase of the site. In June 1925, the LCC Housing Committee was prepared to recommend that the land be acquired and developed with five-storey accommodation for 2,700 persons.[94] Nothing further was done, however, and in 1926 the William Sutton Trustees appear to have begun to discuss the possibility of acquiring the land itself. It seems likely that Cecil Levita initiated these discussions, but the Trustees' minutes are very sparse at this point and do not refer to the issue. In February 1927, though, the minutes of the new Trustees note 'further discussions' on the St. Quintin site. They also report a visit by the chairman and deputy chairman to a similar LCC scheme in Wandsworth which Levita arranged. Throughout the next few months, Levita continued his efforts to move the Trust forward on the matter.

Apparently some Trustees had different priorities, in particular a desire to shift the emphasis of the organisation's activities away from London. At their next meeting in March 1927, the Trustees resolved that further discussion of St. Quintin Park should be

shelved until the 'policy to be adopted in the future as to allocation of funds between London and the Provinces' had been
considered further.[95] In the meantime, William Balmain (now
General Manager and Secretary) was instructed to prepare 'a
statement on a population basis showing the position as between
the Metropolis and the Provinces'. He was also to make an assessment of the likely future activities of the Peabody, Guinness and
Samuel Lewis Trusts in London.[96] Consideration of the St.
Quintin site was again adjourned in April, but Levita pressed the
matter on. He presented his own statement showing two possible
schemes for the site – one with five-storey tenements and 1,350
habitable rooms costing £274,200 and the other of three-storey
blocks with 900 rooms at £177,450. At their next meeting, Levita
again took the initiative circulating his views about 'the apportion-
ment of building work between London and the provinces'.[97] The
Trustees then took a decision to apportion their outstanding
capital of £638,233 between London and the provinces. The basis
for the division of resources is not recorded. Crucially, however,
the Trustees went on to instruct Balmain to open negotiations
with the LCC about the St. Quintin site. Subject to price and
suitability, the Trustees agreed to purchase the site, with the
important proviso that cottages as well as flats should be included
in the scheme.

The pressure on the Trustees to commit themselves to a very
large investment in North Kensington clearly came via their LCC
representative at a crucial time. It coincided with the period when
the Court was about to grant their independent scheme of
management. Their decision to develop the St. Quintin site helped
to meet concern about housing conditions in this part of London
while underpinning the preferred indirect approach of both the
LCC and Kensington Borough Council. It was not a development
that the Trustees felt was best suited to their objectives at the
time. They agreed to it to consolidate the achievement of their
goal in the organisational arena – independence from the Court
and the interventions of the Ministry of Health. The decision to
buy the site did not end the compromises, however. Pressure from
the borough council to keep rents down resulted in a high density,
low quality flatted estate that lacked many of the features found in
the Trust's other estates.[98] No cottages at all were included in the
final scheme. (See Plates15–17). Furthermore, the LCC, the

borough council and Kensington housing trusts sent deputations to the Trustees seeking to influence the allocation of tenancies through the established 'chain of relief' system of nominations.[99] This was a difficult request which the Trustees resisted. Although they were praised by the Town Clerk of Kensington for accommodating 'suitable and deserving Kensington families', they also erected a notice on the Estate inviting individual applications for tenancies; in the event, only 50% of the families who took up tenancies on the new St. Quintin estate came from within Kensington.[100]

In the mid 1920s, St. Quintin Park saw the William Sutton Trust playing a game that was in tune with the needs of the local authorities concerned, at the expense of its own priorities. The episode took place at a period when the rules of the game were again about to change. The Ministry of Health and the local authority representatives on the Advisory Committee were in the process of agreeing to free the William Sutton Trust from formal, legal constraints. They believed that the Trust had been routinised into a non-threatening role. The competence of the Trust was no longer in doubt and its unusual nature no longer feared. For its part, the William Sutton Trust was anxious to achieve independence from the control of the Court of Chancery after twenty-five years. To achieve this, compliance was required for the time being. The acquisition and development of the St. Quintin estate provided the test to demonstrate that the William Sutton Trust had learned the necessary 'rules of the game'. Once having gained its independence, however, the Trust went on to assert its own objectives quite distinctively, but within broad limits that reflected previous experiences.

Right from the beginning in 1900, the legal exchanges and political interactions which the William Sutton Trust had experienced had shown that its objectives could only be achieved by cooperation with, and by satisfying the needs of, other agencies concerned with housing. Its long and short term behaviour in relation to local authorities and the voluntary sector, had been structured under the discipline of the Court, the Government's legal officers, the Local Government Board and the Ministry of Health. Once freed from their tutelage by its independent scheme of management, the William Sutton Trust opted to turn away from London and to build predominantly cottage estates on the outskirts of provincial towns. After 1927, the balance of its activities swung decisively to the provinces. In 1929 a list of towns with populations between 100,000 and 200,000 was prepared to guide future decisions about provincial development. Sites in London, on the other hand, were repeatedly rejected on the grounds that 'no funds (for London) are available'. Indeed, apart from a one acre extension to the St. Quintin estate in 1934, the Trust avoided building in the London housing arena for fifty years.

The experience of St. Quintin Park underlined how different the William Sutton Trust was from other housing trusts, whether the 'model' companies like Peabody or the 'Octavia Hill' agencies operating in places like Kensington. Indeed, the decision to remove the term 'model' from the name of the William Sutton Trust in 1927 symbolises its distinct character. The St. Quintin Park episode emphasises that the role the William Sutton Trust had been groomed to play was that of a responsible public body, nested within the priorities of national housing policy. The rules that it had internalised placed it closer to local authorities than to the voluntary housing sector. The most powerful player in the game, the Ministry of Health, no longer had to rely on threats to secure the Trust's compliance. The Ministry could have confidence in the 'rules of the game' developed in the political arena and reinforced by repeated encounters between the agencies involved in housing provision. How this *institutional design* fared in the second half of the twentieth century is the subject of the final chapters of this study. First, though, the following two chapters adopt a different focus. They explore the consequences for tenants of the 'remodelled' William Sutton Trust during the period 1909–1939.

CHAPTER 5

Housing the Poor – Rents, Subsidies and the Market before 1939

The William Sutton Trust granted tenancies in rapidly growing numbers in the decades before the Second World War. In 1920, the Trust provided 1,447 dwellings housing a population of 5,400: by 1939, the total number of dwellings was 7,829 and the population housed had reached 32,000.[1] This chapter considers how tenancies affected the financial well-being of occupiers. Using several different measures of poverty, previous chapters have shown that during the period 1909 to 1939 a substantial proportion of Sutton tenants fell below even the strictest definition of the poverty line.[2] In what respects, and to what extent, did the William Sutton Trust lift the tenants concerned out of poverty and improve their standard of living? Were its tenants better off as a result, or would they have enjoyed a better quality of life had they avoided contact with the Trust? Questions about the nature of poverty, its relation to standards of living and the quality of life have been matters of considerable debate among historians, economists and social scientists – today they remain highly charged, and contentious issues.[3] These debates will be reviewed to establish the main concepts and approaches to be employed in the analysis that follows. The effects of living on a Sutton estate for tenants' resources, utility, and social capability will then be explored. This chapter will deal primarily with rents, while Chapter 6 will be concerned with the William Sutton Trust's broader effect on tenants' standard of living.

THE QUALITY OF LIFE DEBATE

Defining the standard of living, and explaining the nature and causes of changes over time has generated sustained academic

argument. Controversies about the impact of the Industrial
Revolution, the First World War and the 'hungry thirties' have
been intense. Much of the conflict has been ideologically charged
and imbued with assumptions about the desirability or otherwise
of capitalist production.[4] Nevertheless, despite the contested
nature of much previous work, some basis has to be established to
underpin an analysis of the effect of a Sutton tenancy. At the
outset, three major developments can be identified – firstly,
between 1914 and 1936, the average wage of semiskilled manual
workers rose by almost 30% in real terms,[5] secondly, hours of
work fell generally to forty-eight per week and thirdly, state
benefits for unemployment, old age, ill-health, retirement, widows
and orphans began to relieve poverty among these vulnerable
groups though they hardly eliminated it.[6] Some caveats must be
set against these positive trends – intense poverty remained in
1939 especially in areas with high levels of unemployment: even in
York, Rowntree concluded that 31.1% of the working class were
unable to attain the minimum standard of living he had set in
1936, and a further 19% attained it only by the narrowest of
margins.[7] Against this background, an evaluation of the impact of
the William Sutton Trust requires us to enter the debate. We have
to define what we mean by the standard of living, quality of life
and well-being and then establish the criteria by which these
aspects of life can be measured. Only then will we have a basis on
which to assess the 'added value' of a William Sutton tenancy.

In determining degrees of poverty, three elements have been
identified – levels of income, access to resources and 'living conditions and functionings': Amartya Sen's formulation of these
elements is illuminating and underlies the analysis that follows.[8]
Sen reminds us that, besides money, income encompasses things
that can be exchanged for income and also things that can be
thought of as income. This is important in William Sutton estates
with their benefits in kind such as cheap coal, rent rebates, fitted
furniture, routine maintenance and regular internal decoration.
Sen also highlights the importance attached to visible resources in
assessing people's standard of living. 'The market' he writes,
'values commodities and our success in the material world is often
judged by our opulence'. In many respects, William Sutton estates
did indeed present an appearance of opulence – architect designed
dwellings, modern shops, tennis courts, gardens and sports

pavilions. While not denying the importance of such resources, Sen argues 'the commodities are no more than means to other ends'. Ultimately, their utility for living standards depends on two things – 'the achievements required by the society in which one lives' and the life they allow people to lead through their influence on 'what we can and cannot do, can and cannot be'.[9] Or as Hawthorn puts it, 'The value of the living standard lies in the living'.[10]

Poverty, therefore, arises in a situation where there is low income, a low standard of living arising from lack of general resources (which may or may not be monetary) and by diminished 'functioning and capabilities' that people ordinarily use for survival and improvement. Poverty by this definition has important subjective elements and also some that can be specified and measured objectively. Improvements in someone's standard of living or quality of life arise from increases in income, resources and/or capabilities – this and subsequent chapters will seek to identify particular aspects of Sutton tenancies that carried identifiable consequences for these three elements. Their significance in comparison with other housing options will also be assessed.

SOCIAL HOUSING AND THE POOR

It is generally argued that between 1900 and 1939, neither local authorities nor charitable agencies succeeded in improving the lives of the poor through the housing they provided.[11] This is because, until the slum clearance schemes of the late 1930s, very few poor people were allocated social housing. The few who were accommodated suffered a reduction in their quality of life through high rents, additional travel costs, reduction in employment opportunities, absence of amenities and authoritarian, paternalistic management regimes. At one extreme stood the Octavia Hill type of housing society, which offered reconditioned lowcost apartments to poor families whose potential for self-improvement was closely monitored and regulated by zealous lady rent collectors.[12] At the other, were the purpose built flats and cottage estates of local authorities and philanthropic housing agencies. Here management was relatively less obtrusive and design more sanitary, but the price was that tenants were generally selected for their ability to pay and for regular habits, including employment. Even for tenants such as these, the impact on their lives is judged to have been negative. 'Truly humanitarian in its pretensions yet depressing in its results' was Pevsner's verdict on the Peabody flats. After 1919, local authority housing became more humane and sensitive in design,[13] but M'Gonigle and Kirby showed that rehousing poor families in new well-appointed estates in the 1930s, far from improving standards of living, actually resulted in rising death rates for those who moved there. This was due to the *reduction in resources* that resulted from increased costs (notably rent, food and travel) and decreased income (from reductions in employment opportunities especially for women).[14] Neither charity nor local government, the conclusion seemed to be, could solve the problems of housing and poverty, not even on their most modern estates.

In important respects, the William Sutton Trust appears to have had the potential to succeed where others failed – it had a very large guaranteed body of funds, and it did not have to seek additional donations, subsidies or outside investment to continue its work. Once freed from the control of Chancery in 1927, the Trust could exploit its secure financial position. Its resources gave it a level of independence and freedom from public scrutiny and approval that set it apart from other elected, charitable and semi-charitable agencies. Its tenants did not have to be advertisements for any good cause or commercially viable venture. Its management was not seeking to display the 'deserving' character of the poor. It did not have to charge fixed rents, but had considerable flexibility in individual cases. The only formal constraints were William Sutton's wish that 'some rent should be paid' and the requirement that the Trust showed a 2.5% return overall. Did the William Sutton Trust, then, succeed where others failed? The impact of Sutton tenancies will be assessed to learn whether disposable incomes, resources and 'functionings and capabilities' of those who acquired them were enhanced or undermined. The evidence for this assessment is drawn from the Trust's archive, further analysis of tenants' registers, and minutes of tenants' associations. This is augmented by interviews with tenants who lived on Trust estates prewar, interviews with Trust employees, and contemporary surveys of housing preferences, notably Mass Observation.[15]

AN ILLUSION OF CHOICE? THE PRICE OF A WILLIAM SUTTON TENANCY

In assessing the cost of a Sutton tenancy, it is important to establish whether the accommodation provided what people wanted. William Sutton estates might accomplish this in various ways – they might make good absolute shortages, or they might supply more appropriate accommodation, especially in relation to size and location, or they might provide accommodation that was better equipped and better designed. The question of rents and affordability is a key issue underlying all these considerations. In making judgments about the comparative cost of Sutton tenancies, particular distinctions will be drawn between pre- and post-World War One developments, between tenants at different stages in their life cycle and between London and provincial estates.

All the evidence suggests that for the whole of the period up to 1939, William Sutton tenancies were in demand both inside and outside London. Unlike Peabody, there are no reports of London estates becoming 'hard-to-let'[16] and unlike Guinness, Sutton did not have to contemplate demolition of blocks in the 1930s because they had become unacceptable in design.[17] One tenant recalled that Sutton's oldest estate at Bethnal Green 'always had a waiting list' and that her mother waited two years before being offered a tenancy there.[18] Potential tenants mostly sought out the estates for themselves – one identified the Birmingham Alum Rock estate 'literally by walking around and looking'.[19] The trustees occasionally went along with the involvement of local authorities or charitable organisations in the selection of some of its tenants but only 'within the limits of tenants acceptable to the Trust'. For the most part, however, outside agencies did not preselect its applicants.[20] Again, the William Sutton Trust was in a powerful position. As long as it operated within the framework set out by the Court and the responsible Government Ministry, it could operate independently. It did not have to ally itself with other interested bodies in circumstances that might distort its own preferred ways of working. In Manchester, the Trust's Secretary was authorised to talk to the City Council about taking tenants from an ongoing clearance or improvement scheme. The clear condition was that 'our work [is] not to be delayed if the Corporation are unable to assist ... (and) the Trust's freedom as to acceptance or refusal of

tenants from slums ... is not compromised'.[21] Sutton's favoured
approach was very direct. On the Dick Lane site in Bradford, one
tenant recalled that in 1932 'a great big notice' was put up in the
corner of a field 'and it said houses were going to be built for poor
people – those were the exact words'.[22] Prospective tenants were
invited to apply direct to Head Office in London, and to do so
was an act of choice, not a matter of preselection or nomination.
Given the importance of home for people's sense of well-being, the
continuing demand for Sutton housing suggests that prospective
tenants themselves saw a tenancy as a desirable benefit.[23]

For a choice to carry positive meaning, other comparable alternatives have to be available. If there are no alternatives, then
applying for a Sutton dwelling cannot necessarily be interpreted as
an indication of greater utility or benefit. How adequate was the
supply of lowcost housing for rent in the areas where Sutton built
before 1939? The availability of housing at rents the poor could
afford was affected by the interplay of several factors – the
fortunes of the private rented sector, especially after rent controls
were introduced in 1915; the availability and character of central
government housing subsidies, first provided in 1919, and the scale
of local authority housing finance, especially politically contentious rate contributions. The interaction between these three
elements of the working class housing market and their effect on
the rents charged for William Sutton Trust accommodation forms
the major focus of the rest of this chapter. Their impact is
explored in three phases – pre-1919, where the emphasis is
primarily on London in an unregulated private housing market;
the 1920s with the introduction of state housing subsidy alongside
private rent controls, and the 1930s with the renewed emphasis on
general housing provision through owner-occupation and slum
clearance by local authorities.

(I) 1909–1919
In the decade before World War One, the private rented sector
was the primary resource for accommodation. Estimates are that
this sector provided 90% of *all* housing, not only working class
housing.[24] Even in terms of London's tenement blocks, more
people were housed by commercial dwelling companies than by
philanthropic ones.[25] The need to protect the private market, as
we have seen, was one element underlying the alarm that greeted

William Sutton's munificence in 'providing housing for the poor'. Liverpool City Council's stricture that no accommodation was to be provided 'in excess of what was required or on terms that will involve loss to ratepayers' was widely shared.[26] Before 1914, the provision of council housing as a normal feature of the housing market was not anticipated: such local authority house building powers as existed were strictly limited and no government assistance with building costs was available.[27] Market forces set private sector rents as landlords sought to maximise their net income.

Building booms in the early years of the century 'restored choices not known in twenty years' in the housing market generally. Pressure on London housing, though, never slackened to the same degree as it did elsewhere.[28] Certainly, compared with the rest of the country, London rents remained high – in 1908, the rent of an average working class dwelling in London was 70% higher than in Birmingham, 200% higher than in Wigan and 500% higher than in Macclesfield. Working class housing in the capital was in particularly short supply. Between 1902 and 1913, 70,000 working class lodgings were demolished but only 15,000 new units were built.[29] Even so some London local authorities, like Woolwich, were permitted to demolish housing without rebuilding. Others were refused permission to build under Part 111 of the 1890 Housing Act on the grounds that private enterprise was fairly meeting demand.[30] Vacancies, it appeared, were increasing in every part of the London housing market.[31] Philanthropic housing agencies, notably Peabody, were beginning to suffer from the easing of the housing situation because their tenement accommodation was seen as poor value – relatively high rents, unpopular dwelling form, poor amenities and intrusive management. 'Model' dwellings with 'their grim colourless walls (rearing) some 70 feet without break or ornament except the windows' had been condemned as 'the embodiment of all that is cheap and nasty ... (the rooms are) no better than pigeon holes'.[32] The hostility of working class tenants towards model dwellings continued even when agencies like Peabody began to develop suburban cottage estates at Herne Hill (1902) and Tottenham (1906). Even with rent reductions, lack of demand for these estates continued despite 'the increased distress from which the poor of London are now suffering'.[33] Designed to attract artisan families, these cottages could not shake off Peabody's previous reputation among social groups that were not accustomed to applying for one of their tenancies. Nevertheless, the need to reduce tenant turnover and rent losses from empty property encouraged both philanthropic agencies like Peabody and the London County Council to change their policies on location and tenant selection. They chose to concentrate on providing housing where tenants were more regular and day-to-day management presented fewer problems. By 1914, as Figure 2.1 has shown, 'the geography of philanthropy no longer coincided with the geography of poverty'.[34] The LCC, the Guinness Trust and Peabody all acknowledged difficulties of 'hard-to-let' property both in the east end and south of the river. These were the very areas where the William Sutton Trust built three of its first four estates. In going against the trend in London social housing, was the Trust able to offer accommodation that was financially and also physically desirable? Specifically, how did its rents compare with others?

In setting the rents of its first flats in Bethnal Green (1909), City Road (1911), Chelsea (1913) and Rotherhithe (1916), the Trustees were required to abide by the requirements of the Court of Chancery and the Advisory Committee. Rents had to be set 'to safeguard the reasonable interests of neighbouring owners' and to achieve a return on capital outlay of 2.5%.[35] The assumption was that these considerations would result in rentals 'not far below ordinary commercial rates'. The rents set for Sutton's four pre-1919 London estates were actually very similar to each other: in all of them, a two room flat cost around 5/6 [28p], inclusive of rates, and a four room flat cost around 8/- [40p].[36] (See Table 5.1) These flats included a private scullery/bathroom besides the number of rooms specified. It would certainly have been possible to find cheaper accommodation – a two room Guinness flat could be had for less than 5/- [25p], for example, while two rooms sublet in a private house might be rented for between 5/6 and 7/- [28 and 35p].[37] The LCC, like Peabody, was responding to its letting difficulties by reducing rents, allowing subletting and offering a rent free introductory week.[38] The prospect of wartime shortages and increasing rents, however, led to the introduction of rent controls in 1915. The controls applied to both individual and philanthropic landlords.[39] In the period before 1919, one has to conclude that it is unlikely that, in themselves, the rent levels of William Sutton Trust blocks offered any significant contribution to the standard

Table 5.1 Cost of Renting from William Sutton Trust 1914–1939

Erected pre 1919 (London) average rents (including rates)

	1914				1924				1939			
	2 rooms		4 rooms		2 rooms		4 rooms		2 rooms		4 rooms	
Bethnal Green	5/0	25p	9.0	45p	7/4	37p	13/0	65p	8/1	40p	14/7	73p
Rotherhithe	5/4	27p	7/10[2]	39p	8/7	43p	11/5[1]	56p	8/7	42p	11/8[2]	58p
Old Street	5/11	30p	9/0	45p	8/4	42p	13/2	66p	8/7	42p	14/0	70p
Chelsea	5/6	28p	7/6[2]	38p	7/6	38p	10/1[2]	50p	7/7	38p	10/6[2]	53p

Erected 1919–1929 average rents (including rates)

	1924				1939			
	2 rooms		4 rooms		2 rooms		4 rooms	
Birmingham	4/0	20p	13/0	65p	6/1	30p	12/4	62p
Newcastle (Barrack Road)	7/10	39p	12/4	62p	7/0	35p	11/5	57p
Islington (London)					10/9	54p	18/6	93p
Manchester Gorton (340 houses)					10/2[2]	51p	12/9	64p
Leeds (York Road)					9/8[2]	48p	11/9	59p
Sheffield					11/7[2]	58p	13/5	67p
Bristol					8/0	40p	11/8	58p
Leicester					9/4[2]	47p	12/5	62p
Stoke (Trent Vale)					9/3[2]	46p	10/10	54p

Table 5.1 Cost of Renting from William Sutton Trust 1914–1939 (*Continued*)

Erected 1930–1939 average rents (including rates)

	1939			
	2 rooms		4 rooms	
St Quintin Park(London)	10/8	53p	16/1	80p
Manchester Gorton (72 flats)	9/4	47p	13/11	70p
Salford	8/3	41p	12/2	61p
Leeds (Selby Road)	5/9	29p	9/3	43p
Stoke (Abbey Hulton)	9/3[2]	46p	10/7	53p
Hull	5/11	30p	12/3	61p
South Shields	7/3	36p	11/0	55p
Bradford	3/6	18p	6/3	31p
Newcastle (Benwell)	8/0	40p	12/3	61p
Plymouth (St Budeaux)	8/0	40p	13/0	65p
Middlesborough	6/6	33p	12/6	63p

Notes: 1. All amounts are rounded to nearest new p.
2. Rent quoted is for 3 room dwellings – no 2 room dwellings were included.

of living of their tenants. The predominant influence on their rents was the private land and property market for working class dwellings in London. The London market was itself modified by the constraints imposed on Sutton by the Court, the Advisory Committee and rent control after 1915. These factors meant that overall Sutton rents offered little if any reduction over those prevailing in the public, private and philanthropic sectors at the end of the First World War.

The exception to this general rule was the situation in London's West End where massive redevelopment for commercial purposes was sharply reducing the supply of private rented working class dwellings. Through the combined action of landowners and metropolitan borough councils, however, philanthropic bodies like Sutton came to play the major role in new housing provision. In 1912, it was expected that local authority and philanthropic dwellings in Chelsea would soon accommodate almost 7,000 people. The Sutton estate in Chelsea was planned to supply one third of this total and the Sutton Trust became the area's largest single landlord. When the estate was completed, the Trust had 50% more tenants than the metropolitan borough council itself. The Chelsea Medical Officer of Health in his annual report commented

Probably there are but few places in the United Kingdom where so many people of the wage earning class, in proportion to population, will be able to find so much accommodation in artizans' dwellings as in the Chelsea that will be in two years' time.[40]

In 1919, the Medical Officer of Health calculated that 'possibly 25%' of the working class population of the borough was living in local authority or philanthropic dwellings. This was the result of public and voluntary building activity, on the one hand, and losses of accommodation in the private sector on the other. Demolitions and other redevelopment had been affecting six thousand people a year. Because of the William Sutton Trust's unusually dominant position, it was able to set rent levels and property sizes that diverged markedly from those that might have been expected had the private sector been operating normally – to some extent the Trust had more freedom to disregard the 'reasonable interests of neighbouring owners' since private landlords were rapidly withdrawing from the working class market. At another level, however, the Trust was undoubtedly cooperating in the schemes of large Chelsea landowners like Lord Cadogan. His interests lay in freeing his estate from the encumbrance of squalid poor houses while maintaining a supply of cheap, local labour. The philanthropic trusts, including Peabody and Samuel Lewis as well as William Sutton largely supplied the necessary 'model' accommodation. Unlike the others, however, the William Sutton Trust did not get land cheaply from large landowners.[41] The Trust's very large Cale Street estate had rent levels very similar to those in the Trust's estates in the cheaper parts of London, albeit for flats that were relatively small. None was bigger than three rooms, and two-thirds were one and two rooms.[42] In Chelsea, therefore, small households stood to gain from a Sutton tenancy, not only because rents were relatively cheap, but because the supply of small units in the private sector was being eliminated and not replaced. As we have seen, many of the beneficiaries in Sutton flats were women in service jobs on low incomes. The losers were Chelsea Borough Council whose tenants left to take up tenancies in the Sutton flats.[43]

Outside London, where cheap suburban sites offered an apparently ready solution to housing shortages, the rent question nevertheless remained difficult and contentious. Negotiations surrounding the development of the Trust's estate in a rapidly expanding working class area of east Birmingham highlight the unexpected difficulties encountered in such areas. The problem was to keep rents of working class property within the ability of tenants to pay, even in low cost areas. The Court approved the Trust's purchase of the site in May 1912.[44] In the years leading up to the outbreak of war in 1914, the Trustees saw a rising need for their proposed houses as the private sector moved up market and regulation of house building by local and central government increased. The city of Birmingham was a pioneer of town planning and an advocate of remedying housing deficiencies through building by voluntary agencies like the William Sutton Trust. Suburbanisation on 'model' lines was seen as the way forward, if necessary through land purchase in suitable areas by the Council and development by 'public utility societies and builders'.[45] In 1910, the City Council had applied to the Local Government Board for permission to prepare a town planning scheme for some

1,400 acres in the Saltley area of Birmingham. The proposed scheme included the site for which the William Sutton Trust was then negotiating. The area was without doubt 'ripe for development'. Early in 1913 the Town Clerk pleaded for a speedy response from the Board since 'Considerable developments have recently taken place in the area by the erection of works and the demand for houses is much greater than the supply'. Delay in approving the plan, he warned, was likely to have 'very serious consequences in East Birmingham, as all building development is at a standstill...and large bodies of workmen will shortly be drafted into the neighbourhood in connection with extension of works etc. on the east side of the City'.[46] The town planning scheme was finally approved in August 1913.

Squaring the circle of poverty and housing on a provincial suburban site subject to town planning regulations was far from easy for the William Sutton Trust. While site acquisition costs were low at £400 per acre, returns were squeezed by planning controls on the number and type of dwelling that could be built. Block dwellings were out of the question and the City Council was limiting develoment to an average of 10 houses per acre. Local builders contended that prevailing bylaws allowed 56 per gross acre.[47] The private sector responded by suspending building except for 'men who could pay 10–12/- [50–60p] a week'. In Ward End, public meetings were held to protest against this 'fanatical exclusion' of workers from Birmingham's new suburbs. A petition was raised to lift density restrictions in the East Birmingham scheme to make possible the erection of artisans' houses 'at rents they can afford to pay – 6/6 to 6/9 [33–34p] for 4 rooms and a bathroom'.[48] 'The attempt to make the Saltley district the preserve of men who could pay 10/- to 12/- a week' protesters said, was 'an invasion of the rights of Englishmen'.[49]

Neville Chamberlain, Birmingham's first Town Planning Committee Chairman, acknowledged that 'conditions in East Birmingham' presented difficulties. Planning standards had previously applied only to more 'select' areas of the city; Chamberlain agreed to make concessions over the widths of roads to mitigate the effect of density restrictions.[50] He claimed that 'all cause for fear' about affordability by working people had been removed, and the Mayor cited an existing similar development by a public utility society, the Harborne Tenants' Estate Company, where the revised restrictions had produced houses 'at 4/- [20p] per week, including rates, with a good return on outlay'. This claim, however, was challenged in a letter to the *Birmingham Daily Post* pointing out that the Harborne estate contained only 55 houses let at this 'affordable' price, while the remaining 253 had rents at 10/6 [53p].[51]

The William Sutton Trust had clearly flown into the eye of a storm in East Birmingham and densities and rent levels were key issues in its first estate outside London. Its plans were considered by the East Birmingham Plans Subcommittee in October 1913. The planned estate included proposals for several maisonettes, which were viewed by the city leaders with some misgivings as a means of avoiding the density restrictions based on single houses. From the William Sutton Trust's point of view these 'house-upon-house' structures, which made up almost 25% of the dwellings to be provided, were a way of keeping rents low. The Town Clerk, however, countered this by reducing the density of land 'to be allocated to dwelling houses proper' thereby ensuring that 'the maximum number of dwelling houses allowed under the scheme' was not exceeded in total.[52] One and two room maisonettes did nevertheless remain in the final scheme. The Treasury Solicitor challenged the resulting rents, however, on the grounds that they were too low. By an order of the Court they had to be raised to provide the 2.5% return that had been imposed on the Trust. Mr Dickinson of the Local Government Board was persuaded that the rents were nevertheless 'low enough so as not to stop private building'.[53] The rents' issue proved academic, however, since under the Defence of the Realm Act, the entire estate was requisitioned. Vickers' munition workers occupied the dwellings 'for the duration of the War and six months after the signature of the peace at a rental of 5 per cent per annum on the capital'.[54] In many ways, the Birmingham Alum Rock estate represented a watershed for the Trust in respect of rent policy. The withdrawal of the private sector from the building of working class homes, the greater involvement of local authorities and the state's increasing regulation of working class rents and housing design were to be major features influencing Sutton rent levels both in the 1920s and the 1930s.

(II) 1920–1929

The 1920s saw the politicisation of housing and the replacement of economic considerations by political ones in fixing rents, not only in the public but also in the private sector. Immediately after the war, it was local authorities who were seen as the best providers of the promised 'homes for heroes'. Faith in the eventual revival of private investors remained, however. The government provided subsidies for private as well as public and voluntary agencies to encourage the building of small houses suitable for the working class. The 1919 Housing Act introduced central government help to local authorities at a level never again matched, provided they built the houses to designs and rents approved by the new Ministry of Health. The assumption was that a vigorous private rented sector would return, allowing the 1915 rent controls to be lifted and local authority rent increases to be phased in, to reach market levels by 1927. Meanwhile building costs remained very high, and after the economic downturn of 1921–23, real wages again increased for those in employment.

The shifting balance between local authorities and private landlords made the rent question an especially volatile one for the William Sutton Trust. Although rent controls held private rents below economic levels for the time being, public subsidies were offered to local authorities on the assumption that the supply of private rented property would eventually be restored. Initially, this expectation led the Ministry of Health to insist on high rents being set for the new council houses. In Durham, for example, rents of council houses in 1922–23 were twice as high as equivalent houses in the private sector.[55] Subsequently, persistence of private rent controls and local authority representations brought some reductions in local authority rents, but they remained relatively high.[56] In 1928, 94% of working class tenancies remained subject to rent control. Local authorities, however, responded to the less generous, fixed subsidies available after 1923 by keeping their rents high and shielding ratepayers against the payment of rent subsidies. This strategy meant continuing to select tenants who could afford to pay the high rents without assistance. The result was that 'The poorer the family, the less chance of its receiving a subsidised home'.[57] In the 1920s, the response of the William Sutton Trust was more akin to that of a private sector landlord than a local authority – it adopted a policy of retrenchment, avoiding building any new dwellings while building costs remained high and rents continued to be controlled at prewar levels. It took modest advantage of the minor relaxations of rent controls when they were allowed, especially in London where tenants were becoming better off as employment prospects improved. Variations in the cost of renting from the William Sutton Trust between 1914 and 1939 are indicated in Table 5.1.

At the start of the War, by contrast, the Trustees had been anxious not to lose the momentum of building despite 'the great loss incurred in various realisations' of investments. They applied to the Court for permission to borrow up to £140,000 on the security of Consols to carry on building at Birmingham, Rotherhithe and Newcastle.[58] In 1915, they acquired another site of 15 acres in Bristol and immediately after the war, four more sites in Islington (North London), Manchester, Leicester, and Sheffield. After the War, the Trust faced the acute dilemma of operating in a rapidly changing private market as regards costs, but without the guarantee of government subsidy and the freedom to increase rents, which was being promised to local authorities. In 1918, the Ministry for Reconstruction consulted the housing trusts about their plans for postwar building and their expectations about public subsidy. As we have previously seen, the William Sutton Trust was not at first included in these discussions, though its assets represented over two-thirds of the whole voluntary sector's resources at this point.[59] The Peabody, Samuel Lewis and Bournville Trusts rejected the idea of subsidy since 'none was expected or required' and Guinness was doubtful because of the 'undue restrictions' that the government might impose. Only Rowntree and the William Sutton Trust argued that subsidy was essential and the restrictions on building form entirely acceptable. The William Sutton Trustees used the example of their site in Gorton, Manchester to show the impact of rising costs on building and borrowing.

> The cost of materials has been progressively rising ever since 1914 and labour has been getting more expensive, more difficult to obtain and somewhat inferior when obtained owing to the calling up of the younger and better workmen. The extra cost of the work has been great ... [and] ... the latest estimate which has been put before the Trustees, viz that for cottages at Manchester, shows an increase of 75% over pre-war prices. The meaning of this is that the future work of the Trust is going to be greatly restricted because not only will the unexpended funds

in hand be reduced by this 75% but the spending value of the accumulation of Surplus Rents will be reduced in a like proportion and although the funds remaining amount to about a million sterling it is felt that unless some outstanding assistance is obtained the programme which the Trust hopes to carry out will have to be cut down.[60]

Without subsidy from public funds, the Trust's case was that rents would become 'excessive'. 'It is quite evident that higher rents will be necessary in the new buildings than have ruled in our dwellings in the past'.[61] Worked examples using Gorton as an illustration showed that post war rent for a 3-bedroom cottage would be 8/- [40p] per week, and if capital had to be borrowed, the cost would rise to 19/1 [95p] per week – a level 'more than could be paid by the ordinary working class tenant and of course very much greater than could be paid by the class the Trust is intended to benefit'.[62] In line with the view expressed by Rowntree, William Balmain advised the Ministry of Reconstruction's Committee that the William Sutton Trust recommended that Government should meet 75% of the difference between pre war costs and post war building prices for housing trusts.

After the end of the War, J. A. E. Dickinson, the Ministry of Health's representative on the Sutton Advisory Committee, advised the Trustees to officially give notice that they 'had acquired sites and were proposing to build, and apply for subsidy'. He further recommended that they should prepare plans and layouts for their sites so that 'the question of subsidy might be gone into with the Ministry'.[63] The Trustees agreed to enter this unknown territory, the outcome of which was not certain, and meanwhile they sought tenders for the Bristol site. 'The general dislocation of industry, restriction on building and other factors connected therewith' however, resulted in tenders that were 'much too high to justify the work being proceeded with'. In April 1921, the Court agreed to postponement of the work.[64] As the costs of the government's 'homes for heroes' campaign escalated, the Ministry withdrew its offer of subsidy at Bristol and Islington, and the Trustees decided not to proceed with building on any of its undeveloped sites.[65] The Trust was facing rent control on its existing estates (Bethnal Green, Rotherhithe, Old Street and Chelsea in London; Newcastle [Barrack Road] and Birmingham), together with unfavourable price movements in construction and erratic government subsidies. Poverty and housing appeared, for the time being, to be an insoluble problem for the William Sutton Trust stranded as it was between the movements of the private and public sectors.

During the 1920s, both rent controls and housing subsidies were modified. As both private landlords and local authorities regained some control over rent levels, it was local circumstances, and especially political circumstances, which began to exert influence over the cost of working class housing. The key Acts affecting the level of government subsidy were those of 1923 (the Chamberlain Act) and 1924 (the Wheatley Act), while those affecting rents in the private sector were the 1919 and 1920 Rent Acts and the 1923 Housing Act. The 1919 and 1920 Acts continued rent controls but allowed first 10% and then 40% increases on prewar rents. In 1923, a degree of decontrol was introduced, taking effect when tenants vacated properties and landlords came into possession. The William Sutton Trust took limited advantage of the lessening of controls and levied only half of the increases allowed. Sutton rents, like those of other private landlords, remained well below economic levels. In 1924, Sutton rents were on average only 25% higher than they had been in 1914. It was 'one of the definite objects' of the 1923 Housing Act 'to make a definite attempt to secure the revival of private enterprise' and legislation linked progressive rent decontrol to reductions in the amount and duration of subsidies to local authorities.[66] Government subsidies changed from open-ended support of building costs to fixed sums per house for a specified period. To encourage other agencies to provide working class houses, central government grants and loans were made available. Agencies got them indirectly, however, through the local authorities. Though originally intended to free local authorities from detailed central control, House of Commons' amendments attached conditions to these loans and grants, particularly in relation to the size of dwellings provided. The aim was to ensure that subsidy was available only for the smaller types of dwelling thought suitable for poorer tenants.[67] The 1924 (Wheatley) Act left the Chamberlain Act on the statute book, but provided more generous subsidies, although in a similar fixed form.[68] It was the 1920s therefore that saw local authorities established as major players in public housing provision. They gained considerable authority over setting their own 'norms' for rents and over other bodies who sought public subsidy to help them in the building of working class housing. Ratepayer pressure kept many local authority rents high, while rent controls kept private rents artificially low. The reaction of the William Sutton Trust was to try to negotiate subsidy via local authorities where this was possible, and to build without subsidy as costs fell or where Councils tried to impose unacceptable conditions.

In November 1923, the Court asked William Balmain to set out the Trustees' position in relation to its building schemes. The Secretary outlined the situation for the six sites awaiting development – Bristol, Islington, Manchester, Sheffield, Leicester and Leeds. In each case work had been suspended, but was now going ahead 'with a view to obtaining financial assistance under the new (1923 Housing) Act'.[69] Plans were being 'carried forward as quickly as possible' to make the houses 'qualify for financial assistance under the new conditions'. Financial support from the local authorities concerned varied from a lump sum of £75 per house in Leicester to £120 in Bristol. The total sums involved were large – 'roughly £25,000' – for Islington and £18,000 for Manchester. Public subsidy therefore contributed 15% of land and building costs in Islington and 20% in Manchester.[70] The condition was that the Trust complete the houses quickly, at a reduced size and with low rents. 'In fact', as the Manchester Guardian reported, the Trust's rents on its Manchester Gorton estate were not low. They ranged from 10/6 to 17/- [53–85p] inclusive, appreciably higher than equivalent private rentals of between 5/9 and 7/6 [29 and 38p] per week.[71]

How significant was the contribution of the new Sutton estates once rents in the private sector were no longer set at an economic level and public subsidies were supporting the Trustees' return on capital? As the William Sutton Trust's building programme accelerated from the middle of the 1920s, its rent levels became increasingly linked to local authority housing priorities. Because of the scale at which the Trust could build, it became in many localities a primary source of new 'smaller and cheaper' houses for relatively poor people who were 'most in need of improved conditions'.[72] They were not, however, in this period housing the poorest nor supplying the cheapest housing. The local situation in Leeds may be used to show how this situation developed.

Leeds experienced severe housing shortages after 1919 – the number of empty houses in the city remained below 500 until 1924 and scarcely exceeded 1,000 before 1930. Furthermore, between one third and one half of these empty houses were judged to be 'in an insanitary condition'.[73] Historically, house building had been buoyant, and the local building form of 'back-to-backs' had sustained low rents. The main political parties – Conservative and Liberal – had seen no reason for the municipality to get involved in house-building.[74] It was unprecedented therefore for the City Council to become the major supplier of new housing in Leeds as happened between 1920 and 1927. The emphasis of this building however increasingly became aimed at the upper end of the market. Leeds' housing programmes included schemes for 'rental purchase' of local authority houses and lump sum payments to reduce the price of privately built homes for owner-occupation. Council housing in Leeds was expensive – 9/- [45p] per week for one of its 4 room 'homes for heroes' (16/1 [80p] with rates). In 1929 it was reported that tenants were leaving new houses on the Council's Hollin Park Estate where rents had been set at 21/- [£1.05] a week, higher than for any other Leeds estate and 'probably a record high rent for Corporation houses anywhere in the UK'.[75] Corporation houses with lower, but still relatively high, rent levels remained in great demand, reflecting Leeds' relative prosperity and the dearth of private housing. In May 1929, the waiting list stood at 5,433 and applications were being received at the rate of 220 per week. Demand for houses and flats let at 8/- to 13/- [40p to 65p] per week was said to be 'extraordinary'.[76] The Lord Mayor of Leeds told a National Housing and Town Planning Conference that 'Many good houses have been provided in Leeds' but he went on to say 'problems for the "bottom dog" remain who cannot afford to pay economic rents'. Some attempt to get over this problem had been made by building 'cottage-flats', four to a block, and there were considerable waiting lists for these also. Demand outstripped supply tenfold with rents of 5/- [25p] (7/- [35p] including rates) for three bedrooms but the appearance of these workmen's flats was described as 'gruesome'.[77] Their rents were comparable with back-to-backs in slums which were available at 5/- including rates. Overall, however, the impact of local authority building on the housing of the poor was minimal – the majority was too expensive and the cheaper cottage flats were built in such small numbers that the vast majority of working class households were bound to remain excluded.

The William Sutton Trust acquired a site on the outskirts of Leeds in 1924. The 20 acres were at Killingbeck, located close to the TB isolation hospital and the city council's 'gruesome' York Road estate, with its cheap cottage flats. The Trust built only houses on its site at densities of between 10 and 12 to the acre: none of them was smaller than 3 rooms and all received an annual Exchequer subsidy over 40 years. In addition Leeds Corporation granted a subsidy from the rates, making a gross subsidy amounting to 2/4 [12p] per week per house averaged over 60 years.[79] On this basis, the weekly rents charged were 9/8 [48p] for a three room and 11/9 [59p] for a 4-room house (including rates). This was considerably cheaper than equivalent Leeds Corporation houses, which had rents of 16–17/- [80–85p] per week (including rates),[80] but more expensive than the cottage flats (7/- [35p] per week, inclusive) and the back-to-back (5/- [25p]). Nevertheless, in 1929, a year when there were only 929 vacant houses in the city, the Trust added a further 220. Furthermore, they were letting their superior houses at rents considered 'reasonable' for workers in the city 'on £2/15 [£2.75] per week to afford'.[81]

In Leeds and the other provincial cities where the Trust began building in the 1920s, the Trust was fulfilling a real need. In this decade, however, as the income data previously discussed has shown, they were not granting tenancies to the poorest sections of the population. Rather the Trust was accommodating those who could afford more space. Such people enjoyed relatively secure wages, especially following the economic recovery which began in 1923, but they found the supply of good quality accommodation severely limited. The private sector had failed to build at all because of rent controls and local authorities were building cautiously, protecting their ratepayers by keeping rents high and selection criteria tight. People at or close to average incomes, therefore, could afford more space, but 'they could not necessarily find it'.[82] This balance of economic and political forces was specific to the 1920s. As world depression hit and unemployment rose in the worst affected areas, the configuration of housing agencies altered dramatically. In the 1930s, in terms of rents, the relative price of a William Sutton Trust dwelling changed once more.

(III) 1930–1939

During the 1930s, private investors switched from providing housing to rent to building houses for owner occupation. Simultaneously, local authorities were redirected away from new house building and towards slum clearance. Deregulation of private rents was extended, but dwellings suitable for the working class remained controlled. It was intended that the market for new low rented housing was to be met by the public and voluntary sectors, while private landlords of existing dwellings were confined to the dwindling, decaying and oldest parts of the stock.[83] Despite the Depression, house builders benefitted from falling costs and interest rates after 1933, so that the absolute housing shortage began to diminish. The expectation was that prices and rents would fall to levels within the reach of most wage earners: only 'the real working class' in the smallest houses needed the protection of rent controls, therefore, and only the slum dweller needed subsidised council housing.[84] Though Exchequer subsidies became more generous, intervention in the slums brought local authorities up against levels of poverty that they had previously avoided. Building cheap houses purely on sanitary principles was the most commonly adopted strategy. Another, adopted by a minority of local authorities, was to subsidise tenants, through rent rebates, as well as subsidising the dwellings. In short, the 1930s posed the issue of housing and poverty in a particularly acute and controversial way – rent policy provided a major focus for debate and the William Sutton Trust was involved in testing negotiations as it sought to find its place in political and property settings as far apart as London's West End and the industrial north east.

What options did the William Sutton Trust have in setting rents after 1930 and how might this have affected the standard of living of 'the poor' for whom its dwellings had been intended? The major considerations for the Trust appear to have been its own financial position, the ability of local people to pay the rents it proposed to set, and the cost of local alternatives, whether in the (controlled) private sector or in the increasingly diverse local authority sector. In 1933, the Trustees reviewed their rent levels in the light of the changed economic and financial situation. They agreed to make general reductions in the rents of their estates outside London of between 6d and 1/3 per week [3–6p].[85] No reason is recorded for this change but one can speculate that it reflects the reduction in costs and the worsening unemployment in many districts outside London. There were no further general adjustments to rents during the 1930s, but particularly in London, the Trust's shops made a significant contribution to the income of estates where they were provided. In 1934, rents from the shops on the London estates equalled between 15 and 20 per cent of the gross residential rental.[86] This cross subsidy was one means of keeping rents low, but demand and the ability to pay were other considerations. In Stoke, for example, the Trustees decided to omit parlours from the houses they were building 'because of lack of demand'. They also reduced the size of the houses to 950 square feet for the same reason.[87] In the 1930s, however, the Trust did not routinely reduce quality or specifications in the interest of lower rents as many local authorities did.

Certainly the Trust was finding that the range of housing options and housing experiences was widening. In assessing changes in York in 1936, for example, Seebohm Rowntree had to add two more categories of housing to those he had identified in 1899 'both consisting of houses superior to any occupied by the workers' in the earlier period.[88] In the 1930s, people in middle class and skilled working class jobs found owner occupation within their reach for the first time. This was particularly true of the more prosperous regions of the Midlands and the South. The pull of owner occupation with the push of slum clearance changed the composition of the group who were renting. It also introduced an element of compulsion into the situation. Those whose slum houses were cleared had to choose between basic, sanitary local authority property whose rent was still beyond their comfortable reach or private accommodation at controlled rents, but often with poor and overcrowded facilities.[89] The problems were particularly severe in the depressed areas of the north of England where low wages and unemployment were compounded by a lack of resources on the part of local authorities which prevented them from undertaking either large-scale slum clearance and rebuilding, or rent rebate schemes. The Trust's 2.5% rule became too crude a guide when comparing housing costs and assessing what rents to set.

In relatively prosperous areas, where slum replacement housing could be let at low rents without undue strain on the rates,

William Sutton rents exceeded those of local authorities. Sutton tenancies for example, were more expensive than council housing in London, Birmingham, Manchester and Plymouth. (See Table 5.2). They were roughly the same in Bristol and Leeds but lower in the northern ports of Newcastle and Hull. In calculating the rent actually paid, the incidence of rent rebates has also to be considered. The William Sutton Trust had from the beginning assumed the right to make 'rent allowances' in appropriate cases, provided that a tenant paid some rent, however small. 'Tempering the wind to the shorn lamb' was how William Balmain described the Trust's policy on rent allowances. Local authorities, by contrast, received limited permission to allow rent reductions in 1930, though their powers were later expanded under the rent pooling provisions of the 1935 Housing Act. Some idea of the limited extent to which the William Sutton Trust used its powers is shown by the fact that allowances for 1928 totalled £174 on a rent roll of £79,575; in 1931 allowances were £250 on £119,337 and in 1936 they had risen only to £314 on £177,917. Given that rent allowances were a few shillings per week to each tenant, something of the order of between 750 and 1,500 instances of individual reductions probably occurred annually in the 1930s. However significant the Sutton Trust's allowances were to the individuals concerned, the absolute numbers are small. In the local authority sector also, the financial impact of rebates was negligible. Only 80 out of more than 1,400 local authorities were said to have operated rent rebate schemes.[90] Most of these involved a sliding scale of rents depending on income, with a stated minimum rent to be paid and a maximum rebate that a tenant could receive. Leeds, however, developed the most comprehensive rebate scheme, and a family of four with a weekly income below 27/- [£1.35] paid no rent at all.[91] The apparatus for means testing all tenants and the rent differentials that resulted provoked rent strikes and bitter electoral opposition, notably in Birmingham and Leeds. By the end of the 1930s, local authority rent rebates 'looked like a failed experiment'.[92] There might, of course, have been other less formal ways of reducing the rent burden such as allowing arrears to mount, or permitting subletting to lodgers. Evidence is hard to quantify, but the William Sutton Trust seems to have been strict on arrears though tolerant, within limits, on lodgers.[93] For the most part, however,

Table 5.2 Rents charged by certain local authorities and the William Sutton Trust three bedroom non-parlour houses (November 1936)

Authority	Rents (including rates), per week			Sutton (average weekly rent, including rates)
Birmingham[1]	8s. 9d. to	13s.	5d.	12s. 4d
Brighton	10s. 4d. to	15s.	10d.	
Bristol	7s. 6d. to	13s.	5d.	11s. 8d.
Cardiff	10s. 9d. to	12s.	8d.	
Croydon County Borough[1]	11s. 1d. to	19s.	9d	
Hull[1]	12s. 8d. to	14s.	0d.	12s. 3d.
Ipswich	8s. 7d. to	9s.	4d.	
Leeds[1] "A" scale-voluntary tenants	11s. 7d. to	12s.	6d.	9s. 3d. to 11s. 9d.
Leeds "B" scale-compulsory tenants	9s. 10d. to	10s.	9d.	
Liverpool	8s. 7d. to	14s.	0d.	
London County Council				
On cottage estates	10s. 4d. to	23s.	4d.	
On block dwelling estates	10s. 0d. to	14s.	10d.	15s. 10d.
Manchester[1] "B" scale	11s. 4d. to	13s.	5d.	
Manchester "C" scale	10s. 3d. to	11s.	8d.	
Manchester "D" scale	11s. 1d. to	11s.	11d.	13s. 4d.
Newcastle-upon-Tyne				
Unassisted schemes	12s. 8d. to	13s.	0d.	
Assisted schemes	7s. 5d. to	14s.	7d.	11s. 10d.
Norwich[1]		8s.	10d.	
Nottingham[1]		9s.	10d.	
Plymouth		12s.	5d.	13s. 0d.
Reading[1]	7s. 2d. to	12s.	7d.	

[1]Some authorities, including those in the above table marked[1], have adopted a rent rebate scheme, under which Government subsidies are spread among the tenants according to their needs and family income, and a reduction in the rent is made accordingly.

Source: B.S. Rowntree, *The Human Needs of Labour*, (1937) p. 93

allowances to offset the rents set on William Sutton estates were of little significance.

South Shields in County Durham and St. Quintin Park in North Kensington, London were two contrasting settings for Sutton Trust estates in the 1930s. Poverty was common to both, and local authority housing had proved too expensive for many local people.[94] Neither the LCC nor South Shields operated a rent rebate system. Overcrowding was an overriding problem, and the provision of cheap dwellings was the compelling need. With the more favourable financial situation of the 1930s, some Durham local authorities were able to begin to build at rents which low income families could afford, but in London council housing continued to be the preserve of 'small clerks and tradesmen, artisans and better off semiskilled workers'.[95] In South Shields, the William Sutton Trust built an estate of mostly three and four roomed cottages with rents of 11/- [55p] per week inclusive. An equivalent local council house built under the Greenwood Act cost around 7/- [35p], so here the rent differential was steep. In North Kensington, the Trust eventually built over 600 flats on its nine acre St. Quintin Park site following years of negotiation with the LCC, Kensington Borough Council and the plethora of local philanthropic societies.[96] This congested, high density and minimum standard estate offered large numbers of tenants accommodation that was amongst the Trust's most expensive and least attractive. A four roomed flat here cost 16/1 [80p], while the equivalent LCC rent was 13/- [65p]. Despite the widely divergent rents on Sutton's St. Quintin Park estate and in South Shields, in both places families were spending an average 20% of their income on housing. These divergent examples illustrate that in the 1930s, the rents of the William Sutton Trust varied considerably despite its own national financial base, depending on local circumstances.

THE VARIABLE IMPACT OF RENTS

Clearly, the simple question – were the rents of William Sutton dwellings low during the period 1909–1939? – raises complex issues that cannot easily be answered. Some tenants were helped significantly: one who moved to the Chelsea estate in the late

1930s saw her rent halved, and in Bradford, tenants were happy to find Sutton facilities better and cheaper than they were accustomed to.[97]

> The place we left, my father owned the house and we were paying 6/- [30p] a week for gas, no bath, old stone sink – we came here into a flat, bath, hot water, electric 3/9 [19p] a week.

Chelsea was the cheapest of Sutton's London estates and Bradford the cheapest of the provincial estates so these examples cannot be regarded as typical. The impact of the Trust's rents varied with time and locality, and affected particular types of tenants in different ways. One may attempt to summarise by saying that before the First World War, Sutton rents were marginally below the market. In the 1920s, prices and government regulations pushed rents for new property higher but held those for existing property down. During the 1930s, as political considerations strengthened, the rental situation became complex and subject to local issues. As the William Sutton Trust began to build in widely scattered places after 1930, its rental structure became very complex. Comparisons made earlier in this chapter suggest that in prosperous regions Sutton rents were higher generally than equivalent local authority rents while in poorer, depressed areas they were lower. This situation resulted above all from the relative ability of local authorities to take advantage of more favourable subsidies and building prices, and to use their rateable income to support rents. One section of the population that the William Sutton Trust served consistently well in the period before 1939 was the elderly – they needed small cheap accommodation of the kind that neither the private nor the public sector readily supplied.[98] As a result they often found themselves over occupying accommodation and suffering the associated high rents, or drifting downwards into poorer, highly inappropriate accommodation.[99] The William Sutton's contribution in providing one room and bedsitter accommodation, not least in London, was considerable. This is underlined by recent research which has shown that in the capital 'the elderly were more vulnerable to poverty than children were'.[100] Finally, perhaps, it needs to be said that loyalty and appreciation of the value of a Sutton tenancy were conditional –

they could be dissolved by changing circumstances. In 1932, the Trustees' Minutes record that an Islington tenant 'who obtained £1,200 from the Irish Sweep ticket gave notice and wanted to leave without paying the week's rent – 11/- [55p]'.[101] It is to the broader issue of how far the William Sutton Trust provided for the non monetary needs and aspirations of its tenants that we must now turn.

CHAPTER 6

Resources and Capabilities – Living on William Sutton Trust Estates 1909–1939

This chapter is concerned primarily with the value of a Sutton tenancy rather than with its price. Leaving rent levels aside, was Sutton Trust housing superior to other housing being provided for 'the poor' in this pre 1939 period? How far did it meet the needs and wants of tenants? The first question invites aesthetic and technical judgements about the design and layout of the Trust's accommodation. The second shifts the focus to the expressed preferences of tenants and to the improved 'functionings and capabilities' that tenants might draw upon while living on a Sutton estate. Given the nature of the debates and of the evidence, any assessment of this kind inevitably has to deal with contradictory opinions and changing views.

APPEARANCES

It does, however, seem clear that the Trust's earliest estates in London – Bethnal Green, City Road, Chelsea, and Rotherhithe – were designed as grand and impressive places. (See Plates 2–6). The London estates were composed of three and five storey blocks of flats, but unlike Peabody, Guinness and Samuel Lewis, they were far from bleak or barrack-like. Bethnal Green was designed by Joseph and Smithem, a leading firm of architects which had previously designed schemes for the Four Per Cent Industrial Dwellings Company and for the Guinness Trust.[1] The other three were designed by E. C. P. Monson (son-in-law of Charles Sutton). The materials used were superior, and included high quality brick, dressed stone and ornamental terracotta. Facades were ornate and decorative. Construction was meticulous, and one employee remembered that 'the pointing throughout the (Chelsea) estate was said to be so perfect that people used to come specially to see it'.[2] Rustication, stone wreaths and swags, Corinthian colonnades, porticos, mansard roofs and dormer windows all added to the liveliness of the architecture. Windows were consistently generous in size: the Rotherhithe estate had bay windows to both living rooms and bedrooms and its stairs were lit with wide arched casements. Every opportunity was taken to give architectural significance to practical features such as chimneys, doors and gates. Externally, these early London estates shared many features with the contemporary 'Queen Anne' style – not the 'highest order of architectural art', perhaps, but fresh, cheerful and attractively diverse.[3] In presenting a remarkably different 'face' to their neighbourhoods, these London estates avoided the uncharitable look of 'grim piles of brick' and the gaunt cliff walls that characterised their philanthropic housing contemporaries.[4] Individual blocks were arranged at right angles to the adjoining streets and appeared rather like wings on a country house. This had the effect of reducing the apparent bulk of the buildings while providing scope for a variety of striking architectural devices. The gable-end walls were used in several decorative ways including inscriptions telling of the generosity of the founder, William Sutton. The centre of the estates had further architectural features of lawns, monuments, trees and shrubs fenced against the attention of children.[5] Nevertheless, the effect was of a humane and positive environment rather than a rigid and depressing one.

The Trust built only two estates outside London before 1918 and they represented a stark contrast both to each other and to the four London estates. The Newcastle estate involved clearing a barrack ground with its dilapidated and insanitary dwellings and replacing them with the kind of featureless three storey flats that had been so completely rejected in London. (See Plate 8). They were designed by Charles Errington, a leading Newcastle architect, but his concept was distinctly utilitarian.[6] He quickly rejected grass in favour of tarmac.[7] Given the levels of poverty reported by the Newcastle Medical Officer of Health and also the degree of opposition to anything that might undermine private landlords in the city, it is perhaps not surprising that such an unremarkable scheme was produced at Barrack Road.[8] To display the kind of architectural playfulness of the London schemes would have been distinctly inappropriate. As one of the most persuasive advocates of housing reform in Newcastle argued.

> He was sure none of us wanted to see slums. We did not want to build castles; we did not want to build great houses; but we wanted to build comfortable homes; ... Without saying anything further, he hoped they would take this matter seriously to heart, and answer the prayer of the petitioners – the prayer that better homes might be built for the people.[9]

Tenants were similarly low key in their assessment, commending the Trust's Barrack Road flats as 'good, quiet places to live in' and 'clean, vermin free and well-built'.[10]

In Birmingham, local expectations were different. Newcastle's opponents of greater housing provision for working people had to be soothed with the thought that 'the housing problem did not begin or end with garden city development'. Birmingham City Council, by contrast, actively promoted model housing schemes as an essential part of the solution.[11] The Trust's Alum Rock estate was included in Birmingham's second town planning scheme – the East Birmingham Town Planning Scheme. The estate layout was spacious, with generous front and rear gardens, plentiful allotments and roads lined with trees. (See Plate 7). Building materials varied, with both brick and render being used decoratively. Roof lines were steeply picturesque and the windows were cottage casements. Even the warm red of the roof tiles offered a colourful contrast to the uniform slate of the surrounding Saltley bylaw streets. The estate's layout, however, remained fairly conventional in structure – the houses were primarily arranged along long straight streets with minimal curves. There were no cul-de-sacs nor artistic treatments of corners to maximise street vistas and enclosures. These and other design features subsequently endorsed by the famous Tudor Walters Report of 1918 were absent from the Trust's Birmingham Scheme.[12]

Except for Newcastle, Barrack Road, the William Sutton Trust estates designed before 1918 were aesthetically sophisticated. Though not in the forefront of architectural innovation, they introduced new dimensions to housing for 'the poor'. They unmistakably gave tenants experience of some of the most popular architectural styles of the day. Their dwellings had features similar to those being incorporated into civic buildings, fashionable apartment blocks, and middle class suburbs. In Newcastle, philanthropic housing continued to wear its previous drab look, but in 1918 the Trustees could claim that for the most part they were

> not only providing first class dwellings for the poor but are also doing work of an educational character and are undoubtedly raising the standard of housing in every neighbourhood they touch.

They stressed that the Trust was entirely in tune with the 'present progressive ideas as to housing' displayed by the Local Government Board and the Tudor Walters Committee.[13]

At the end of World War One, the William Sutton Trust was lining itself up with progressive and enlightened housing designers. It could legitimately claim to have more in common with the London County Council and Birmingham City Council than with other housing trusts or conservative city councils like Newcastle. Aesthetically, the appearance of its estates and dwellings added pleasure to the urban scene and greatly improved the environment of the residents. In the interwar period, by contrast, the Trust's contribution was less striking. Only two of the seventeen locations where it built were in London. The vast majority were suburban cottage estates located in provincial towns as far apart as Plymouth and Manchester, Bristol and South Shields. In design, they were conventional, unspectacular, even dull. (See Plate 19.) The architectural freedom of the pre1919 period had been replaced by cost cutting, standardisation and constraints associated with local authority regulations and Government subsidy rules.[14] Increasingly, local town planning schemes affected estate layouts. In Leeds, the Trust's Selby Road estate was reduced from 12 to a mere 10 houses per acre, a 'compromise' it seems in view of the limit of 8 houses to the acre set out in the Borough Engineer's existing town plan for the area.[15] The limitations meant that the number of cottages provided had to be reduced from 297 to 265 – a ten per cent reduction that the Trustees reluctantly accepted.[16]

Town planning regulations, however, meant that estate surroundings were spacious. Even the dwellings were still often superior in style to many built alongside them, whether for owner occupation or local authority tenants. A *Manchester Guardian* reporter described the setting of the Trust's Gorton estate where 'one can see on a fair day the whale-backs of the Pennines rising out of the plain'. The houses themselves were 'simple and pleasant' in appearance, arranged in short blocks or as semi-detached pairs and 'better than usual in houses of this class'. They had 'rustic' rough brick exteriors, and generous sized windows, some with bays. For decoration, 'a course of vertical bricks divides the ground from the first floor'.[17] The Trust's Middlesborough estate incorporated the more expensive red tiled roofs for the houses, and also the kind of vistas, varied building lines, crescents and cul-de-sacs advocated by Raymond Unwin but notably absent from the earlier scheme in Birmingham.[18] These design features are all the more surprising since the Middlesborough estate was one of the last undertaken before the outbreak of War in 1939 and the architect was Charles Errington, designer of the Barrack blocks in Newcastle.

Evidence suggests that Sutton tenants were themselves well pleased by the appearance of their estates. The style certainly struck the daughter of the first superintendent on the Dick Lane estate in Bradford who had been transferred there in 1934 from one of the London estates.

> It was very wide, very well laid out. Everybody had a garden and there was all this grass at the front. It was really spacious, wide roads with grass verges and trees.[19]

Bradford tenants themselves thought their estate was like 'a new world'.

> I remember having lots of playmates and a garden, and a door at the front and a door at the back which was something we'd never had.[20]

This regard for 'openness, the trees and parks' was an important part of housing satisfaction in the interwar period, according to a contemporary survey carried out by the newly formed *Mass Observation*. Disliked were ' "ugly", built-up districts containing drab, monotonous streets'. Indeed, the Mass Observation report

stressed, 'Aesthetic factors emerge in this survey as more important than has often been supposed'.[21] The Trust's low density
cottage estates of the 1920s and 1930s, while not in the first rank
for the design of individual houses or for layout, nevertheless
could convey a 'village like' appearance that met important
contemporary housing desires and preferences.

On the interwar flatted estates in Islington and North
Kensington in London, and in Salford and Newcastle in the
provinces, the local architects used by the Trust seldom attempted
design initiatives. The LCC was the point of reference for the
Trust, even when the estate being designed was in a distant conur-
bation.[22] In Islington, the Trust did pursue important technical
innovations – steel frame construction, flat roofs and a central
boiler delivering hot water to every flat. (See Plate 10) The estate,
however, proved problematic and unpopular with constant trouble
from smoke, fumes and infestation in the ducting.[23] The infill
block of flats on the Manchester Gorton estate in turn made some
small gestures towards modernism with its curved balconies and
metal framed windows. Despite these attempts, the Trust could
not claim to be meeting the challenge

> to mould these standardised units into good architectural
> groups, well gardened and well planted and to avoid the barren
> barrack like appearance of earlier tenement buildings[24]

While most of the Trust's interwar designs were plain rather than
progressive, there was one estate that was decidedly retrogressive.
This was the North Kensington St. Quintin Park estate completed
in two stages between 1930 and 1934.[25] Built on a very large site
of nine acres, this was the Trust's last London estate and it seems
to have been a development undertaken with considerable reluctance. Both the LCC and Kensington Borough Council urged the
William Sutton Trust to play its part in developing the last empty
site in North Kensington. Yielding to their pressure to 'provide
accommodation to relieve overcrowding', the Trust seemed to step
back into the nineteenth century. It built 642 dwellings at a
density approaching 70 to the acre. The unbroken lines of flats
had almost no decoration and no structural beauty. (See Plates
15–17) Rising virtually straight up from the surrounding streets,
the three, four, five and six storey blocks were gripped by tarmac,

and the yards behind sprouted only washing posts. Trustees themselves criticised the original layout prepared by the architects, Sir Henry Tanner and Son, as showing 'no imagination and might be improved' but little was actually changed.[26] Sir Henry suggested that the blocks facing the park and the main roof should have Roman tiles though the internal ones should keep their flat roofs.[27] Commentators at the time heavily criticised the estate's layout. They bracketed the William Sutton Trust with Peabody (building on an adjacent site), and compared them both very unfavourably with the approach of progressive local authorities in England and Europe, notably Vienna, the LCC and Liverpool.

> The Peabody and Sutton Trust alone are responsible for the building of 13,600 dwellings, and their joint capital amounted at the end of 1932 to well over six million pounds.
>
> It is terribly depressing to realize that the housing exhibitions, propaganda for Town Planning and good examples at home and abroad should not yet have penetrated to the people in whose power it lies to take active part in the slum clearance problem. Hardly ever do these people, either as local governing bodies or as private individuals, take advantage of the knowledge of trained town planners.[28]

The bad publicity relating to the St. Quintin Park estate certainly undermined the Sutton Trust's previous claims to be leaders among philanthropic agencies in architectural terms. Their desire to rank with the country's most progressive designers had certainly been compromised.

Whatever their lack of architectural quality, however, all the Trust's houses and flats provided many tenants with what they most wanted – privacy. They agreed that

> It doesn't matter what the flat looked like. I put my two hands together and said 'I've got my own front door'.[29]

To be able to opt for privacy was a very important achievement. One Barrack Road tenant quoted her mother's advice that 'When you get a flat of your own, keep your door shut, and keep yourself to yourself.'[30] The degree of privacy available in the home, the

Mass Observation survey found, was 'one of the paramount factors affecting people's feelings' about the place where they lived. '"The own front door" which can be shut, figures largely in people's ideas about the home'. Deplored above all was 'sharing a house with another family or even with one person, as many have to do'.[31] Before 1939, 'I wanted my own house' was above all a statement about not having to share. The William Sutton Trust provided this to many poor tenants who could not otherwise have achieved this goal.[32] The desire to *own* one's own house, to become an owner occupier, was growing but was not yet the norm.

AMENITIES

Although the first four decades of the twentieth century saw 'a striking improvement' in housing conditions in England generally, the situation of those at or near the Trust's wage limits remained at best dreary and very often detrimental to health.[33] As late as 1939, one prospective Sutton tenant described a series of downward moves from a back-to-back house to overcrowded lodgings with a cold tap in the scullery and a shared outside toilet. Fearing for the 'corruption' of her children, she applied for a tenancy on the Trust's Alum Rock estate. The Superintendent who visited her accommodation was sympathetic and said 'You'll have to get out of here. It's terrible with the children'.[34] She was housed after only six weeks. All the Newcastle Barrack Road tenants interviewed had come from 'Tyneside flats', where terraced units were divided horizontally into two dwellings, one at ground floor and one at first floor level. Each flat had its own front door, but there was no indoor toilet, no bath and no running water if it was an upstairs flat. Separate toilets were provided in the back yard and originally were earth closets ('netties'). There was a cold water tap in the downstairs flat but only one in the back yard for the upstairs flat. To these tenants, their Sutton flats were 'a gift from heaven' or, more prosaically, 'a big leg up'. The feeling above all was one of relief – 'As soon as I got through that gate I'd think "Thank goodness I'm home!"'[35] Compared with what they had left behind, the contrast was immense. The Bethnal Green flats, even twenty years after they had been built

Plate 1. Bethnal Green Estate from Cornwall Avenue (Joseph and Smithem, 1909)

Plate 2. Bethnal Green Estate (Aerial View). The low building adjoining the estate in the top right hand corner is a pub. It was already in existence when the site bought. There was no direct access between the two, however.

Plate 3. Birds Eye View of the Chelsea Estate: Cale Street (E.C.P. Monson, 1914)

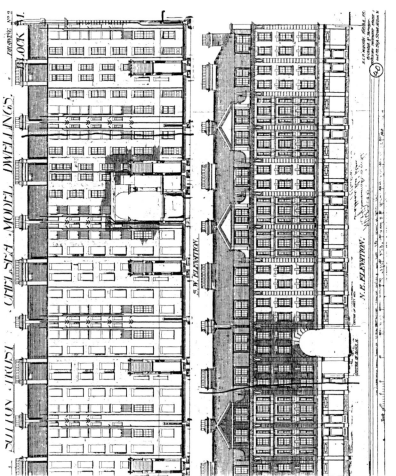

Plate 4. Chelsea Model Dwellings. Architectural details, showing shop fronts at ground floor level.

Plate 5. Birds Eye View of Rotherhithe Model Dwellings: Plough Way (E.C.P. Monson, 1916). The long low buildings to the top left are alongside the docks.

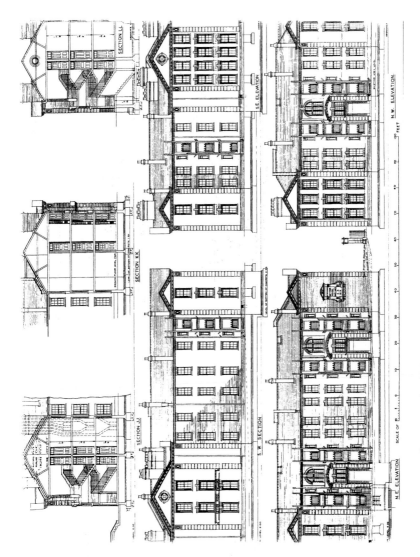

Plate 6. Rotherhithe Model Dwellings. Architectural details.

Plate 7. Birds Eye View of Birmingham Model Dwellings: Alum Rock (E.C.P. Monson, 1916)

Plate 8. Newcastle Upon Tyne, Barrack Road Estate. (Charles S. Errington, 1920)

Plate 9. The William Sutton Trust Estate Office, Manchester Estate, Gorton. (Henry Fairhurst and Son, 1929)

To us kids, they were like little palaces ... when you think, seventy years ago, how many people had tiled kitchens and tiled toilets? Even though the toilets were on the balcony, they were lovely little balconies – you could hang your washing out there, it was really nice.[36]

Tenants seem to have savoured, not only their personal good fortune, but also the envy of those struggling in alternate types of housing. As one London tenant said

This was a 'des.res.' and people would bend over backwards to get here....When we got our own place here it was like comparing a rabbit hutch to Buckingham Palace – and it was our own![37]

In Bradford, the point of comparison was the growing owner occupied sector, but even here Sutton was felt to be superior.

We were envied by other people because there was a list a mile long of people wanting to come on the Estate. We were getting all the same facilities that people that had more money and buying their own houses were getting, but as I say for 5/- [25p] a week (for a 3-bedroom house).[38]

Tenants with memories like these are inevitably drawn from those resident on estates for long (though not necessarily continuous) periods. Such tenants, as we have seen, were in a minority. In assessing how far their views are likely to have been generally shared, we have to try to establish what 'the basic needs' of housing were thought to be during this period. These 'basic needs' have to be set alongside William Sutton Trust estates to see how far they were designed to meet them and also people's more general housing requirements and preferences. Leaving aside the question of aesthetics, housing reformers like Seebohm Rowntree continued to stress the importance of internal layout and amenities as fundamental requirements in working class housing. Rowntree summarised working class housing essentials in *The Human Needs of Labour* (1937) as

a properly constructed house, with three bedrooms, a fair-sized living-room, a scullery-kitchen, and a bathroom.[39]

In the period 1909-1939, the William Sutton Trust was operating against a background of rising expectations regarding housing so that not only the design of new dwellings but also the upgrading of existing ones presented a considerable challenge. What policies did the Trust adopt for the amenities of its houses and the facilities of its estates before the Second World War?

There is no doubt that its early London estates provided better amenities than those of any other philanthropic housing trust. In particular, the William Sutton Trust provided completely self-contained flats with kitchens, fixed baths, hot water and individual toilets to each flat. The only exception was the original Bethnal Green scheme where twenty-one of the smallest flats had no fixed bath. Where baths were provided, they were not in a separate bathroom, however. They were fixed in the scullery, covered with a hinged wooden flap, which served as a work table. On the Bethnal Green and City Road estates, individual WC's were installed on balconies rather than within the flats. By contrast, Peabody, and other agencies including Guinness, the East End Dwellings Company, and the Artisans', Labourers' and General Dwellings Company all built minimal-standard blocks. Many of their flats were 'associated' rather than self-contained. In these blocks, facilities like baths, WCs and sculleries were shared between several dwellings.[40] It was only after some discussion, that the William Sutton Trustees agreed to provide individual fixed baths in the Newcastle Barrack Road flats. Furthermore, in Birmingham, although they were building houses, the Trustees also sanctioned baths in sculleries and toilets outside. As in estate layout, so in house design, the Trust's Alum Rock estate was an intriguing mix of old and new. It was a low density cottage estate, but it was undoubtedly lacking in progressive sophistication as the design of its toilets clearly shows. One tenant remembered her WC 'in the rear porch with the pantry facing'.[41] Nevertheless even before 1919, Sutton tenants were free of the continual regulation and supervision that other agencies exercised over the use of communal facilities.[42]

After 1919, as we have seen, the Trust shifted its emphasis away from high density London flats to cottage estates in the provinces. This move was accompanied by a reliance on a variety of individual architects, who might be influenced on the one hand by Ministerial subsidy rules, and on the other by local building forms and requirements. The Trust did not manage to secure any subsidy under the 1919 Housing Act, so it did not build any 'Homes for Heroes' to Tudor Walters' designs. The criteria required for subsidy under the 1923 and 1924 Acts related primarily to house size. These restrictions bore particularly on the vexed question of the provision of a second living room – the parlour. The Acts prescribed a minimum and a maximum size for subsidised houses – between 620 square feet and 950 square feet respectively for two-storey cottages and 550 to 880 square feet for flats. The provision of a second living room was difficult within these constraints, as was back access, internal circulation space, and use of good quality materials. Most important, however, was the strong imperative to produce small, non-parlour type housing. Even the Ministry's 1927 *Housing Manual*, suggested that any parlour provided need be 'little more ... than a recess opening from the living room'.[43] While separate living spaces were discouraged, separate sanitary facilities were insisted upon. To qualify for subsidy after 1924, it was not sufficient to provide a fixed bath – it had to be placed 'in a bathroom'. As we have seen, the William Sutton Trust incorporated both central government subsidy and local authority rate contributions into its developments. It was also prepared to use its own resources to provide nonstandard accommodation where this seemed in accord with its original aims.

Between 1927, when the Trust's building programme revived after the First World War, and 1939, over 6,000 dwellings were provided. They were built on estates in London, Bradford, Bristol, Hull, Leeds, Leicester, Manchester, Middlesborough, Newcastle-upon-Tyne, Plymouth, Salford, Sheffield, Stoke-on-Trent and South Shields. How far did the interior design of these dwellings reflect changing housing demands and in particular the pressure of subsidy arrangements? The Minutes of the Trustees for 1923 and 1924 show urgent activity in altering plans for Bristol, Islington, Manchester, Sheffield, Leicester and Leeds 'with a view to (Government) assistance ... Plans are again being altered to make the houses (and as many of the tenements as possible) qualify for financial assistance under the new conditions.'[44] All the dwellings, except for Islington and St. Quintin Park, had separate bathrooms. For St. Quintin Park, however, the Trustees instructed the architect 'if necessary, make some kind of partition around the bath to comply with the requirements of the Ministry.'[45] (See Plate

18.) This arrangement was criticised in a contemporary architectural review and compared unfavourably with the Kensington Housing Trust that was building blocks of flats on an adjoining site. Their tenants, it was pointed out, 'will be the only inhabitants of the Dalgarno Estate (St. Quintin Park) to possess private bathrooms, as the Sutton Trust's tenants bathe in the scullery.'[46] Generally, however, internal design was more enlightened than this. Cooking was separated from living rooms and confined to kitchens. The solid fuel ranges previously installed gave way to hot water boilers behind the fireplace and gas (or more rarely electric) cookers. (See Plate 13.) Individual rooms were designed to be more specialised and were required to fulfill fewer functions. In Stoke, however, toilets were put in bathrooms in some smaller houses 'on account of saving'.[47] Rooms were designed to have their own entrances and exits – front lobbies were provided to the stairs while bedrooms no longer opened out of living rooms, for example. Circulation space consequently took up a greater proportion of general floor area, a feature apparently more a cause for concern among architects than householders.[48]

At Gorton, the *Manchester Guardian* noted 'wider staircases and higher ceilings than usual in houses of this class.'[49] Nevertheless, the Trustees had been forced to restrict the number of parlour houses to reduce average costs. Parlour houses contained two separate living rooms, but here

> ... in view of the demand for smaller and cheaper houses, the numbers of the various types to be altered to about 20 parlour type, 80 3-bedroomed type and 78 2-bedroom type[50]

This meant that only about one in ten of the Gorton houses included a parlour. After discussions with Raymond Unwin at the Ministry of Health, floor areas for the three types were also reduced to 750, 850 and 900 square feet.[51] At Leicester, the Trustees considered the possibility of simply 'eliminating parlour-type houses for the western half of the site'[52] and a further overall reduction in the range of sizes in future schemes was agreed in the summer of 1927.

A2 Living Room and 2 bedrooms   650–720 square feet
A3 Living Room and 3 bedrooms   780–820 square feet
B3 Parlour, Living Room and 3 bedrooms   900–940 square feet[53]

The Trustees did not, however, abandon the parlour type design. In 1932, for example, designs for the Stoke estate included them. Subsidy was refused, however, and the Ministry

> advised omission of these unless the (local) authority could justify demand for them. These houses to be reduced in area to 950 square feet. Mr. Scott at the Ministry states that the prices are slightly higher than usual, but justified on the superior specification.[54]

The evidence is that the Trustees were trying to keep abreast of developments in house interiors, and to maintain standards of finish, but they had limited room for manoeuvre if they were seeking Government subsidy. In 1931, the Trust Secretary and General Manager, William Balmain, joined the Garden City and Town Planning Association at the request of the Trustees. Despite the Charity Commissioners raising 'some objection to the Trust being a member' of the Association, Trustees made visits to new housing schemes in Britain and Europe 'to see the latest thing of the kind'.[55]

The Trust's pursuit of State subsidies meant that only one in eight houses that the Trust built before 1940 included a parlour. (See Table 6.1) Rowntree was one leading housing reformer who would have approved. He saw parlours as inappropriate symbols of achievement and respectability in working class houses. Yet Mass Observation found that by 1940, people wanted kitchens big enough to be eating places, and two living rooms, one for everyday activities and 'another where visitors may be entertained and which they like to keep for best'. Indeed, demand for these requirements is reported to have been 'fairly strong, especially on Housing Estates.'[56] There is little evidence, however, that the Trust's tenants missed parlours. As one of them who was 'thrilled to bits' to move onto the Birmingham estate in 1938 put it,

> You didn't keep up with the Jones' because the Jones had got no more than we'd got[57]

COMFORT

Pride in aesthetically pleasing designs and in an estate that was 'the latest thing of the kind' certainly need to be allowed for in

The Conduct of Philanthropy

Table 6.1 The William Sutton Trust: Analysis of Schemes by Room Size, 1940

Estate	1 room		2 room		3 room		4 room		5 room		Totals		
	F	H	F	H	F	H	F	H	F	H	F	H	T
Birmingham	32	–	32	–	–	48	–	152	–	30	**64**	**230**	**294**
Bradford	28	–	30	–	–	50	17	154	12	17	**87**	**221**	**280**
Bristol	–	–	16	–	–	–	–	88	–	88	**16**	**176**	**192**
Hull	24	–	–	–	–	162	–	268	–	46	**24**	**476**	**500**
Leeds (YR)	–	–	–	–	–	96	–	74	–	50	**–**	**220**	**220**
Leeds (SR)	28	–	30	–	–	38	14	135	15	6	**87**	**179**	**266**
Leicester	–	–	–	–	–	42	–	128	–	76	**–**	**246**	**246**
Bethnal Green	24	–	66	–	73	–	12	–	–	–	**175**	**–**	**175**
City/Olds	65	–	123	–	94	–	2	–	–	–	**284**	**–**	**284**
Chelsea	115	–	331	–	227	–	1	–	–	–	**674**	**–**	**674**
Rotherhithe	24	–	91	–	78	–	1	–	–	–	**194**	**–**	**194**
Islington	–	–	30	–	144	–	24	–	1	–	**199**	**–**	**199**
Kensington	39	–	130	–	321	–	139	–	–	–	**629**	**–**	**629**
Manchester	6	–	18	–	36	102	12	164	–	74	**72**	**340**	**412**
Middlesborough	–	–	40	–	4	109	–	179	–	33	**44**	**321**	**365**
Newcastle BR	18	–	80	–	52	–	27	–	–	–	**177**	**–**	**177**
Newcastle BE	30	–	58	–	125	–	56	–	7	–	**276**	**–**	**276**
Plymouth	–	–	15	–	30	50	15	200	–	27	**60**	**277**	**337**
Salford	59	–	56	–	332	–	96	–	22	–	**565**	**–**	**565**
Sheffield	–	–	–	–	120	–	180	–	36	–	**336**	**–**	**336**
South Shields	–	–	48	–	4	157	–	240	–	7	**52**	**404**	**456**
Stoke Trent Vale	–	–	–	–	108	–	172	–	30	–	**310**	**–**	**310**
Stoke Abbey	24	–	–	–	164	12	188	–	13		**36**	**365**	**401**
Total	**516**	**–**	**1194**	**–**	**1520**	**1246**	**428**	**2322**	**57**	**533**	**3715**	**4101**	**7816**

Key: F Flats
H Houses
T Total

assessing the value that tenants ascribed to their Sutton dwellings in the decades before the Second World War. More fundamental, however, is the question of the level of comfort they enjoyed. Above all, this is a matter of the impact of such a tenancy on people's total resources. The study of local authority housing in Stockton – on – Tees in the late 1920s and early 1930s has already been cited. It showed that living on a model estate could undermine tenants' quality of life very severely. The mean death rates of tenants rehoused on the new local authority estate was almost

50% higher than that of tenants who remained in slum housing.[58] High rents leading to malnourishment were the primary factors in this situation. The other costs of a new tenancy, however, such as furnishing, heating, travel and shopping also played their part. Given the very low incomes of Sutton tenants, such considerations were crucial. An early Birmingham tenant recalled that her mother, with four children, 'was given a 3-bedroom house, but was too poor to furnish all the rooms'.[59] Seebohm Rowntree recognised the problems and emphasised that in calculating his poverty line he had assumed that the 'home has been got together'.

> It does not allow for capital expenditure for the provision of furniture, bedding, etc., but only for the necessary repairs and replacements. In the case of the lowest-paid workers, however – and it is with those that we are primarily concerned – it is usual to begin housekeeping with a very meagre equipment, and to add to it gradually during the earlier years of marriage, before all the children are born. Thus a portion, at any rate, of the sum which might have been saved against the period of special stress will, quite rightly, be absorbed in the furnishing of the house.[60]

Given that so many of the Sutton tenants were low paid or unemployed and were going through periods of 'special stress' in their lives, such as family building or old age, the problems of making and maintaining a new home were severe.

The Trustees seem to have been conscious of tenants' difficulties in these respects from the beginning. The pre1919 London flats and the Birmingham estate were all fitted with 'green venetian blinds'. Financial problems after the War, however, meant that these had to be 'struck out' from the schemes in Newcastle and Manchester.[61] From time to time, the Trustees discussed the question of 'supplying furniture to certain poor tenants' but they always agreed that 'nothing further could be done'.[62] From the earliest scheme in Bethnal Green, however, some built-in furniture such as 'a capacious dress cupboard' in the bedroom was included.[63] They installed built-in wooden dressers, ventilated larders, draining boards and plate racks in most of the kitchens. (See Plate 14). Such facilities provided what 'many a housewife asks for' according to the Mass Observation survey.[64] The problem of drying washing in flats was also considered: some estates relied on posts or pulleys with lines between them but others including Chelsea and Islington had heated drying rooms with cabinets for individual flats. (See Plates 12 and 15) These facilities were of more than individual importance, however, since there were no formal restrictions on their use for doing other people's washing, if such use was discrete.[65] The fittings provided on Sutton estates, therefore, stopped short of 'getting a home together' in every essential, but in major ways provided resources that were both directly and indirectly beneficial.

A warm, dry house with convenient and reliable means of cooking, heating and lighting was then, as now, a highly desirable resource. In the period up to 1939, the Trust regularly reviewed the provision it was making in these respects. It tried to balance installation costs against running costs, to allow for changing tenant expectations and to deal with pressure from gas and electricity suppliers. Over the four decades, coal gave way to gas for cooking, and electricity was installed, though usually for lighting only. For the most part the Trust moved in line with contemporary preferences, and many of its initiatives matched the findings of the Mass Observation survey. The Trustees' remained concerned, however, to exercise some discipline over tenants' total spending and to ensure that their ability to pay the rent was not impaired by additional energy costs.

Cooking and heating were initially combined in the cast iron range located between the scullery and the living room and fuelled by coal. (See Plate 11). Managing one of these, it has been said, 'required a number of skills of no mean order',

> estimating future needs (for coal), budgeting for these, assessing the quality of different types of coal, laying, lighting and tending the fire in different weather conditions, regular cleaning – much of it in the form of vigorous black leading – and getting to know all the various shutters, dampers and idiosyncrasies of any particular appliance.[66]

Indeed, since originally the only cooking appliance in the Sutton flats was the coal range, the day could not properly begin for tenants until the hearth had been cleaned out, laid and lit.

Furthermore, having the chimney swept (for if this was neglected, it might catch fire) was a major domestic event which was estimated to take over nine hours of the housewife's labour.[67] Several of the Trust's practices, however, brought positive relief. Most obvious was the supply of coal at cost to the London estates. The Trust bought coal wholesale and stored it in specially constructed cellars beneath the blocks of flats. Porters delivered it to coal bins in the individual flats. Tenants were thus ensured a cheap and reliable supply of coal right to their doors. This was not only a considerable convenience, but at times it meant Sutton tenants could get supplies when others could get nothing at all. In the First World War, for example, merchants ceased supplying coal to small dealers. In the severe winter of 1916–17 large parts of East London, including Bethnal Green, were said to be almost entirely without coal.[68] Sutton tenants, however, were protected because of the Trust's established position as a large-scale purchaser. Though the war-time crisis passed, routine deliveries to flats became generally difficult through the 1920s and 30s. and Mass Observation found 'there are complaints that tradesmen, especially the coal merchant, will not deliver to top floors unless bribed.'[69] The onerous chimney sweeping was also organised and carried out by the Trust, though a small charge was levied on each tenant.[70] The policies of the Trust for the supply and delivery of coal and the cleaning of chimneys represented a major saving of resources to its London tenants before 1939. In flats that were chiefly machines 'heated by coal ... and powered by women', resources were saved that might otherwise have been spent on securing more expensive supplies, scavenging for fuel, bribing tradesmen, or organising chimney sweeps.[71]

The comfort of the coal-fired range continued to be greatly appreciated by tenants well into the interwar period. Some saw practical advantages in heating the home, providing hot water, and cooking all from the same source. Others regarded it as symbolic of homely warmth and well-being. Mass Observation found that among the people it interviewed 'people are attached to (ranges) in a sentimental way, and like them as a means of heating a room and for boiling a kettle now and then.'[72] A tenant on the Trust's oldest estate in Bethnal Green recalled

It was so cosy ... the kettle always boiling and the coal oven used regularly. There was some kind of arrangement whereby the actual fire could be swung round from the kitchen to face into the living room. All the rubbish was burnt on the fire.[73]

The original ranges' combination of practical and spiritual significance dwindled and they became increasingly unsatisfactory as they aged. In 1928, the Trustees decided to 'bring the supply up to date (at City Road) by providing hot water to the sink, bath and scullery copper by means of a boiler in the kitchen range'.[74] In 1930, the Trustees became concerned that 'the [Bethnal Green] stoves having been in use for 20 years and there being no hot water supply' improvements should be sought.[75] The ranges at Bethnal Green and Chelsea were upgraded in the early 1930s. 'After experiment', the Trustees agreed to install new back-to-back ranges between the living room and sculleries 'as and when possible'. The cost was estimated at £19 to £20 per tenement – a figure equivalent to eight weeks' wages for tenants, based on the Trust's guideline for earnings. The new ranges were said to be very efficient in providing hot water even with a minimum of coal, and new ovens were provided in the scullery. The change was not universally popular – some tenants compared it unfavourably with the old, while others felt the 'improvements' were insufficient to meet new expectations. New ovens were said to be 'so big nobody used them.'[76] Another tenant, arriving on the Chelsea estate in 1939, found it 'very dreary – bath in the kitchen, hot water from the coal fired boiler, gas lighting and a gas cast-iron oven – very greasy'.[77] Nevertheless, from the early 1930s, no Sutton tenant had to rely solely on a range for cooking, which Mass Observation found was very unpopular. They also had access to hot water – a rare but greatly desired amenity according to Mass Observation.[78] Compared with Peabody tenants, their situation was indeed remarkable. On Peabody's Hammersmith estate of 284 flats and 36 cottages, built in 1926,

> The superintendent ... was very proud of the washing arrangements. These consist of (1) cold water laid on to each flat (2) three hot water taps for the whole population (3) a communal bath-house which each tenant may use twice a week (4) a communal laundry and drying room for the use of tenants.[79]

'I wonder', the commentator J. Fletcher, concluded, 'whether some tenants might not have preferred ... individual hot water ... (or) electric light instead of gas which is turned off at the main at 11p.m.'

The question of gas and electricity supply was a difficult one, particularly as the interests of landlord and tenant were in conflict. There is no doubt that electricity increasingly became identified with 'modern' living after 1914. In the country as a whole, wiring went on most slowly in the private rented sector and most rapidly in newly built suburban houses, both local authority and owner occupied. Invidious comparisons between 'backward' and 'progressive' sectors of the housing market only increased the desirability of electricity. After the 1926 Electrical Supply Act set up the National Grid, the Central Electricity Generating Board vigorously promoted the new source of energy. Some Labour local authorities cabled streets in working-class areas and helped the wiring of individual homes through credit schemes.[80] The William Sutton Trustees were wary of these new consumer temptations and tried initially to resist, then to moderate, them. They were fearful of their effect on their own budgets and on those of their tenants. Houses on the Birmingham estate were originally gas lit, with coal fired coppers and kitchen ranges. In 1928 tenants petitioned for electric light. The Trustees, however, 'in view of the heavy capital cost and the heavy arrears ... decided to do nothing at present.'[81] Where a local authority was involved, the decision was less clear cut. In the same year, the Trustees received a letter from Councillor A. Beavis of Shoreditch Borough Council, 'one of our tenants'. He asked the Trustees 'whether they would have any objection to the Council installing electric light in the (City Road) tenements at the Council's expense?'[82] The Trustees agreed to cooperate if the Shoreditch Electricity Department 'converted the flats free, while the Trust financed the lighting of staircases'.[83] Cost to the Trust was the overriding factor: when 75% of the Islington tenants applied for installation of electric light, the Trustees were lukewarm – 'the Trustees not inclined to go to much expense in the matter'.[84] Furthermore, in the financially difficult years of the early 1930s, the Trustees were particularly conscious of how stretched tenants' budgets were. When a private company applied for permission to install loudspeakers in flats to amplify wirelesses, the Trustees refused, noting 'it was difficult enough to collect rents at present without encouraging tenants to undertake a charge of this nature'.[85] By 1939, two in three households nationally had an electricity supply and it was difficult for the Trustees to maintain their opposition. Where gas lingered, it served to make dwellings dreary – Chelsea, one tenant said, only 'came up' when it got electricity in 1953.[86]

The estates built after 1927, whether suburban cottages or flats, usually operated on a mixture of fuels, though with only limited electricity. Most kept the coal fire in the living room, still 'very definitely preferred to any other means of heating living rooms'.[87] There was gas for cooking and electric lighting, though at St. Quintin Park lighting was by gas also.[88] At Salford it was agreed only 'after full discussion to have electric lighting, but gas for cookers and wash boilers'. The difficulty in the way of using electricity, it was noted, 'being the question of quarterly payments by tenants'.[89] Cooking by electricity was thought to be particularly unsuitable, because of the bills that could accumulate and undermine the household budgets of 'our class of tenant'.[90] Nevertheless, some of Sutton's cottage estates were 'all electric', a rarity in the 1930s but something that was vigorously promoted by the electricity industry. In Hull, the local authority recommended electric cookers on the Marfleet Lane estate. The Trustees first sought advice from the LCC, 'there being a doubt as to the suitability of such cookers' on the basis of the Council's recent experience with the Ossulston Street flats in central London.[91] Hull Corporation kept up the pressure, however, and sought 'full electrification of the estate for lighting, cooking and heating including copper (hot water also to be supplied from living room fire).'[92] After further investigation, the Trustees agreed unanimously to go ahead with the 'electricity experiment'. Other 'all-electric' estates followed, including the one at Middlesborough. Such estates must have been something of a marvel compared with the 'dreary' unimproved Chelsea and the newly built but old-fashioned St Quintin Park. The servicing of houses changed very rapidly from the late 1920s and the Trustees evidently tried to regulate such changes in the light of their perception of 'our class of tenant'. They were, though, prepared to experiment where circumstances were favourable, and to help tenants to meet costs by renting the necessary appliances.[93]

The maintenance of the dwellings themselves and of the common areas was very significant for tenants' quality of life and for the reputation of the estate locally. These factors bore directly on the resource that a Sutton tenancy came to represent. In these respects, the estates do seem to have been 'model'. One tenant remarked that in the 1920s, her estate was 'the "Pride of Bethnal Green" ... people used to come to see it, it was so well kept'.[94] The quality of the day-to-day care depended on resident estate superintendents and their porters. From the lighting of gas lamps to yard and drain cleaning, and from cleaning windows to mending washers, their activities were highly visible. One tenant of the Barrack Road flats in Newcastle recalled that in the 1930s 'You got everything done'.[95] The Superintendents also regulated behaviour likely to cause standards to slip – washing had to be removed before 10.30 am; children had to be indoors by 7.00pm; lights around the flats were turned off at 11.00pm and 'You wouldn't dare chalk on the walls' or climb over the fences.[96] Staff were 'very, very strict' – 'He'd just point his stick at us and we'd freeze'. Longstanding tenants at least, judged this to have been 'a good thing'.[97] While much of their influence was informal, 'like parents', one Chelsea resident recalled that the porters were known as 'the guards'.[98] It is important to note, however, that the resident staff were in fact front line representatives of law and order, since the police were excluded from Sutton estates. Tenants themselves spoke of this situation which was officially confirmed after incidents in London and the provinces. The Trustees were advised that police 'were excluded by service regulations from patrolling private property but would continue to give assistance to prevent disorder when called upon'.[99] Without any police presence, the disciplinary part of the superintendents' duties is more understandable. They also explain, in part, the Trust's preference for ex-military men as superintendents and its dismissal of staff for 'lack of control' over their estates, however satisfactory they were in other respects.[100] In the words of one tenant, 'The Superintendent was God'.[101]

Nowhere, perhaps, was the authority of the superintendent seen more clearly than in the round of annual inspections. Each dwelling was visited and tenants graded according to cleanliness and care of their property. One tenant described these occasions as 'as strict as any army kit inspection'. 'When the list went up', reported another, 'that number 16 to 32 was going to be inspected everyone was out washing, scrubbing and painting'. On the day, '[The Superintendent] he'd come in and sit down ... and his eyes were all over – if you had dirty net curtains he'd say "take those curtains down and have them washed"'. The inspections must have had a powerful cumulative effect, since though they affected individuals only once a year, they were going on almost continuously. As one tenant remarked, they were ' a constant feature ... every day except when he was taking the rent'.[102] Over time, some accommodation between superintendent and tenant might be reached – 'They didn't bother every body ... they knew who was likely to cause problems'.[103] Either way, the effect was the same – to ensure compliance with expected standards of cleanliness and care inside Sutton dwellings. Apart from the annual inspections, tenants were aware that Superintendents 'had a key to every flat'.[104] The intrusion on personal space had positive as well as negative consequences. For transfers, finding tenancies for other family members, and job opportunities, 'knowing and being known' by staff could have distinct advantages.[105]

While maintenance at grass roots or tarmac level was a matter of daily concern, planned maintenance and repair were conspicuously absent. Minor defects were often noted on estate visits by Trustees and the Secretary, but these were usually superficial rather than structural. In 1919, for example, the Trustees visited the estates at Rotherhithe, Bethnal Green, Chelsea and City Road. They reported that they 'looked over the places generally', finding that things were doing 'fairly well'. They were concerned, however, with untidiness especially of yards at Bethnal Green and gardens at Chelsea. They gave instructions that yards must be swept every day, 'all chalk marks to be obliterated, and the glazed bricks round entrances to be washed down, women to be employed for this purpose'. In addition, 'instructions were given for the gardens to be dug up more frequently to give the shrubs a chance'.[106] Very little was spent on the fabric of the dwellings. In 1914, it was agreed that external painting should be carried out to City Road, but this was delayed by the outbreak of War and completed only in 1920. Bethnal Green was painted in the same year and James Collin, one of the Trustees, agreed to inspect its progress. It was only after the Trust finally achieved an independent scheme of management in 1927 that a sinking fund and reserve fund for repairs were set up. Apart from structural repairs to the Birmingham estate in the late 1920s costing £18,000, repairs generally continued at a low level. In 1930, the water pipes at City Road were reported as in a dangerous state because of corrosion from condensation. Previous remedial measures had been superficial and restricted to painting. Similarly at St. Quintin Park, painting was recommended 'as it might do some good' in remedying reported condensation in the sculleries.[107]

FUNCTIONINGS AND CAPABILITIES

Besides the facilities offered within the Trust's flats and houses, there were amenities on the estates that could bear quite directly on tenants' personal resources. On the flatted estates, sheds were provided at a small weekly rent.[108] (See Table 6.2) Some were intended for prams and cycles, but others were termed 'barrow sheds'. This provision for the tools of the costermongers' trade reflects the kind of employment pursued by Sutton tenants in places like Bethnal Green and Chelsea. It also suggests that the Trustees were prepared to be flexible in meeting the needs of their tenants. In early LCC and Peabody estates, by contrast, costermongers and their untidy trade were regarded as unsuitable tenants in newly built blocks. Housing reformers like Seebohm Rowntree thought such sheds 'a serious blot ... they look like privies', but Sutton tenants found them 'very handy'.[109] Mass Observation commented that 'sheds for prams and bikes are only rarely provided and are very much missed'.[110] In Hull, the Trustees went further and provided a workshop 'with a w.c. for men'.[111]

On Sutton's provincial cottage estates, gardens and allotments were available which offered the possibility of recreation, but they were primarily 'a valuable addition to the family food supply'.[112] The working class, generally, were said to take a 'utilitarian approach' to their gardens. Indeed, one Birmingham tenant described her father keeping chickens, a billy goat and pigeons in his garden, and every tenant also had an allotment.[113] More whimsically, another described annual estate garden shows, where the emphasis was on more decorative aspects and that added to the 'village atmosphere'.[114] In supplying most of its new tenants

Table 6.2   Sheds

The following table shows the number of perambulator or barrow sheds provided on the Block Dwellings Estates named

Estate	Number of pram sheds	Number of barrow sheds	Estate	Number of pram sheds	Number of barrow sheds
Bethnal Green	58	–	*Brought forward*	642	61
Chelsea	126*	21	Newcastle:		
			Barrack Road	51	–
City Road	44	33$	Newcastle:		
			Benwell	92	–
Islington	88	7	Manchester	48	–
Rotherhithe	70†	–	Plymouth	30	–
St. Quintin Park	256¥	–	Salford	223	–
Carried forward	642	61	*Total*	1,086	61

---

* Chelsea – 50 sheds removed for air-raid shelters.

$ City Road – 3 sheds demolished by enemy action.

† Rotherhithe – 8 sheds removed for air-raid shelter.

¥ St Quintin Park – 27 sheds demolished by enemy action.

(1948 Sutton Dwellings Trust Annual Report).

with gardens, the Trust was meeting a 'strong desire' but they were also creating potential management problems. As Mass Observation noted, 'The most neglected gardens (58% neglected) are found where households contain one or more children under fourteen'.[115] This was precisely the group that the Trust housed on its provincial cottage estates. Sutton conditions of tenancy required gardens to be cultivated and in 1929, to maintain interest, the Trustees voted annual gardening prizes of £6 to each estate.[116] Here again, the estate superintendent's role was central – he set the standard by his maintenance of the common garden areas, organised the annual shows and arranged for mutual help among tenants when ill-health or old age made gardening difficult. When successful, such efforts could make an estate 'like living in the country' and 'a picture to live in'.[117] (See Plate 9) The gardens and allotments, therefore, had both practical, individual significance for tenants and also a collective psychological value. They helped to promote a sense of well-being and status both within and beyond the confines of the estate for tenants whose individual resources were often very small.

Concern for the resources of tenants also influenced the Trustees' attitude to shops on their estates. Shops were incorporated into the City Road, Chelsea and St. Quintin Park estates in London and the South Shields (Cleadon) and Middlesborough estates. (See Plates 4 and 17) Two shops were originally considered on the Leeds (Selby Road) estate 'for the benefit of tenants on the estate'.[118] All tenants benefitted indirectly from these commercial developments since the income from them helped to keep rents down. The estates where they were actually located had the bonus of new, purpose built shops. Furthermore, the Trustees restricted their trade to providing basic services and especially food. The five shops at St. Quintin Park, for example, were to be 'grocer, baker, confectioner, greengrocer and chemist, subject to offers received'.[119] Proposals for changes of use were carefully considered, and the Trustees consulted the St. Quintin Park butcher over the possibility of converting the greengrocer into a cooked meat shop. They wanted to make 'the best arrangements possible'.[120] The importance that the Trustees attached to accessible shopping is shown by their refusal of sites which were 'too far out for our class of tenants' especially if 'there is no good shopping centre near'.[121] The emphasis again is on practicality and convenience for tenants, but it is likely that tenants benefitted in additional ways also. They gained from the possibility of building up credit facilities with the estate shopkeepers, based on mutual confidence. They also enjoyed the enhanced status that these estate facilities brought along the neighbouring streets.

Sutton tenants' social functionings were frequently expanded by estate facilities such as social halls, sports pavilions, tennis courts and bowling greens. (See Table 6.3). What is important, however, is the manner in which these amenities were provided and run rather than their mere physical existence. The Trustees did not routinely provide facilities like meeting rooms and sports facilities, nor did they form part of the Trustees' philosophy about what made an estate suitable 'for our class of tenants'.[122] In taking this detached view the William Sutton Trust stood apart from many contemporary social reformers. There were many who feared for community life on housing estates if such facilities, staffed by

Table 6.3 Recreational Amenities

Amenities are handed over rent-free for management and maintenance by the Estate Tenants' Association or similar body. The amenities marked "x" are maintained by the Trust.

Estate	Institute	Sports pavilion	Tennis courts	Bowling greens	Groups of children's playing apparatus	(a) Playing fields or (b) Ball-games enclosure (c) Social room
					x	x
Bradford	1	1	2	1	2	–
Hull	–	1	–	–	1	1(a)
Leeds: York Road	–	1	1	1	1	–
Leeds: Selby Road	1	1	2	1	1	–
Manchester	–	–	–	–	1	–
Middlesbrough	–	–	2	–	–	1(a)
Plymouth	1	1	1	–	1	–
Rotherhithe	–	–	–	–	–	1(c)
Salford	–	–	–	–	1	1(b)
Sheffield	1	–	–	–	–	–
South Shields	1	–	1	1	1	–
Stoke: Abbey Hulton	–	1	1	1	1	–
Stoke: Grent Vale	1	–	1	–	1	–

(1948 Sutton Dwellings Tust Annual Report)

properly trained workers, were not provided from the start. The ideas of bodies like the New Estates Community Committee have recently been condemned as 'misdirected'. It is argued that their views strongly reinforced prevailing negative stereotypes of the working class and were out of touch with the kind of lives actually lived by tenants on local authority estates.[123] The evidence is that community facilities on Sutton estates were not implanted but were selfgenerated. They were created as part of a process of tenants' adaptation to life on an estate, combining self-help with collective associations and sharing networks. The role of the superintendent (and his wife) was fundamental, while the Trustees' concern was primarily financial. Such a robustly practical attitude, it could well be argued, contributed to tenants' well-being to a far greater degree than the lofty but misplaced civic ideals of contemporary charity workers in other housing associations and social work settlements. While the New Estates Community Committee undermined the very values they intended to foster, Sutton estate institutes and their organising committees meshed existing informal links with the new, more formal ones.

While the promotion of community activity on Sutton estates was undoubtedly seen as part of the superintendent's job, the responsibility 'depended on the residents themselves being involved'.[124] The Trustees agreed to provide recreational facilities that were of a type more often associated with private suburbs and included bowling greens and tennis courts. Though the Trust might bear the initial cost, the facilities were then leased to tenants. They had to pay an annual rent with agreed repayments of the principal 'until the debt was cleared'.[125] In Sheffield, the Trustees agreed to provide a meeting hall, 'subject to agreement with a representative committee of tenants, superintendent and deputy superintendent to be members of the committee. Tenants to pay £15 per annum, and to be responsible for maintenance, cleaning, heating, lighting and rates'.[126] On the Leeds Killingbeck (Park Road) estate, a piece of land for a bowling green was identified but tenant members of the organising committee did 'all (the) work necessary'.[127] In Bradford, the Trust agreed to build an institute 'If they found we were making the job financially a success after 12 to 18 months'.[128] The emphasis was clearly on financial rectitude rather than civic ideology but the social effect was nevertheless positive. On several estates, the need to secure a regular income led to the formation of a group of tenants who acted as 'roundsmen'. They collected individual weekly subscriptions of a penny to support estate activities from a 'round' comprising a street or part of a street. In Bradford, one roundsman remembers

> 'I used personally to do mine on Sunday mornings, and it wasn't a case of just knocking on the door and taking a penny and marking a card – we used to go in, and I got used to spend probably half an hour with them and get really interested with the people. I remember one old dear who'd been laid in her bed for years and years, and she used to be looking forward to when we went'.[129]

The Bradford estate tenants' association seems to have been particularly successful. The *Yorkshire Observer* called it 'the most enthusiastic and progressive body of similar organisations in the city'. As well as special celebrations like the coronation of 1937 when 'over 500 children on the estate enjoyed a party in the open air' there were regular activities.

> A tennis court and a bowling green are provided; there is a swimming club and a harmonica band; an interest is taken in the welfare of all – if people are sick hospital gifts are sent along, if sickness occurs at home appliances for the sick room may be loaned to their families – each year the association gives Christmas treats, and each year the children are taken to the seaside.[130]

Such a successful and progressive association could not be replicated on every estate. Leeds Killingbeck (Park Road) estate caused considerable initial concern when it was reported that the tenants' committee 'was apparently composed of the worst element of the estate'.[131] Things improved, however, and tenants' efforts in creating their bowling green eventually showed that the organisation had been restored 'on a proper footing'. In some cases, routine financial concerns subsumed the wider community benefits. The Benwell Association, for example, was said to be 'financially a success' but 'socially a disappointment' with members 'showing little interest apart from paying their penny a week contribution'.[132] Nevertheless, the available evidence suggests that Sutton tenant associations brought significant tangible and intangible benefits to residents. As well as access to facilities and activities, associations offered advice from the 'super' on dealing with everyday hazards like burst pipes and woodworm infestation; cheap deliveries of mineral waters and beers, gardening advice and supplies of lime, manure and 'all your garden goods'; coal; tennis racquets and balls on credit; hire of invalid chairs; use of piano; and death benefits.[133] Many tenants must have felt that their social life 'was self-contained. We didn't need to go off the estate'.[134] The organisers of the frequent events and competitions gained experience in handling large sums of money (the Stoke Trent Vale Association had assets of over £800 by 1946). They also found the management skills to shepherd hundreds of children on the annual seaside visits and to order Saturday night socials and dances to the satisfaction of all the participants. In Stoke, for example, the organising Committee felt the need for a notice 'to be placed in the Institute notifying dance patrons that permission must be had from the M.C. to sing at the microphone on dance nights'.[135] An important part of the Committee's role was indeed to establish boundaries of appropriate behaviour, and their discussions on the issues could be sophisticated. The Stoke Trent Vale Association Committee debated a proposal to set up a first aid station at the approach of war. Their view was that 'the people on the estate and the district looked upon the Sutton Committee as the leaders of social welfare ... to safeguard the people in the vicinity'. Despite this, they concluded that an ARP post and first aid station was properly 'a local government or national responsibility'. They agreed therefore to seek the collaboration of the council and the St. John's Ambulance in setting up the station.[136]

The level of activities sanctioned and promoted by the Sutton Trust Associations were closely attuned to tenants' own notions of self-help and mutual assistance. In their everyday lives, tenants have reported 'having an eye for each other'. Births and deaths were times of mutual support. People were 'buried with ham' and sharing of food – even if only bread and dripping or a large and cheaply made stew – was part of neighbourly behaviour.[137] Playing whist or sharing a pea and pie supper could just as readily occur in individual homes as in the tenants' meeting hall.[138] The emphasis was on mutual benefit and above all personal enjoyment.

Not for Sutton tenants the high-minded emphasis on citizenship, moral welfare and training espoused by community centres run by social reformers. Indeed, the Trustees specifically ruled such centres out. They only agreed to include a welfare centre in association with the St. Quintin Park estate after pressure from well-connected North Kensington welfare groups.[139] One advantage of the Sutton strategy was that its estates were integrated with their surroundings rather than set apart. Consequently, a Sutton estate was seen as a resource across space and time – local organisations rented estate facilities 'at normal retail price'; people from neighbouring areas came to be entertained; children 'played on the Sutton's'. Frequently such contacts led to applications for tenancies there.[140] Through family links and across the generations, contact with 'the Sutton's' were experienced and recounted. Familiarity with the Trust often ultimately resulted in one or a series of tenancies being taken up on individual estates. The superintendent often reinforced these links, recognising a potential applicant as 'one of "x"' and 'cherry-picking' likely tenant activists from among existing tenants and applicants.[141]

The organisation and operation of recreational facilities and tenant associations were undoubtedly distinctive and positive features of Sutton estates between the wars. The activities accorded with the commonly accepted values of the society in which Sutton tenants lived. Because of this, they reflected and strengthened the social habits of their tenants, helping them to survive and make the most of their extremely meagre resources. While expressing themselves 'in sympathy with social movements on all estates', the Sutton Trustees emphasised communal and financial rectitude above any moralistic or ideological concerns for moral welfare or civic duty.[142] The evidence is that the benefits to tenants added to their resources, and improved their personal and collective capabilities. It also gave residents 'special status' in the eyes of their neighbours that emphasised 'the big leg up' that a Sutton tenancy was held to represent.[143] As the Mass Observation survey report noted, the reputation of a neighbourhood rested on its physical characteristics – particularly shops and entertainments – and on the standing of the residents. Respondents' views of community activities were found to involve 'functional rather than "citizen" interest'.[144] This chapter has shown that in these key respects – physical character, recreational opportunities and communal life – Sutton estates accurately reflected widely shared views of a 'des. res.' and of a neighbourhood in tune with contemporary aspirations and needs. The William Sutton Estates were seemingly ignorant of, and were ignored by, bodies such as the New Estates Community Committee. The result was that the Sutton estates escaped the label of failure that was being attached to their local authority counterparts by the outbreak of the Second World War.

CHAPTER 7

New Games in Old Arenas – Poverty, Charity and Housing after 1945

In the postwar period, provision of a comprehensive welfare state and the commitment to full employment brought the role of voluntary agencies into question. Dire poverty on the scale of the prewar period was no longer encountered and wage packets came to be regarded for the most part as 'adequate'.[1] In 1948, a public opinion poll showed the virtually unanimous belief that philanthropy had nothing further to do.[2] Even when poverty was rediscovered in the 1960s, it seemed a specific phenomenon associated with personal or social 'stress' rather a widespread feature of society as a whole.[3] Periodically, there were reviews of the need for voluntary activity in this new 'never had it so good' society. William Beveridge, architect of the welfare state, remained committed to a robust role for the voluntary sector, alongside the market and the state. The Prime Minister Clement Attlee appointed the Nathan Committee to review charitable trusts in 1950. Its remit was to examine the value of this 'vital strand' of the voluntary movement 'in the social fabric of the modern state'.[4] Much debated, though not acted upon until the Charities Act of 1960, the Nathan Committee's reassessment was taken further for housing associations. The Cohen Committee, a Subcommittee of the Central Housing Advisory Committee, was set up in 1968. It considered the function and permissible influence of voluntary provision in the 'topsy turvey' housing world of the late 1960s. The most glaring anomaly in that world was the existence of a vast public housing sector that was nevertheless inaccessible to those experiencing the desperate plight of homelessness.[5] In the thirty years following the Second World War, voluntary agencies were widely condemned as patronizing, outdated, 'odious' and superfluous.[6] Even their supporters emphasised their 'frail and delicate but gracious' character in contrast to the 'robust and forceful' local authorities.[7] In the 1940s and 1950s many voluntary organisations became moribund and subservient. In the 1960s, however, the presentation of different forms of poverty and especially new types of housing need led to the formation of new societies. Changing demands also led to the reorganisation of some old established societies, with a particular emphasis on campaigning and community action. *Shelter*, born out of a homelessness campaign, led the vanguard of this reformation. It held up a critical mirror to state housing provision, while successfully pioneering fund raising and supporting a diverse range of alternate providers. The purpose of this chapter is to analyse how the William Sutton Trust responded to the changes of the early postwar decades. The concepts of game theory and especially nested game theory will be used in considering some of the Trust's fundamental strategies.

In many respects the William Sutton Trust conformed to the pattern that one might have expected in the prevailing political and social circumstances. Chapter 2 has outlined the Trust's acceptance of its 'displaced' status following the establishment of a central role for local authority housing after 1945. It accepted the need to redefine itself, and to forge a new subordinate relationship with government agencies.[8] Through the late 1940s and 1950s, the Trust favoured retrenchment onto its existing estates with small infilling schemes. Even the grand project of Crownhill was focused on the elderly, a group not then a priority on the agenda of the welfare state. In other words, a modest, supportive and complementary approach typified the Trust's initial response. The Conservative administration appeared to endorse this and in 1961 it invited the Trust to pioneer a new form of housing for the middle classes at rents that covered costs. This initiative required the diversification of the structure of the Trust, displaying again the organisation's pragmatic and flexible approach. There is no doubt that the years after 1945 were difficult ones for the voluntary sector. The Trust's initially cautious policy of retrenchment, marginal activity and positive response to government initiatives and experiments appears to be a rational one in the circumstances. What on the face of it is much more difficult to explain is the decision to buy almost the entire housing stock of the General Electric/English Electric Company in 1970 – some 1,500 tenanted dwellings spread over ten estates. Although the estates were recently built, they did not obviously meet the Trust's location criteria, nor did their tenants meet its selection criteria. Their acquisition might well have placed the Trust's charitable status – already under some scrutiny – in jeopardy. How is this move to be explained? I shall suggest that it has to be seen as an outcome of the William Sutton Trust's operating position. The Trust continued to operate at the intersection of the three arenas identified in nested game theory, namely the political, market and organisational arenas. The experience of repeated games played out in previous decades had made the William Sutton Trust very sensitive to changes in these arenas. In particular, the political arena was evidently the key. Experience had shown that developments here could ramify unfavourably into the other interconnecting arenas. In the late 1960s, the William Sutton Trust was seeking to protect its future financial and legal position in the face of renewed political debates about charitable status, housing and the poor. It will be argued that the Trust's acquisition of the General Electric/English Electric stock was an important element in this strategy.

Issues that arose in the debates of the 1960s are remarkably reminiscent of the arguments that surrounded the original challenge to William Sutton's will and to the initial operation of his trust. The categories of 'charity', 'the public interest' and 'the poor' were again contested terms. Issues coming under scrutiny were whether providing housing was in itself a valid charitable purpose, whether housing the poor constituted a public benefit, or whether it could be accepted only if 'the poor' could be appropriately defined. Before 1919, it had been the local authorities and the Local Government Board who had been seeking to affirm their position. It was they who used the case of the nascent William Sutton Trust to establish their preferred 'rules of the game'. By the 1950s and 1960s, however, the William Sutton Trust was a mature and experienced organisation. It was very sensitive to its own interests, not only in relation to the public sphere but also vis a vis other voluntary housing bodies. Nevertheless, the William Sutton Trust had to fight once more to ensure that it was not 'written out of the game', legally and financially, by proposed changes in the status of housing charities. The acquisition of the General Electric/English Electric housing stock makes sense in this context because it increased the Trust's organisational resources and added to the diversity of its estates. The Trust's expansion and diversification were deployed to counter efforts likely to restrict the charitable status of housing agencies. 'Ageing' may have neutralised some long established housing societies and trusts as circumstances changed. The William Sutton Trust, by contrast, responded by actively seeking to modify its operational setting.[9] The renewed contest over housing and charitable status will first be explored. Subsequently, the response of the William Sutton Trust, including its decision to acquire the General Electric/English Electric stock will be examined in detail.

CHANGING THE OBJECTS OF CHARITY

Threats to the status of the William Sutton Trust came from an interconnected series of political, legal and financial initiatives, intended to modernise the apparently outmoded and moribund voluntary sector. On the one hand, changes in the law were proposed to allow the objects of charities to be brought up to date where necessary. On the other, government departments like the Inland Revenue and the Ministry of Housing and Local Government sought to review the legitimacy of claims to charitable status from their particular points of view as guardians of the 'public interest'. This was a complex set of developments whose significance for the William Sutton Trust was grasped from the outset by Charles Baker, then its General Manager and Secretary. Baker had worked for the Trust since 1935. He calculated that the Trust's ability to keep a major role in housing was related to the maintenance of its independence and of its charitable status. Securing these features required not only judicious intervention in legal and political spheres, but also tactical moves to counteract potentially harmful policy initiatives by government departments. This section will deal first with the legal and political debates and then with government policy. It is important to remember that in practice these components did not operate as self-contained elements but were closely interrelated. The Courts have developed a doctrine that political activities are not charitable in law. The experience of the twentieth century has repeatedly shown, however, that when charity operates as a mechanism of welfare it has an inherently political quality.[10] This interrelation between philanthropy and politics has been clearly shown at work in the early history of the William Sutton Trust.

The rapid social changes experienced after the Second World War undermined not only many ancient trusts but also ongoing philanthropic activities. Speaking in the 1959 House of Lords debate on charitable trusts, the Bishop of Sheffield commented:

> We have seen in the span of our own lives the whole pattern of our society alter very much. So, I believe, looking to the future, that a wise and charitable man today will not only wish to give his money to this or that object for which he has great care and concern, but will also want to be sure that, in the changed situation which he cannot really foresee, when the need which he did see no longer exists, his money will be transferred by some intelligent persons to meet some other object or need fairly in line with the spirit and intention of his original gift.[11]

In the same debate, Lord Nathan himself argued that many charitable objects had been overtaken by the speed with which society had changed, and that trusts had to 'keep in step'. 'It is the business of charitable trusts to pioneer', he said, 'not to stagnate in the backwaters of social change, and the law must put nothing in their way'.[12] It was argued therefore that ways had to be found to prevent the philanthropy of individual founders from becoming outmoded, while also making trustees publicly accountable. At issue was the balance to be struck between the freedom of the philanthropist to give money for the purpose originally identified and the concern of society that charity should make the best possible contribution to its needs.[13]

This heightened public and political interest in reviewing and updating charitable purposes was disturbing to the William Sutton Trust, marked as it was by earlier conflicts around these very issues. Two particular concerns were, first, the linking of private philanthropic intent with requirements of public benefit and, second, the reexamination of the issue of poverty. Furthermore, the explicit involvement of the state in what had formally been a matter for legal determination seemed likely to challenge the status quo that had operated since the Trust's scheme of management was agreed in 1927. A debate about the desirability of modifying the *cy pres* doctrine to widen the grounds on which the objectives of an existing charity could be changed, led inevitably to a reconsideration of the principles that underlay charitable purpose itself. Lord Nathan's Committee reported in 1952. It had sought to define the circumstances in which charitable objects should be modified and the new principles that should apply if *cy pres* were overthrown. Lord Nathan regarded the consequences as fundamental and wide ranging. The social and legislative changes of the last fifty years, he said, had 'outstripped very many trusts in every county and town in the country'.[14] Furthermore, as Lord Beveridge commented, a commitment to amending charity law according to 'views of social justice or social progress' transformed it into 'an administrative and, in the last resort, a political task'.[15]

THE DOCTRINE OF *CY PRES* AND THE PUBLIC INTEREST

The doctrine of *cy pres* and the need to reform it had been at the heart of the deliberations of the Nathan Committee. Under the existing doctrine, a trust's objects could only be altered when they became 'impossible of fulfilment' and then 'only to objects as near as possible to the original'.[16] Lord Nathan argued, and the Government was said to 'broadly agree', that the original objectives of any trust should have a 'life' of only 35 years. After that, they could be changed under certain conditions. These conditions were to be either changing circumstances (including changes in the scope of public or local services) or obsolescence in the original charitable purposes. The aim was, primarily, to ensure that 'laggards' in the charitable sector could be forced to reform their trusts 'if it was called for in the public interest'. It was also intended that charitable gifts whose original purpose could no longer be pursued, could be redirected to current needs. Lord Nathan tempered his recommendations by stressing that any such changes had to have regard above all for 'the spirit of the intention of the founders'.[17]

We have seen from the legal and political reactions to the establishment of the William Sutton Trust that 'the public interest' was already an important consideration in bestowing charitable status in 1900. The term, however, had acquired a distinctly different character by the 1950s. It had become less a legal abstraction and more a social ideal or political goal. The Nathan Committee, therefore, wanted to change the nature of the body that had responsibility for reviewing the performance of charitable trusts. In place of the quasi-judicial Charity Commissioners, it proposed that there should be

> a part-time body of men and women of standing in public and charitable affairs – a body of the same kind as the Governors of the British Broadcasting Corporation – backed by an advisory body and served by a permanent staff like, for example, that of the Director-General of the BBC.[18]

This proposal proved very controversial. There were fears that the balance between public and private interest would shift too far. In particular, the Nathan Committee envisaged that local and central government would take the initiative in applying for changes in charitable purposes. Such a system, it was feared, would open the door to 'interference from central quarters'.[19] Even worse, it seemed local authorities were being authorised to intervene in matters where 'there is no place' for them. Many argued that individual charitable intent was paramount and

> testators would intensely dislike the idea that local authorities could lay their fingers on the money they had labouriously accumulated in their lifetime.[20]

Several peers defended the *cy pres* doctrine and warned of the 'inflationary tendencies of the state' if it were relaxed. They challenged the right of third parties to divert funds from the purposes for which the original donors gave them, however inappropriate.

> A great many purposes may seem to us foolish, but it is their money that the donors gave … it is not for us to say they are foolish – this is the donor's right.[21]

The Government shelved the Nathan Report and the subsequent White Paper.[22] It promised only to clarify and reenact the existing charity statutes, while maintaining the role of the Charity Commissioners. It explicitly rejected the notion of a replacement 'public service' body and opposed any increase in the influence of local and central authorities over charity trustees. The Charity Commissioners were to act as 'friends and advisors' for charity trustees and should not have 'any general policy to enforce' upon them.[23]

Throughout the 1950s, the William Sutton Trust responded by keeping an active watching brief on possible changes in charity law. The Trustees liaised with the other larger trusts – Peabody and Guinness – to approach the Nathan Committee and explore whether 'trusts of our type' should prepare evidence.[24] Neither Peabody nor Guinness, however, was planning to take any action though they agreed that the Committee's proposals could be 'detrimental to the efficient running' of the larger trusts. The Sutton Trustees then instructed Charles Baker to keep directly in touch with the Secretary of the Nathan Committee. The Secretary agreed to let Baker know 'if the Committee's enquiries began to touch upon matters of special interest to housing charities and this Trust in particular'.[25] Charles Baker also made use of Sir Edward Forber's contacts within Whitehall generally and especially the Ministry of Housing and Local Government. Forber – 'a man of much influence in high circles'[26] – had joined the Sutton Trustees in 1927 as the Ministry of Health nominee. He chaired the Board of Trustees from 1940 until 1956. Forber's advice was that the Committee's proposals, though potentially alarming, were unlikely to be acted upon because they were time-consuming and expensive to implement. He was particularly contemptuous of what he called that 'extraordinary fantasy, the new Charity Commission'.

> Apparently instead of a quasi-judicial body concerned primarily with seeing that the testator's wishes are respected and the trustees behave themselves, the Committee contemplate a new body of men and women who will be concerned with Policy. ... If this monstrosity were to come to birth I do not think that it could fail to be made up of planners, thinkers, nosey parkers, welfare faddists and what all. A dreadful prospect. ... It would be quite possible for them to say, that as local authorities can provide – (and have a duty) – all the houses necessary, the money of the Sutton Trust should be diverted to the provision of television sets for lonely spinsters, or some other vital service.[27]

Forber concluded that the Government was likely to dismiss the proposal as 'typical of much of the shoddy thinking' that marred the Nathan Report. His judgement was that Prime Minister Churchill's 'guarded statement' meant that action on the report was unlikely. He added, 'It doesn't look to me like the makings of an attractive legislative venture for any Government'.[28]

Charles Baker, therefore, on the advice of Sir Edward, merely laid a memorandum before the Trustees to inform them of the major features of the Nathan Report. He alerted members to the possibility of changes in the *cy pres* doctrine and to the

> real danger of the Charity Commissioners being brought into the picture to a much greater extent than they are at present, if only on the grounds that it is necessary to ensure that trustees are acting within the terms of their trusts.[29]

Charles Baker went on to warn of several potential difficulties in demonstrating that the William Sutton Trust was still adhering to its own original objectives. The Trust, he pointed out, had not been building dwellings in any number since the War, nor were all its tenants poor. The Rent Restrictions Acts, he said, were 'a serious discouragement to fresh building' and he acknowledged 'the impossibility of keeping the dwellings entirely occupied by "the poor"'.[30] On the proposal that local authorities should have the power to initiate changes in trusts operating in their areas, Charles Baker recommended that 'large trusts operating over the whole country should be excluded from any such new powers'. These pointers are significant for the Sutton Trust's later moves, particularly over the General Electric/English Electric estates. The General Secretary was emphasising the importance of maintaining charitable status in the new political environment. He strongly implied that the Trust's charitable status was dependent on its ability to show continuing expansion of housing across a broad geographical area and for people of limited means. Furthermore, he drew a clear distinction between very large trusts such as Sutton, administered by people with wide experience of public affairs, and most of the very small organisations where greater control by Charity Commissioners might be appropriate. The need for the William Sutton Trust to expand and to distinguish itself from the bulk of housing associations underlay many subsequent

Plate 10. Sutton Dwellings, Islington: Upper Street. (Henry Tanner, 1926)

Plate 11. A Living Room Range, City Road Estate.

Plate 12. Drying Rooms, Islington Estate (Photograph by
Jonathan Barry, 1998)

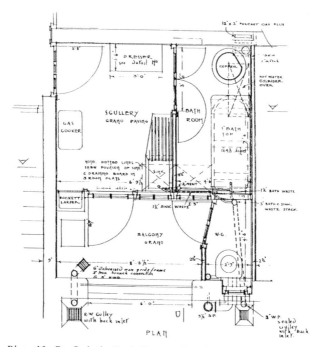

Plate 13. St. Quintin Park Estate, showing the arrangement of scullery, bath and WC.

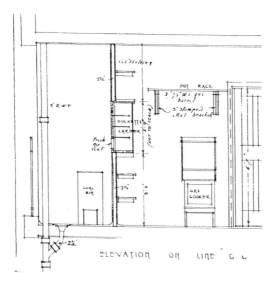

Plate 14. St. Quintin Park Estate, showing scullery and its fittings

Plate 15. Drying yards, St Quintin Park Estate.

Plate 16. The St. Quintin Park estate under construction. The area was said to be the last open site in Kensington that was available for housing. (Reproduced by permission of the Kensington Public Library)

AEROFILMS LTD. HENDON, LONDON

Plate 17. Birds Eye View of St. Quintin Park Estate, North Kensington. (Henry Tanner, 1930–1934)

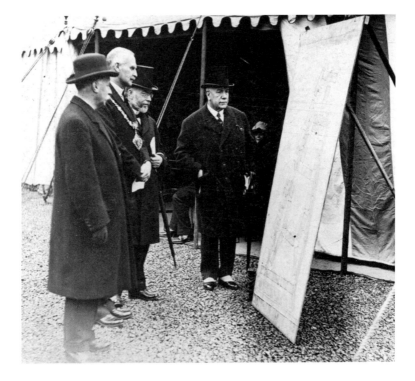

Plate 18. The Mayor of Kensington and other local figures at the opening of the St. Quintin Park Estate in 1930.

Plate 19. The Cleadon Estate, South Shields. (Charles S. Errington, 1932–35)

moves, not least the acquisition of the General Electric/English Electric estates.

POVERTY AND CHARITABLE STATUS

The debates of the 1950s produced little change in the existing structure of charitable organisations. In the 1960s, the issue of poverty reemerged in ways that threatened to renew the arguments between the sector's reformers and defenders and to give them greater potency. A particularly disruptive influence was the Inland Revenue, concerned about the generous tax exemptions enjoyed by charities. In the interest of the public purse, officials wanted to establish more stringent criteria for deciding charitable status. Politicians, on the other hand, were increasingly deploying voluntary bodies, whether charitable or non-charitable, to tackle problems that public authorities wanted dealt with but which they were unwilling to undertake themselves. From a policy perspective, therefore, the Government had much to gain by keeping rules fluid and flexible. Flexibility maximised the ability of the voluntary sector to respond to changing circumstances and helped to secure the sector's compliance with public policy objectives. This section examines the renewed attempts to revise charitable status. It also evaluates their impact on the strategies of the William Sutton Trust both in relation to Government and to other voluntary housing agencies.

After 1960, fewer and fewer new charities cited relief of poverty as the primary purpose for their establishment.[31] The inclusion of poverty in the charitable objects of bodies like the William Sutton Trust, however, raised serious problems. Its legitimacy was queried by Inland Revenue officials and the consequences were potentially very damaging, especially for a trust operating on the scale of William Sutton. The William Sutton Trust was 'at the top of the charity tree' which was still predominantly made up of bodies with small incomes.[32] In 1968, the Trust had an annual income of over £900,000 and assets worth £7 million. During the twentieth century, charities have been granted exemptions from nearly all the major taxes, notably income tax, capital gains tax and local rates. The Nathan Committee estimated that their privileged tax position doubled the income of every charitable trust in the country.[33] A price could, however, be exacted for these privileges as the Archbishop of Canterbury reminded his fellow peers in the original Lords debate on the Nathan Committee Report.

> It is said that it (tax exemption) deprives the State of a large amount of money, and the State is always likely to demand a *quid pro quo*. And all this is held powerfully to reinforce the need to provide means ... to compel trustees "to put their trust to the best possible service of the community".[34]

Deploying charities to carry forward political policy initiatives represented a challenge to the independence of trustees and to the primacy of their founding objectives. The Inland Revenue, on the other hand, was concerned above all with the legal and financial rectitude of those claiming charitable status, irrespective of their wider 'service of the community'.

In 1969, the Inland Revenue raised these questions in an acute form in relation to housing charities. If, because of changing circumstances, charitable housing no longer universally housed the poor, did it still satisfy the criteria for charitable purpose and tax exempt status? What meaning did 'poverty' have in contemporary charity? From the point of view of charity law, did any 'public benefit' remain if the housing provided no longer necessarily benefitted the poor? These were exactly the issues that Charles Baker had already trailed before the William Sutton trustees in the early 1950s.

The particular circumstances that prompted the Inland Revenue's questions related specifically to the Leeds Jewish Housing Association. The episode, however, seems to have been part of a wider review by the Department of Inland Revenue of tax exempt charities. Indeed, officials claimed that despite the position of the Charity Commissioners, the Inland Revenue had 'a distinct and equally valid role' in making enquiries about the principles on which charities operated. In claiming this supervisory role, they asserted that the issue was not so much the safeguarding of revenue as 'keeping charitable trustees within the terms of their trust'.[35] Responding to the Leeds Jewish Housing Association's tax return for 1967-8, the tax inspector posed a series of questions designed to reveal how the charity was currently being operated. She asked the Association to satisfy her on the following points:

1. How the existence of the charity is bought to the attention of the public who are entitled to benefit from it? May I please see copies of any publications or any literature via which this is done?
2. How many homes are at present available and what rents are charged? Is the amount of rent ever varied and if so in what circumstances?
3. By reference to what criteria the trustees select the beneficiaries. If any rules have been drawn up ... may I be supplied with a specimen copy...?
4. Whether the trustees ascertain the total annual amount of income of any applicant before granting a tenancy and how they accomplish this.
5. At what upper annual income limit the trustees would cease to consider an applicant as qualified to receive the bounty of the charity?
6. Once the accommodation has been granted whether the continued occupation depends on the means of the occupant. How often do the trustees review the circumstances of the occupants to ensure that he or she continues to qualify to receive the bounty of the charity?[36]

These questions 'appeared to raise quite new issues of principle'[37] and Lewis Waddilove, Chairman of the National Federation of Housing Societies commented to Charles Baker that 'this is the first time I have seen an enquiry from the Inland Revenue so clearly intended to disturb' the position of housing associations in relation to the income of their tenants. Waddilove alerted both the Charity Commissioners, who were 'equally concerned about this' and the Cohen Committee then looking at the role of housing associations.[38]

'SOME CLARITY ON CHARITY'

The National Federation of Housing Societies and the Charity Commissioners combined to try to bring 'some clarity on charity'. They aimed to remove the threat to housing associations' charitable status that had arisen from the Inland Revenue's 'narrow view of what constitutes poverty'.[39] Clarity, however, proved both elusive and disruptive. Pursuing it revealed even more clearly than before the different interests at stake between government departments and between members of the National Federation. What the National Federation was asking the Charity Commissioners to clarify was who the legitimate recipients of the 'bounty of charity' could now be – the poor, the elderly, disabled, or another special group, or the homeless? Special groups, including the homeless, the Federation acknowledged, might not necessarily be poor in an absolute sense. The Charity Commissioners were therefore asked to rule whether those who were 'poor' only in relation to the cost of providing a home in the area where they lived could be included in the definition.

Case law on these matters was inconsistent. The principles set out by Lord Macnaghten in *Commissioners of Income Tax v. Pemsel* (1891) still formed the basis for establishing charitable status. There were four categories, (a) relief of poverty, (b) advancement of education, (c) advancement of religion and (d) other purposes beneficial to the community that the law recognises as charitable. In addition, all charities must (with certain exceptions) entail benefit for the public at large – that is they must contain 'public benefit'.[40] As the early history of the William Sutton Trust has shown, 'this seemingly objective notion (of public benefit) has actually been highly responsive to the particular judicial and administrative contexts in which it has been employed'.[41] The relevance of the 'relief of poverty' and 'public benefit' in relation to housing has perhaps been the most problematic issue of all. The boundaries of the first of these categories will be explored next, and the ramifications into the realm of public benefit will then be assessed.

By the end of the 1960s, there was a prolific amount of case law relating to the notion of 'relief of poverty'. Within certain boundaries, the interpretation appeared very wide. It certainly did not confine the term to absolute destitution, and terms such as 'of limited means' and 'needy' were as acceptable as 'poverty' or 'poor people'. Furthermore, by this stage, 'relief of poverty' was deemed to be automatically in the public interest and 'is scarcely affected by the public benefit requirement'. Housing, however, was a complex area. As recently as 1954 in *Re Harman* Justice Harman had ruled that a trust to provide dwellings for 'the working class and their families' was not acceptable. Such a trust would not contribute to the 'relief of poverty' since the tenants would not necessarily be poor. Housing for the elderly remained an area where clarity was particularly difficult to find. In *Re Cottam* (1955) the provision of housing for the over 65s at economic (ie nonprofit) rents was held not to be charitable because there was no evidence that they would house only people who were needy. No clear or coherent guidance, however, had emerged from case law about what constituted poverty among tenants of existing housing charities.

The use of the terms 'poor', 'needy' and 'of limited means' suggested that both absolute and relative measures of poverty might be accepted. In the pre1939 period, the William Sutton Trust and many other large housing trusts had selected tenants according to an absolute level of income, but the tendency of case law after 1945 was to accept a relative concept. The dictum of Evershed MR in *Re Coulhurst* was frequently cited as support for the notion that poverty was a relative matter. He spoke of the need to accept that poverty meant

> persons who have to 'go short' in the ordinary acceptation of that term, due regard being had to their status in life, and so forth.[42]

This relativity, both as to general standards of living, and a person's prior status potentially broadened the idea of poverty considerably. Whether the idea of poverty used was an absolute or a relative one, however, the problem of where to draw the line remained. In 1967, a report of the Charity Commissioners had set out several examples of acceptable provision for the poor. These examples were based on the principle of 'topping up' the state's basic income maintenance while still forming 'relief of poverty'. They mainly consisted of 'special help' in unforeseen emergencies, such as sickness, 'sudden distress' or infirmity. Help might range from travel grants, special food or the loan of televisions, to personal services like laundry or decorating, and convalescent care.[43] There was no explicit attempt to define or implement an income limit for these 'charitable bounties' though the principle of an absolute measure of poverty based on state benefit levels was clearly implied. Furthermore, the items listed were relatively small-scale and transient in character. They stood in marked contrast to housing, which conferred a high-cost and permanent good on recipients.

Two years later, in 1969, Lewis Waddilove sought clarification of the position of housing charities from the Charity Commissioners. The Commissioners advised that

> Basically, a person may be regarded as poor if he has not the means to provide for himself those things that are necessary to maintain a very modest standard of living for himself and those dependent on him. ... The Charity Commissioners consider that trustees are entitled to regard as 'poor' for the purposes of their trust any person who cannot afford to pay the rent demanded (presumably a fair rent) for such satisfactory but modest housing for himself and his dependants as may be available in the area in which he reasonably has to live.[44]

Clearly, the Charity Commissioners were here accepting a relative view of poverty, and one that was subject to the vagaries of the market in rented housing. They stressed, however, that trustees had the duty to review the financial situation of their tenants periodically. They had to remain aware of 'any important change in the tenant's circumstances'. This did not mean that all tenants should be monitored but when tenants became 'obviously more wealthy' they should be asked about their new financial circumstances. The Commissioners recognised that such tenants could not be evicted, but attempts should be made to persuade them to leave and make the accommodation available 'for those who are really poor.' Failing that, the Commissioners advised that the house should be regarded

> as ordinary income-producing charitable endowment until such time as the tenant leaves or becomes poor again. Thus, if the tenant has been paying a rent less than the fair rent for the district and below any maximum fixed in an agreement with the local authority, the trustees should seek so far as they lawfully may to raise his rent to a level which will yield a reasonable profit.[45]

Lewis Waddilove regarded this compromise over rents as 'not altogether successful' but as nevertheless providing 'a firm base on which these smaller associations can conduct their affairs'. It rescued many smaller charitable housing bodies from the trouble they had been in. The Inland Revenue agreed (after pressure from the Charity Commissioners) not to press its points any further.[46]

As the Director of the National Federation of Housing Societies, Waddilove acknowledged that the compromise was 'not a satisfactory outcome' for large old trusts like his own, Rowntree, or Sutton. Indeed, the compromise opened some fundamental disagreements within the Federation in which Charles Baker took a prominent part. The agreement over rent adjustments, Baker said, was a case of 'the tail wagging the dog'.[47] It met the interests of smaller associations but jeopardised existing rental policies without resolving any of the basic issues about the place of housing in charitable activity. The threat of 'a progressive diminution in the scale and usefulness of the work of charitable bodies' had not been lifted.[48] Throughout the negotiations, Baker had tried to secure prior consultation between the National Federation, the Charity Commission and bodies like Sutton that had 'a substantial interest' in the outcome. He had also tried to coordinate the views of the large housing trusts, particularly Peabody and Guinness. In many respects, however, the special situation and historical development of William Sutton Trust undermined the common cause that Baker sought to build.

The course of the negotiations over charitable status and its resolution revealed a significant cleavage between the National Federation and the William Sutton Trust. The differences centred on the nature of housing as a 'public benefit'. Both wanted to see all types of nonprofit housing accepted as a 'contribution to the general benefit of the community'. Waddilove, however, went on to argue that housing for the poor should now be specifically *excluded* from recognised charitable purposes. He contended that it had become 'socially undesirable' to develop one class housing estates.

It is clearly no longer tenable to extend charitable status to an entire housing estate. Even if it were possible permanently to ensure that all the residents on an estate were 'in necessitous circumstances' it is doubtful whether it would be good social policy to act in this way.

Baker regarded this as a dangerous argument that would invalidate the purpose of the William Sutton Trust. It seemed that the

wheel had come full circle. As in 1900, housing the poor – in itself
a valid criterion of charitable purpose – was being condemned as
incompatible with the requirement of 'public benefit'.

Waddilove's views have to be seen in the specific context of the
Joseph Rowntree Trust of which he was director. The Rowntree
Trust had a wide remit for 'building up genuine communities' not
exclusively for the poor. It had recently been forced to reorganise
its work, however, to keep within the definition of a housing trust
for the purposes of the Rent Acts. This experience influenced
Waddilove's conviction that for legislative purposes charitable
status 'should be equally applicable to nonprofit making housing
trusts whose work is distinguishable only in relatively technical
terms from that of some charitable bodies.'[49] There was already a
de facto example of this broader basis. The Finance Act of 1965
empowered the Ministry of Housing to make a grant to an
approved housing association equal to the tax concession, even
though the association did not have charitable status. This provision brought not clarity but confusion to the issue.

> It could, therefore, be that a charitable organisation could be
> denied tax relief on the grounds that its activities were not
> charitable when a similar housing association not having chari-
> table status obtained the same relief from the Ministry of
> Housing.[50]

To many newly formed associations, this situation made the
question of charitable status of little consequence. To a long established and wealthy trust like William Sutton, however, status
conferred by parliamentary legislation and tied to government
policy priorities was a poor substitute for the Charity Commission
and accumulated case law. Furthermore, the Inland Revenue
maintained its view that 'the provision of housing per se is not
regarded as a charitable purpose unless it is clearly directed to the
relief of those who are in poverty'.[51]

The William Sutton Trust was on the horns of a dilemma – to
maintain its existing charitable status and the associated tax privileges, it had to house the poor. Housing the poor on its traditional
kind of estate, however, was under attack by the leading figure of
the voluntary housing sector as an undesirable social policy that
was unacceptable in a body enjoying charitable status. Such incon-

sistency was destabilising, and the situation was being compounded by the proliferation of 'quasi-charitable' housing associations spawned by the Ministry of Housing. It was the appearance of *Shelter* on the scene, however, which really threatened to rewrite relations between government, local authorities and the voluntary sector, much as the William Sutton Trust had done seventy years before. It added a new dimension to the debate about charity and public benefit that further complicated the standing and future strategy of the William Sutton Trust. Shelter – the National Campaign for the Homeless – had been founded in 1967 largely by church-based groups. It immediately launched a special appeal to help associations that were housing the homeless. The fund raising efforts were remarkably successful, and by 1970, Shelter had raised over £3 million in donations, which it used primarily to fund the provision of accommodation for homeless families in 'stress' areas.[52] The value of its work, however, was not universally accepted.

The dangers of the Shelter phenomenon were set out by a Labour MP, Douglas Houghton, in evidence to the Cohen Committee.[53] Houghton himself was a member of a housing trust. Disturbed by reports of 'Shelter's first million', he asked the Minister to explain 'the whole basis of what associations like mine are supposed to be doing'. Houghton clearly expressed the view that 'the whole basis' of housing provision had come to rest on an 'apparent absurdity'. People who were in desperate need of accommodation were regarded as 'appropriate for some kind of charitable help while many thousands with a weaker claim to Government and local authority subsidy are municipally housed or re-housed.' The Minister replied that he hoped the Cohen Committee would provide the new evaluation needed. The Committee, however, chaired by a protagonist of local authority housing, was then struggling with large amounts of contradictory evidence. The Minister's hope was not to be fulfilled. Nevertheless, he emphasised

I should like to feel more certain that we can make ever increasing public provision for bodies that are subject to very slight controls, and are not responsible to anyone, without attracting the wrong kind of people and undermining the work of local authorities instead of helping them.

The desire to protect local authorities from invidious comparison with housing associations is significant. Nevertheless, the Minister went on to say that he regarded 'top up' donations as 'a suitable place for private initiative and private generosity'. Charitable gifts could bridge the gap between what ordinary statutory housing subsidies could provide and the specialised housing management that homeless families might require. Houghton explicitly challenged this presentation of the situation. To represent the work of housing trusts as 'topping up' state provision was unacceptable. In practice, trusts had become the first resort of the most desperate cases, he insisted.

In subsequent correspondence between Douglas Houghton and Des Wilson, Director of Shelter, in the columns of the *Guardian*, Houghton raised some pertinent, related questions namely:

(i) the function of 'charity' in the public sector of housing provision and (ii) the kind, size and permissible influence of charitable help.[54]

Unlike the Minister, Houghton felt that it was precisely the 'rigid framework of administration' surrounding central and local housing bureaucracy that had to be tackled.[55] The current situation could not be sustained since 'notwithstanding the millions of pounds, devoted effort and imagination going into public sector housing provision', 'the most grievous needs of all' could not be met. Pressures were being put on local authorities to follow their established and publicised system of allocations. These systems were responsible for putting housing associations in the position of 'salvage squads' for 'the casualties of local authorities housing programmes'. Houghton pointed out that such a situation would be unacceptable in any other public service.

Is this the result of social and political pressures in the localities from people who put 'fairness' of treatment of those on the housing lists higher than urgent need? If we ran our hospitals on a similar principle we should be shunting emergency cases off to charitable hospitals.

Local authorities and housing associations both colluded in this situation by giving 'tipoffs' and accepting cases which

by any test of humanity should be housed (by the local authority) but they don't fit the local authority rules for allocating
available accommodation.

Houghton argued that overhaul of local authority housing priorities was necessary *before* charity was asked to come to the rescue.

It is not the role of housing associations but the whole of
public housing policy which requires fresh thought and fresh
courage.

Without such reform, Houghton's fear was that the charitable
sector could grow to unmanageable proportions, fuelled by the
success of Shelter. 'How big', he asked, 'will the scale of their
activities have to be to put a safety net under the shortcomings
and rigidities of local authority housing policies?' The danger was
that these organisations were not now filling 'gaps' but were
building bridges across chasms large enough to jeopardise the
stability of the whole system. In 1900, it was William Sutton that
appeared to pose this kind of threat. In 1970, it was Shelter.

Given the size of the task facing them, Houghton's fear was that
housing associations would be driven 'into the arms of this new,
aggressive and growing charity called Shelter'. 'It is not desirable
that one body like this should become the financial power behind
the whole movement', he wrote. Houghton's disapproval of
Shelter's fund raising methods probably led him to exaggerate the
dependency of housing associations on its money, but his unease
led him to advocate, at the very least, the urgent need 'to regulate
and supervise' the function and use of charitable help. Charles
Baker received a copy of Houghton's evidence to the Cohen
Committee and read it with some irritation and disquiet. He seemed
to feel that this was less a case of 'the tail wagging the dog' and
more that Shelter, through its agitated wagging, would provoke
unwarranted legal and political restrictions across the whole pack
of housing associations, including the William Sutton Trust.

There is no doubt that by 1969, questions were being asked and
answers were being proposed which threatened the position of the
older surviving housing trusts. It is also true that the controversies
were revealing conflicts of interest in government and housing
association circles that threatened to disrupt existing patterns of

behaviour and established alliances. Even within the 'big four' charitable housing trusts, alliances were difficult to maintain. For example, Charles Baker sought to unite the 'big four' behind the argument that even if their estates no longer provided uniquely for poor tenants, they still formed a 'public benefit' because of their superior amenities and design. His counterpart in the Peabody Trust, however, countered this view and candidly remarked

> Our estates ... tend to be somewhat unaesthetic, functional Estates deliberately catering for the lower paid element, and if they were, in fact, filled with the rich, would cease to have any special justification at all.[56]

In game theory terms, the arenas in which the William Sutton Trust was operating were in flux – the rules of the game were no longer understood nor consistently applied. Considerable uncertainty prevailed. The rectitude of the Trust's legal status as a charity and its viability as a large-scale provider of housing were both being threatened. The involvement of the Ministry of Housing in conferring 'quasi-charitable' status on housing associations willing to deliver housing objectives set by government further clouded the basis of charitable purpose in housing. Greater precision in definition, however, was likely to lead to the questioning of charitable status where it was impossible for everyone to win. Equally, without reform, Douglas Houghton argued, the role of local authorities in housing would be undermined. In the political arena, the conflict was widening. Central government wanted to keep the rules of the game fluid, to maximise the scope for using housing associations in policy initiatives. Local authorities and their supporters, however, saw their role jeopardised by the burgeoning voluntary sector under its aggressive 'leader', Shelter. This situation underlines the significance of the political arena and its payoffs into the administrative and legal arenas. It also reveals that maintaining charitable purpose in the face of legal and political challenges has been a dynamic process during the twentieth century. Moreover, the William Sutton Trust was repeatedly at the heart of the encounters. In the uncertain situation that prevailed in the late 1960s, how does game theory suggest that a player like the William Sutton Trust would respond?

The basic assumption is the Trust would try to maximise its payoffs, here to retain its charitable status. The Trust had taken steps to secure the cooperation of those most similar to itself in the voluntary sector, though not altogether successfully. Indeed, defection rather than cooperation was the most likely response of other members of the voluntary housing sector. The Trust had tried to keep the National Federation of Housing Societies 'on-side'. Experience showed that the large number of very small associations in the Federation's membership made this difficult. Threats to charitable status were being linked to questions about the legitimacy of voluntary housing in relation to the public sector. The government was being asked to redefine 'the rules of the (housing) game'. The William Sutton Trust and Charles Baker its General Secretary was certainly not suffering from 'limited information' nor 'imperfect cognitive capacity'. Its information channels were good and it possessed a political sophistication built up over many decades. It could therefore assess risks and it was also powerful enough to restructure the available choices. The Trust could attempt to exploit the uncertainties and itself redefine the rules of the game, thereby generating a new set of options. The possibility of acquiring the General Electric/English Electric Kingsway estates offered the William Sutton Trust such an opportunity.

THE WILLIAM SUTTON TRUST AND KINGSWAY HOUSING ASSOCIATION LTD.

The prospect of the William Sutton Trust acquiring the stock of the Kingsway Housing Association appears to have been raised first in the spring of 1969; the Sutton trustees took the decision to go ahead in principle in September 1969 and the conveyance of the property was finally signed in December 1970. The episode therefore almost exactly coincides with the debates on charitable purpose and charitable status between the Inland Revenue, the Charity Commissioners and the National Federation of Housing Societies. It is important to understand the nature of the Kingsway Housing Association and its stock to assess the significance of the William Sutton Trust's decision to acquire it.

Kingsway Housing Association had been set up in 1946 by the English Electric Company on the initiative of the then Chairman,

Sir George Nelson. It provided housing for workers in various parts of the country. Between 1947 and 1953 estates had been built in Liverpool, Preston, Rugby, Stafford and St. Albans. Between 1953 and 1956 there were three more in Luton, Chelmsford and Kidsgrove and between 1958 and 1962 others in Newton le Willows and Bradford. Sir George Nelson laid down 'a social policy' for the estates – to provide labour saving and pleasant houses wherever possible in 'a good natural setting'.[57] The estates represented a total capital expenditure of over £3.5 million. Most of the dwellings had been built using government subsidies and there were some 1,500 dwellings in all in 10 towns.[58] Despite the use of subsidies, none of the local authorities concerned exercised their nomination rights. The English Electric Company itself remained closely involved with the day to day management of the estates. Company personnel staff made all the lettings and the officers of the Kingsway Association had 'no say at all'.[59] The turnover of tenants was high (between 20 and 40%) – the result of company moves, resignations or transfers into owner occupation using financial help from English Electric. By 1969, not all the tenants were still employees of the parent company – some worked elsewhere, some were retired and some were 'widows of former employees'. Though English Electric claimed that there was still 'a big demand' for the Kingsway houses, evidently the housing shortage was far less acute than it had been. In this and other ways, the houses no longer represented 'a great asset to the group'. Rents were low – about 35/- [£1.75] per week – whereas most tenants were said to be earning between £17 and £25 per week. This was an unattractive rent roll for English Electric. Furthermore, although the Association met some management costs, the parent company was responsible for maintaining the extensive open spaces.

It is not, therefore, surprising that the takeover of English Electric by the General Electric Company (GEC) in March 1969 prompted a decision to dispose of the residential estates. Kingsway was 'instructed to make early repayment' to the parent company of outstanding loans amounting to approximately £1 million.[60] Initially, the Director of the Kingsway Housing Association approached Charles Baker with a tentative suggestion that 'Your trust may be interested in taking over either some of the houses or the estates, or the Association itself as a running concern'. He suggested that the Bradford houses might be of interest because of the Trust's existing estates in the region. He also expressed the view that 'I am sure our parent company would be delighted if another housing association or trust could be found to take over the Association as a running concern'.[61] The pressure on Kingsway to find a buyer quickly is obvious. The Sutton Trust's decision to buy, and to purchase virtually the whole stock of the Kingsway Association is less clear. Other parties were also drawn in, including the Charity Commissioners, the various local authorities and the Ministry of Housing and Local Government. Did the acquisition fulfil charitable criteria? Was it in the public interest? The resolution of these questions here throws further light on these issues, and in particular clarifies the role played by the William Sutton Trust.

On the face of it the William Sutton Trust's decision appears neither wholly rational nor charitable. Individually, the estates in question were reported to be 'attractive' and 'spacious' with a generally high standard of maintenance especially in the public areas. Spending on house improvements, however, had become very restricted. The 1969 budget was only £2,000 over all the estates. Even modest improvements to kitchen sinks and fires had dwindled to very small numbers so that waiting lists had built up on most estates.[62] It is not clear whether, or at what stage, the Trust had structural surveys of the estates carried out. 'All the evidence we have, visual and otherwise,' reported Baker, 'points ... to the unlikelihood of there being any undisclosed defects on a scale which would have serious financial consequences'.[63] Nevertheless, rents had not been raised for ten years and no repairs reserve fund had been established. While 'touching up' had taken care of minor problems, the age of some properties might have suggested that the need for more extensive work would soon arise. Not surprisingly, the level of arrears did not generally give cause for concern, but there were rather more 'empties' than the Sutton Trust was accustomed to seeing. The total purchase price to the Trust per house was estimated as about £1,750, roughly half the price of equivalent properties offered with vacant possession on the open market.[64] These practical points, however, had to be weighed alongside broad principles that bore on the purpose and character of the William Sutton Trust.

Charles Baker set out for the Trustees' consideration what he saw as the case against purchase.

Against the transaction, the following points may be fairly urged:

a. The business of the Trust is to provide new dwellings. The proposed takeover does not add one house to the Country's present stock.

b. The £230,000 in cash which the transaction would call for would provide roughly 57 new houses without borrowing or 192 if 70% of the cost is borrowed....

c. The houses do not provide the spread in sizes which experience has shown to be desirable. There are insufficient small houses suitable for older people.

d. The Trust would be taking over the houses as they stand and where they stand and with some existing tenants of a type which the Trust would not probably have selected itself. Although they are all in towns with a fair amount of industry it is improbable that the Trust would choose these precise locations for its operations if it were providing an equivalent number of new houses at the present time.[65]

Apparently the initial response of the Trustees to the approach from GEC/English Electric had been hostile. The 'case against' outlined by Charles Baker probably summarised the sources of their disquiet. A major practical consideration was the fact that Kingsway had to wind up its affairs without profit or loss, repaying all outstanding loans including those to its parent company. These obligations meant that Kingsway needed to generate a cash sum of £1.25 million from the disposal of its estates. The prospect of providing such a sum in cash seems to have been unacceptable to the Trust, whatever the general principles involved. The Director of Kingsway responded by offering to sell independently certain groups of houses 'mostly of the more expensive type' for ready cash. After paying off outstanding loans on these houses, it was hoped to raise £900,000 in cash. The advantage of this scheme, Charles Baker explained to the Trustees, was that it would reduce both the amounts of cash needed from the Trust, and the total purchase price for the remaining 1,442 houses. Baker had suggested that Kingsway should pass on to the Trust any 'profit' on the sale of the 'more expensive' houses over their book value. Furthermore, Baker had agreed that the maximum cash transfer that the Trust would make to Kingsway as part of the purchase would not exceed £200,000. This sum was much lower than the original amount but still caused the Trustees concern, in view of other outstanding commitments. Baker, however, drew their attention to the possibility of using other reserves. He suggested making transfers from the Repairs Reserve Account and from a fund set aside for lump sum payments under the Staff Pensions Fund. Including this immediate cash outlay of £200,000, the 'total consideration' for the acquisition amounted to £2,492,000.

The stakes were undoubtedly high – here was a very large stock of houses but they did not meet the Trust's operational criteria. Previous management practices had resulted in rents that were 'a disincentive to any purchaser' and in high rates of turnover.[66] Little provision had been made for improvement or long-term maintenance. Nevertheless, negotiations for purchase went on 'without even a sample structural survey' and based on possibly diverting Trust funds already earmarked for quite different purposes.[67] Furthermore, the proposal was that the stock bought from the Kingsway Association would be incorporated into the William Sutton Trust without distinction. Kingsway would not become a subsidiary of the Trust and the properties would not be shown separately in the Trust's annual accounts.[68] Indeed, the Trust ultimately went as far as agreeing that existing Kingsway tenants would have rights of transfer to other William Sutton Trust properties. Following existing practice, no enquiries about a tenant's financial circumstances would be made when a transfer was sought.[69] Given the simultaneous debates that were taking place in Government and legal circles about how far trusts like Sutton still fulfilled their original charitable purpose, one needs to ask whether a decision to acquire any, let alone nearly all the Kingsway dwellings and their tenants, was rational.

It is, in fact, possible to argue that such a decision *was* indeed essentially rational. The decision can be justified because of its potential to build support for the William Sutton Trust in the legal and political arenas and to consolidate its reputation for capability and stability in the turbulent housing world of the late 1960s. At this time, charitable housing bodies were being threatened with a progressive reduction in the scale of their operations, and the backlash from the aggressive activities of Shelter was building up. Nevertheless, Charles Baker steered the negotiations over Kingsway to secure *more* options for the William Sutton Trust. He used the Kingsway case to test out the rules on 'charity' and 'poverty' by requiring the Charity Commissioners to apply them to the Trust's particular case. He sought to secure judgements that would set favourable precedents for the future, not only by the Charity Commissioners, but also by the Ministry and local authorities concerned. The views of the Charity Commissioners were obviously crucial. As a first step, Charles Baker succeeded in getting the Charity Commissioners to confirm that the Trust's 1927 scheme allowed it to provide housing by acquisition as well as by building.[70] The Trustees' power to act by acquiring sites with buildings 'for the purpose of those buildings being used to house the poor' was confirmed in August 1969. The Trustees gave their approval to negotiations going forward with Kingsway in September, but subsequently the Charity Commissioners raised some further questions bearing on the central issues of poverty and charity. In January 1970, they asked 'whether all the tenants of the properties to be purchased are poor tenants, so far as can be ascertained at this stage?'[71] Somewhat disingenuously, Charles Baker replied that 'no information was available as to whether all the tenants of the properties to be purchased are poor persons.'[72] The Charity Commission recommended that

> all of the tenants should ideally be persons entitled to benefit under the trusts of the Charity, but it is appreciated this will take some time to accomplish. In the meantime, the trustees should ensure as far as possible that those tenants who would not be qualified under the trusts of the Charity pay fair rents for the properties occupied by them.[73]

This was the same formula that the Commissioners were proposing for dealing with the case of people who prospered after they became tenants: it was a face-saving device, legitimising a situation that might otherwise have threatened the charitable status of many trusts, including Sutton.

The Charity Commission had therefore confirmed that a large scale acquisition of property neither designed for, nor presently accommodating, the poor, was a legitimate activity for the William Sutton Trust. The Commission was persuaded that changing circumstances had not invalidated the 1927 scheme. In addition, Charles Baker skilfully bought the negotiations with Kingsway to the attention of the Ministry of Housing and Local Government to enhance the reputation of the William Sutton Trust in the political sphere. The opportunity arose because a number of local authorities who had a financial stake in Kingsway houses, resisted their purchase by a non-public sector body. They felt that houses built with public subsidy 'properly' belonged in the public sector, and they argued that the estates would deteriorate in the hands of a trust like William Sutton. Baker turned these arguments to the Trust's advantage. He pointed out to his contact in the Ministry that if Sutton acquired the properties they would be preserved 'in the hands of a reputable landlord' with no further call on public funds.[74] While Baker argued that this factor alone might be sufficient to sway Ministry officials, he also drew attention to the contentious issue of poverty. Stafford Corporation had argued that 'the extremely attractive estate at Stafford might deteriorate when managed by the Trust'.[75] They argued that the estate at Stafford should be transferred to the Corporation, which 'housed all types' whereas the Trust 'will only house the poorer tenants'. Echoing the message of Shelter, Baker underlined the assumptions behind Stafford Corporation's views.

> As the [William Sutton Trust] rents are lower than Council house rents for dwellings of a similar size, surely it is a good thing that they should be made available, as they become vacant, to poorer people of good character? There must be poor people in Stafford who ought to be better housed but are deterred by the rents they would have to pay?[76]

Whereas the tactics of Shelter were a destabilising factor, however, those of the William Sutton Trust were presented as reassuring.

Charles Baker presented Sutton's purchase of the Kingsway properties as a viable solution to a pressing problem that was not only cheap in financial terms but also valuable in social terms. On both counts it compared favourably with the option of local authority acquisition. Negotiating for Kingsway gave Baker a fortuitous opportunity. It enabled him to influence the broader debate about charitable status and charitable purpose. At the same time, it enabled him to secure decisions that set precedents on which to base a future strategy for the Trust. No wonder he rejoiced that the 'Trust can now consider the present project and any similar proposition in the future free from any uncertainty about the trustees' power to act'.[77]

In game theory terms, the William Sutton Trust was powerful enough to use the Kingsway episode to influence the rules of the game and to generate new options. Without incurring Ministerial opposition, the Trust secured permission to acquire property on a very large scale, though the tenants were not poor, would not be removed and could transfer freely into the Trust's existing 'charitable' property. Charles Baker explained the significance of the purchase for the Trust.

> The Testator's intention, which is reiterated in the High Court Scheme of 1927, is that the Sutton Trust shall be an ever-expanding body. Whilst hitherto expansion has in the main been achieved by the building of new dwellings there does not seem to be any fundamental objection to expansion by acquisition. The Charity Commissioners certainly seem to take this view...
> The Trust is nowhere near its optimum size, nor would it be if the number of its houses doubled. Therefore any development which increases the stock of houses in the pool...is to be welcomed from this point of view. The opportunity is now presented of increasing the size of the pool at a stroke by roughly a sixth.[78]

Kingsway had both a particular importance for the William Sutton Trust and a wider significance for the current debates about housing policy. The episode endorsed the validity of William Sutton's charitable gift and confirmed that it could make a real contribution to current needs. It blocked challenges to its own charitable status and by increasing its already dominant size, made it more difficult for general issues of housing charity to be raised. Any pursuit of greater precision in the definition of charitable purpose might lead to the questioning of the status of a range of other bodies, including William Sutton, that were proving themselves useful in the government's wider housing strategies. The Trust had underlined its viability as a large-scale national provider of housing: it was no 'salvage squad' riding on the coat tails of Shelter, but a wealthy and resourceful alternate provider in its own right. Kingsway was a 'quick fix' offered on very favourable terms. Buying it restored the initiative to the William Sutton Trust at a time when the position of the old charitable housing trusts was being seriously threatened.

CHAPTER 8

The William Sutton Trust at the end of the Twentieth Century

CHANGING THE CONDUCT OF THE GAME

This book set out to explore the conduct of the William Sutton Trust in the twentieth century. It has done this through an assessment of the Trust's policies and its wider impact. Using ideas derived from game theory, it has examined the Trust in terms of its place in the interconnected arenas of politics, markets and organisational structures. The analysis has shown that it is too simplistic to characterise the Trust's conduct as dependent either on 'the state' or 'the voluntary housing sector'. The Trust's role has not been the reactive one that such explanations imply. Sometimes consciously, but often unconsciously, the William Sutton Trust has followed policies and produced results that were different and unexpected. Some examples of its distinctiveness are its pre1914 location policy, the poverty of its tenants before 1939, its expansion in the 1930s, the acquisition of Kingsway in 1971 and its close relations with local authorities and central government. The book has shown the importance of these highly individual features. In particular, it has shown the significance of the William Sutton Trust in the history of housing policy in Britain since 1900. The Trust has repeatedly been the 'wild card' in the housing pack – the card that has made sense, or nonsense, of the games other agencies were playing. Even more notable is that the William Sutton Trust has also played the 'joker' – the card that can change 'the rules of the game' – altering the timing and modifying the pattern of alliances and defections between players. Above all, it is the unprecedented scale and stability of the Trust founded by William Sutton's original bequest that has brought this about.

Will this combination of financial stability and independence of conduct survive beyond the Trust's first hundred years? The recent history of the Trust suggests that it continues to adopt its own detached view of changing housing priorities. Stability, autonomy, and a sense of continuity have certainly persisted as distinctive features of the Trust during the last twenty five years. In the 1970s, many voluntary organisations expanded rapidly following the favourable financial arrangements of the 1974 Housing Act. The William Sutton Trust, however, adopted a policy of containment. It did not follow up its acquisition of Kingsway with further growth or diversification. Other associations, by contrast, chose to take on the role of house renovation in improvement areas (GIAs) and action areas (HAAs). By 1980, one-third of all rehabilitation in England and Wales was being carried out by housing associations.[1] The William Sutton Trust continued to concentrate on small infill schemes on existing estates, including some of those acquired from Kingsway. Managing the Kingsway estates did, however, lead to the establishment of regional offices, a rarity before 1980 even for large national housing associations.[2] This reorganisation was not an exercise in delegating power from the centre, however. The emphasis was on conformity with long-established procedures, enshrined in the codified manual supplied to every estate manager. Provided that compliance was displayed, the Trust's regional and estate offices were largely left alone, apart from an annual visit from head office staff to carry out one of the weekly rent collections.[3] One estate manager at the time regarded these visits as 'a kind of audit' but head office staff thought them 'a real event'.[4] Modernisation of the Trust was limited to a change of name – the term 'dwellings' was dropped from the Trust's title in 1973, because of the 'unfortunate connotation' which it appeared to carry.[5] There was no development department either centrally or regionally. The emphasis at the top of the organisation through the 1980s was on maintaining control using the old systems in the belief that changes were neither necessary nor agreeable. A tight rein was kept on tenants' groups in case they provided a platform for undesirable elements. The job specification of the Deputy General Manager included responsibility for 'monitoring' tenants' associations', 'attending meetings where necessary'.

Bob Poulter (1971–1978) and Ian Butcher (1978–1992) were Charles Baker's successors as General Manager and Secretary.

Both pursued cautious policies on both internal management and development. Job descriptions for senior staff emphasised checking, reporting and control of the existing structure. There was little emphasis on budgeting or planning and more on the importance of presenting 'a clean set of accounts' to the Trustees. In the 1970s and 1980s, management was seen as an administrative activity rather than a strategic exercise. Radicals like Richard Best and Harold Campbell joined the Trustees in the early 1970s as Ministerial appointments. The aim was to try to stimulate innovation, but the struggle to maintain existing concerns continued. Social and political changes, however, were threatening to make these concerns obsolete. In particular, government provision of rent rebates and later Housing Benefit appeared to make Sutton's building for tenants on low incomes unnecessary. The response, however, was not to seek new roles or new ways of delivering services, as both Best and Campbell favoured. It was to emphasise the paternalistic notion of the 'Sutton family', embracing both staff and tenants. Estate superintendents were given enhanced status and renamed estate managers. They continued their annual inspections of tenants' homes until 1990. The aim was 'Discipline kindly done' – a notion that summed up the ideal of relations between staff and tenants and between staff themselves.[6] At the heart of this idea was the continuing commitment to estate based management. 'The key to good housing management' it was emphasised, 'is the resident estate manager'.[7] Equally important was the provision of schemes for elderly people, many of whom were longstanding Sutton tenants.[8] Feelings of loyalty could undoubtedly be very strong. One estate manager told his colleagues on his retirement that

I have only served two people in my lifetime as a working man: they were His Majesty (in World War Two) and the Sutton trust. In my view, they were comparable in the way I was treated.[9]

Turning in on itself in this way and espousing its own version of 'family values' eventually brought the Trust into conflict with the Housing Corporation. There were many indications that the old methods were no longer appropriate. Community halls survived on most of the pre-1939 estates but support was low; garden competitions failed for lack of interest and in 1978 the total

annual income from allotment rents was £3.04. Housing Corporation rules and performance indicators undermined the Trust's
traditional allocation policies and led to a polarisation between
old and new tenants on its estates. Trustees wrestled with the need
to forge new relationships with their increasingly diverse body of
tenants. The forms of consultation they proposed, however, fell
short of extending greater rights to tenants. Trustees were looking
for a framework for 'practical tenant participation' which would
work well 'with the minimum of disruption to our present structure'.[10] In the early 1990s, the Trust was losing its place in the
'super league' of housing associations to those who embraced the
Corporation's new competitive financial arrangements. It did not
enter the world of mergers nor did it succeed in acquiring local
authority estates. Instead, it found itself a 'supervision case' of the
Housing Corporation which was critical of its unreformed procedures and remoteness from current concerns.

FUTURE PROSPECTS

By the time the Trust appointed a new chief officer in 1992, the
choice of keeping things the way they were or engaging with the
new games that were emerging in the provision of housing still
had to be made. A 1993 audit of the Trust's political profile
showed that it was barely recognised any longer as a player on the
housing field.[11] Other similar trusts such as the British Legion,
Shaftesbury and especially the Peabody Trust had distinctly higher
profiles. They had achieved this by improving their image,
updating their operations and engaging in what were seen as
positive and imaginative schemes. The audit had been conducted
for the Trust on a broad basis, involving 'those in Westminster
and Whitehall who have reason to be aware of the housing
association movement in general and Sutton in particular'. Its
findings show how successful the insulation of the Trust since the
1970s had been. Where the Trust *was* found to have a discernible
profile, it was 'low key' at best – a 'sleeping giant'.

> Sutton does not have a high profile. Many questioned have
> never heard of it and most of those that have are not aware of
> the scope of its operations. . .

The Housing Corporation does not believe that Sutton is very innovative, especially in comparison with other similar housing trusts.[12]

It was particularly striking that neither the Housing Minister, Sir George Young, nor Nick Raynsford, then a Labour MP with a longstanding interest and expertise in housing issues, had much knowledge of the Sutton Trust. Indeed, they and many other respondents expressed surprise that they knew so little about the organisation. They warned that such a low profile was a distinct handicap in the prevailing financial climate.

Early in the 1990s, therefore, the William Sutton Trust found itself in an unprecedented position. It was no longer 'wild card' nor 'joker'. There was scarcely even a shadowy recognition of its existence outside its own territory. Only those who were in direct contact with it as employee or tenant responded to its image. How had this transformation come about and what elements were responsible for the subsequent changes? After 1971, the Trust had chosen to play a game of its own, cushioned by the recent confirmation of its continuing charitable status and its expanded stock of estates. Over the next twenty years, however, the character of housing and the nature of housing need changed dramatically. These changes undermined the credibility of the Trust's traditional role. Its status as an organisation that *by its very existence* could force change in the housing sphere declined rapidly.

Some changes affecting housing were social, but others were economic and ideological. Social changes included the intensification of poverty for restricted numbers of the population. Poverty was not the lot of most working people as it had been in 1900 but was confined to relatively small and distinct disadvantaged groups. Sutton's 'market' therefore had been greatly reduced. The poor were only one of several groups in housing need. The tenure balance nationally had also radically altered. Before the First World War, fewer than 10% of households owned their own homes: in 1994, it was 67%. As a charitable housing trust, the right to buy did not apply to Sutton tenants, and the Trustees had agreed not to extend the right voluntarily. Their estates could be seen as 'sinks' of single tenure dwellings where many disadvantaged and unambitious tenants increasingly concentrated. Furthermore, most demand for new housing was occurring in the prosperous south, and the Trust's inheritance of large estates in northern areas posed problems both managerially and financially. Policy makers who were interviewed as part of the political audit painted images of a 'fortress' Trust that had retreated from the real world. The tendency was for the Trust to emphasise its history and 'tradition' and to hide behind the terms of its 1927 scheme of management whenever change was mooted.

Changes in the housing scene intensified after the 1988 Housing Act was passed following a major review of housing policy by the Conservative government. The reforms brought a reduction in grant levels to housing associations, the phasing out of fair rents leading to rent rises, the introduction of private finance to supplement capital costs and the transfer of development risk from public funds to housing associations themselves. As Housing Corporation allocations became openly competitive, the initiative passed to those associations willing to adopt more dynamic, aggressive and commercial approaches. The 'audit' of 1993 was one of the first steps taken by the new Chief Executive, Mike Morris, to redress the balance between these new associations and 'the sound and established associations, like Sutton.' Mr Morris, previously Chief Executive with Hanover Housing Association, was only the sixth chief officer to be appointed to the William Sutton Trust and the first to come into the post from outside. Previous chief officers had all served lengthy apprenticeships in the role of deputy.[13] His initial judgement was that the 'existing organisational culture was unhelpful to the new opportunities that were available'. He considered the Trust 'introverted, highly centralised in decision making and with a prevailing sense of drift in the regions.' His sense was that new directions were felt to be 'not for us'.[14]

The political audit was a means of bringing in ideas from well connected and well-informed people outside the Trust's usual circle. Though there was a certain amount of recognition that the Trust would have difficulties with the sale of its existing dwellings, many of those interviewed saw the sale of new houses and even whole estates as desirable. The idea of managing the property portfolio, rather than particular estates, was novel. It was reinforced by another suggestion that instead of modernising individual dwellings on its older estates, the Trust should take a different approach. It should see its task as one of redesigning whole estates in an imaginative and innovatory way. Apart from political issues such as these, there were several proposals for maximising the impact of the Trust's activities. The Sutton Trust was advised to form partnerships with some smaller specialist housing associations 'to combine strengths and achieve a local foothold'. It was also recommended that the Trust should keep in close touch with the policy making network in central and local government – responding systematically to policy documents and consultation papers and attending appropriate political and professional conferences. What the audit showed was that at the end of the twentieth century, the Sutton Trust no longer had the inside track to the arenas where housing policy was discussed and made. The housing field had changed radically. It was larger, more diverse and more dominated by both ideological and commercial values. To succeed here, housing organisations had to learn more self-conscious, deliberate and calculated tactics. The need now was to anticipate and engage with the future, rather than to look to the past for focus and direction.

Under its new chief executive, the William Sutton Trust began to apply the language of corporate planning, devolved budgeting, team briefing and human resources management. The structure of the organisation was redesigned explicitly to show the importance attached to setting objectives and disseminating strategies. To promote development, the development and technical services merged. The Trust targetted a few specific local authorities and expanded the development and acquisition programme to 400–450 dwellings per annum. The modernisation programme doubled and by 1998, private finance facilities totalling £140 million had been negotiated with major lenders including Halifax plc, Abbey National and Barclays Bank. This sum should be set alongside the sum raised by Peabody between 1993 and 1997. During these four years, Peabody borowed £200 million from City sources, to fund housing development and modernisation, often tied to community development and regeneration in cooperation with local authorities.[15] Nevertheless, to coordinate and carry this expansion forward, major changes were introduced in the Sutton Trust's regional structure. In 1996, the five existing regions merged into three larger operating divisions, each under a Housing Director. With wider responsibilities devolved from the centre, the Housing Directors became 'full members of the Chief Officers' team'. They were given a key role in developing and disseminating general strategies.[16] The role of head office was redefined. Its role was to foster best practice in the regions, to market and promote the Trust, to maximise development, to establish corporate objectives and to assess future risks and opportunities. "Investment in People" was another key aspect of the work of the centre and this involved not only employees, but also Trustees and tenants. A newly appointed Tenant Participation Officer sought to involve new kinds of residents' groups in the life of their estates. Trustees now expect to engage with tenants face to face on their extended annual estate visits. The hope is that these initiatives will gain recognition in both 'Housing Plus' and in the Labour Government's 'Best Value' agendas.

Over the next decade, the Trust considers that limited resources, more demanding 'customers' and the 'Best Value' agenda will dominate. These elements will mean that the Trust is more dependent on private funding, while public funding will diminish. Public funding, itself, will be much more competitive, specific and targeted. Securing public finance will depend on effectiveness in carrying out policy and on successful strategic leadership. More precisely, the Labour Government has said that it wants to see local authorities assessing housing need in their localities as a whole, and allocating public resources to secure regeneration on the widest possible scale. At the same time, the Trust recognises that those whom it houses will also become more demanding – this is likely to be a general feature and one heightened for tenants with specific needs. A few residents are expected to be 'particularly antisocial'. Nevertheless, the Labour Government has made it clear that a major strand in its approach to housing is greater tenant involvement in deciding management priorities and evaluating management success.

The William Sutton Trust's most recent Corporate Plan (December 1998) envisaged both the cooption of a tenant trustee and also the exploration of a new group structure to adapt to possible business ventures. In reviewing 'risks' over the next decade, the prospect of selling properties and of losing tenants to competitors has been mooted. Income streams, especially from Housing Benefit and prevailing rents, were seen to be at possible risk from political and general economic forces. In such a climate, the likelihood of more mergers, group structures and strategic alliances was recognised. One such strategic combination has been the Trust's compact with the black-led housing association, Ujima. The agreement is that over a period of five years, the William Sutton Trust will lend Ujima £6 million. The two will promote joint developments at affordable rents. By this means, Ujima gains access to the Trust's capital funds which will help it overcome the marginalisation that it has experienced under the new Housing Corporation funding regime. In return, the Trust hopes to gain entry to Ujima's extensive network of contacts in London. While undoubtedly an altruistic move, this imaginative alliance has 'added value' for the Trust. It confirms its commitment to equal opportunities while opening contacts with key local authorities.

NEW PROVIDERS – HOUSING ASSOCIATIONS 2000

There is no doubt that the world now occupied by housing associations is fast changing and volatile. Sociologists and political scientists have offered several formulations of the character of this new world.[17] Some welcome it as more pluralist and less monolithic, where partnerships between responsive, voluntary housing associations and reformed, enabling local authorities deliver democratically agreed housing solutions. Others detect in it a voluntary sector penetrated by the state, and doing its bidding. Because the voluntary sector is not part of the state, however, it operates as a 'shadow state', with the danger that it is neither representative nor accountable. Yet others see both the government and the voluntary sector as imbued with commercial values and goals, while the commercial sector, in turn, is structured by the state. From this perspective, the market does not exist as an independent force, but is subject to regulation and management by political interventions. In such a situation, the voluntary sector will operate according to the logic of these hybrid 'quasi-markets'.

As we have seen, however, theorising about the voluntary housing sector as a whole is likely to be confounded by its uneven geographical spread, its lack of coordination and its variability in size, resources and responsiveness. There are strong signs, however, that the sector has become increasingly enabled, regulated and subsidised by the state. There is no doubt that in the 1990s, Government has adopted a much closer supervision of the Housing Corporation. A recent report cites the view that the Housing Corporation is at best a reluctant, and at worst a willing tool of the Government.[18] Without the Corporation, and ultimately the central state, many housing associations could not operate. The performance indicators that determine access to public funds are set and monitored by the Housing Corporation in line with current government objectives. On the other hand, the interpenetration of state and market is clear from the mechanism of 'HAG-stretch' – getting most units for lower housing association grant. To achieve this government objective, associations must embrace volume building, design and build deals, and reductions in space standards. All these are favoured tactics of private estate developers. The need to stretch HAG further with private finance, means that associations who wish to develop must further hitch themselves to the wagon of the market. The Labour Government has yet to show the precise differences between its 'best value' criterion and those of the Conservative 'value for money' regime. It seems, likely, however, that Labour's measures of effectiveness will continue to reflect both political priorities and market values. They will also stress the need for greater tenant assessment and self assessment by the organisations concerned.

What is the position of the William Sutton Trust in this setting – must it embrace the (politically structured) new housing markets? Can it avoid the grasp of the 'shadow state'? Will it be able to retain its independence and show the sense of social significance, continuity and creativity that have characterised its past? Several arenas in which the William Sutton Trust conducts its affairs have already been identified. Each one – political, market and organisational – has undergone substantial change. Of the three, there seems no doubt that the market is now predominant, although shaped by central government priorities. Legal considerations may also yet come back into play if current concerns about charitable status achieve political salience. In the political arena itself, the 'shadow state' is not likely to take hold of the William Sutton Trust as much as it has many other housing associations. Since the Trust's borrowing capacity is large, it has the capacity to subsidise and pool rents. It can therefore act with greater independence and avoid becoming merely a tool of government policy. Its established practice of estate management through a local presence is well established and some communal facilities exist or can be provided. Its stock is diverse, which enables it to house a greater range of households than current funding permits. Despite this, it has lost a considerable degree of control over the selection of its tenants because of Housing Corporation targets and local authority allocations. If the Trust is to fulfill a truly democratic role in the future, contributing to a society where power is more widely shared, it must address the issues of tenants' rights and public accountability.

In the future, as in the past, those who seek to understand the conduct of an organisation like the William Sutton Trust must study both actions and their outcomes. Statements of intent and principle are merely starting points. Moreover, this account of the Trust's first century has shown that when the rules of the housing game are in flux, it is the *irrational* actions that deserve the closest attention. These are the settings where the important game is probably being played – the places where new rules are being formulated and the patterns of future play are being worked out.

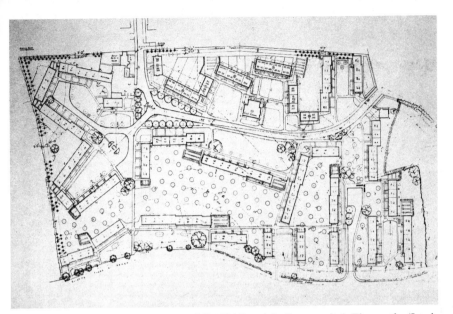

Plate 20. Proposed layout for Crownhill 'Old People's Community', Plymouth. (Louis de Soissons, 1954)

Plate 21. Miles Mitchell Village, Crownhill, 1958.

Plate 22. Miles Mitchell Village, Opening Ceremony, 1958.

Plate 23. Jura House, An Extension Scheme at the Rotherhithe Estate (Frederick MacManus and Partners, 1972). The scheme has six flats for disabled people on the fourth floor and a play centre. Jura House was commended for its good design by the Ministry of Housing and Construction.

Plate 24. Infilling on the William Sutton Trust's Birmingham Estate, 1967.

Plate 25. Sketches for the Conversion of Alfred Schofield House and Flats for Single People, Hull. (G. Alan Burnett and Partners, 1983)

Plate 26. Modern Resources (i) Shops on the Chelsea Estate (Jonathan Barry)

Plate 27. Modern Resources (ii) Marlborough Arms, Chelsea Estate (Jonathan Barry)

Plate 28. Modern Resources (iii) Play in Birmingham (Jonathan Barry)

Plate 29. Modernisation Scheme, Islington Estate, 1990. These houses in Evelyn Denington Court are the first ever to be built by the William Sutton Trust in London.

Plate 30. Modern Resources (iv) Spring in Chelsea (Jonathan Barry)

Notes

CHAPTER 1: THE PHILANTHROPY OF WILLIAM SUTTON

1 A series of affidavits sworn for the purpose of probate saw the amount of William Sutton's estate rise to £2,126,195. (11th Corrective Affidavit, sworn 19 February 1909) London Metropolitan Archives Acc 2983 010/ 1–8. The calculation of the 1997 value of the Sutton bequest is based on the index given by P. Johnson, ed., *Twentieth Century Britain* (Longman, 1994) p. 6 Table 1.2, updated by reference to the Central Statistical Office, *Annual Abstract of Statistics* (HMSO) 1996–99.

2 Throughout this account, the Trust is referred to as the William Sutton Trust, a title formally adopted in 1973. The previous name, Sutton Dwellings Trust, had been used since 1927, and before that the Trust's estates had been identified as Sutton Model Dwellings.

3 A recent audit carried out for the William Sutton Trust showed that the organisation did not have a high profile among MPs and civil servants. There was little awareness of its operations among national decision makers. (August 1993).

4 W. De L'Hopital, *Westminster Cathedral and its Architect* (Hutchinson, 1919).

5 Notes and Comments, *The City Press*, 27 July 1901.

6 B. Gidron, R. M. Kramer and L. M. Salaman, *Government and the Third Sector: Emerging Relationships in Welfare* (San Francisco: Jossey Bass, 1992) p. xii.

7 F. K. Prochaska, 'Philanthropy' in F. M. L. Thompson (ed) *The Cambridge Social History of Britain, 1750–1950*, Volume 3 (Cambridge, 1990), pp. 360–361 Prochaska points out that in modern times, the bulk of philanthropic giving in Britain has been by the working class for the working class, springing from a mixture of motives including humanitarian, religious and family.

8 Ibid, p. 359.

9 For a critique of the state/market dualism employed in explaining housing outcomes, see J. Barlow and S. Duncan, *Success and Failure in Housing Provision. European Systems Compared* (Pergamom, 1994).

10 Some examples of the former are S. Merrett, *State Housing in Britain* (Routledge and Kegan Paul, 1979) and ibid *Owner Occupation in Britain* (Routledge and Kegan Paul, 1982). M. Daunton's study of *House and Home in the Victorian City* (Edward Arnold, 1983) is an examination of the predominant private sector, where he argues that

there was 'no inevitability' about the emergence of state subsidised public housing. (pp. 2–3) Daunton also collected a number of studies of local authority estates in *Councillors and Tenants: Local Authority Housing in English Cities, 1919–1939* (Leicester University Press, 1984). Andrezej Olechnowicz's *Working Class Housing in England between the Wars* is primarily concerned with the Becontree estate at Dagenham. Jim Yelling, on the other hand, has treated housing under both public and private landlords in *Slums and Redevelopment. Policy and Practice in England 1918–1945* (UCL Press, 1992) but this is particularly concerned with London. Some authors have attempted comparative housing history, notably M. Daunton, *Housing the Workers 1850–1914: A Comparative Perspective* (Leicester University Press, 1990); A. Power, *Hovels to High Rise: Social Housing in Europe Since 1850* (Routledge 1993) and M. Harloe, *The People's Home? Social Rented Housing in Europe and America* (Blackwell, 1995). Many of these comparative accounts are empirical, and, as Barlow and Duncan point out, lack any theoretical basis for explaining why differences exist.

11 *Statistics of Middle Class Expenditure*, British Library of Political and Economic Science HD6/D267 (nd ?1896, Table x).

12 J. Harris, 'Political Thought and the Welfare State 1870–1940: An Intellectual Framework for British Social Policy', *Past and Present*, 134–135 (1992), p. 116.

13 See for example K. Waddington, 'Bastard Benevolence: Centralisation, Voluntarism and the Sunday Fund 1873–1898', *The London Journal* Volume 19 (2) (1994). He claims that for many Victorians, voluntary action 'symbolised the antithesis of state intervention by creating a 'benevolent economy' where welfare was rooted in charitable agencies and personal action'. (p. 152).

14 B. Harrison, *Peaceable Kingdom: Stability and Change in Modern Britain* (Oxford University Press, 1983) and most recently F. Prochaska, *Royal Bounty: The Making of a Welfare Monarchy* (London, 1995).

15 D. Owen, *English Philanthropy* (Cambridge: Cambridge University Press, 1964) p. 6.

16 J. N. Tarn, *Five Per Cent Philanthropy: An Account of Housing in Urban Areas Between 1840 and 1914* (Cambridge University Press, 1973) p. 31; G. Stedman Jones, *Outcast London: A Study in the Relationship between the Classes in Victorian Society* (Peregrine Books, 1984) p. 267, 270; A. P. Donajgrodzki (ed), *Social Control in Nineteenth Century Britain* (1977); R. J. Morris, *Class, Sect and Party: The Making of the British Middle Class Leeds, 1820–1850* (Manchester University Press, 1990) p. 167 and Donald Fisher, 'The Role of Philanthropic Foundations in the Reproduction and Production of Hegemony: Rockefeller Foundation and the Social Sciences', *Sociology* 17 (1983) p. 224.

17 This trend is clear in the USA as well as Britain, see J. Sealander,

Private Wealth and Public Life. Foundation Philanthropy and the Reshaping of American Social Policy from the Progressive Era to the New Deal (Baltimore: The Johns Hopkins University Press, 1997).

18 More information about William Sutton and his business enterprises can be found in P. L. Garside and S. Morris, *Building a Legacy. William Sutton and his Housing Trust* (The William Sutton Trust, 1994) pp. 2–12.

19 See Court of Exchequer Reports, 21 November 1865, Sutton *v* The South Eastern Railway Company, pp. 32–41.

20 See for example House of Lords Record Office, House of Commons Select Committee on the London and North Western Railway (Additional Powers) Bill and the Midland Railway (Additional Powers) Bill, 4 April 1879, William Richard Sutton, pp. 189–195 (I am grateful to Susannah Morris for drawing this case to my attention); Obituary, *The City Press*, 23 May 1900.

21 Sealander, *Private Wealth and Public Life*, pp. 17–18, and pp. 101–102.

22 Ibid, pp. 17–18.

23 Ibid, pp. 18–19.

24 On Lord Ashton, for example, and his benefactions to Lancaster and various local and national charities see P. J. Gooderson, *Lord Linoleum. Lord Ashton, Lancaster and the Rise of the British Oilcloth and Linoleum Industry* (Keele: Keele University Press, 1997).

25 William Sutton supported Thomas Lewis, the organ builder who was the elder brother of his first wife, Anne Eleanor Lewis. He also employed J. F. Bentley, architect of Westminster Cathedral to design his house on Sydenham Hill, 'Sunnydene'. For details see Garside and Morris, *Building a Legacy*, pp. 13–15.

26 Rate Book for the Ward of Finsbury East in the Parish of St Luke's 1873–1892. For an account of Sir Sydney Waterlow's Committee for the City's Hospital Saturday Fund, see Waddington, 'Bastard Benevolence'.

27 William Sutton Trust, Head Office Archive (York) GN 421 Part 1 History of the Trust. Notes of reminiscence by Mr Collin about Mr Sutton, 8 June 1949.

28 The full text of the Will is given in Appendix 2.

29 See M. Curti, J. Green and R. Nash, 'Anatomy of Giving: Millionaires in the late Nineteenth Century', in J. M. Lipset and R. Hofstadter (eds), *Sociology and Historical Methods* (1968) pp. 268–291.

30 G. Finlayson, 'A Moving Frontier: Voluntarism and the State in British Social Welfare 1911–1949', *Twentieth Century British History*, 1 (1990), pp. 183–184.

31 F. Prochaska, *The Voluntary Impulse: Philanthropy in Modern Britain* (London, 1988).

32 The role of the model dwelling companies is discussed further in Chapter 3.

33 Bremner, *American Philanthropy*, p. 111.
34 Ibid, p. 112.
35 The three trusts, set up with about half of Joseph Rowntree's property were the Village Trust, the Social Service Trust and the Charitable Trust. The latter two were very similar in aim, though separated for legal reasons. Both supported research into social problems and the formation of public policy. A. Briggs, *Seebohm Rowntree 1871–1954* (Longmans, 1961) pp. 92–93. B. Seebohm Rowntree published his first study of York, *Poverty. A Study of Town Life*, in 1901. E. Macadam, *The New Philanthropy* (1934) identified 'research and experiment' as one of the 'most enduring' if controversial possibilities for voluntary action. pp. 32–33.
36 Helen Meller, 'Philanthropy and Public Enterprise: International Exhibitions and the Modern Town Planning Movement 1889–1913', *Planning Perspectives* Volume 10 (3), July 1995, pp. 295–310.
37 Bremner, *American Philanthropy*, p. 99.
38 For a comparable American situation see Sealander, *Private Wealth*, pp. 30–32.
39 The idea of "de-centred" power has been proposed by M. Foucault, *Discipline and Punish: The Birth of the Prison* (London, 1979).
40 The development of charity law is analysed in Michael Chesterman, *Charities, Trusts and Social Welfare* (Weidenfeld and Nicholson, 1979).
41 High Court, Chancery Division, Buckley J, 23 July 1901. In re Sutton. Lewis *v*. Sutton For a report of the proceedings, see *The City Press*, 27 July 1901.
42 Chesterman, *Charities*, p. 7.
43 Chesterman, *Charities*, p. 66.
44 Ibid, pp. 55–58.
45 High Court, Chancery Proceedings, 23 July 1901, p. 645.
46 Letter dated 19 August 1949 from Assistant Secretary, Sutton Dwellings Trust, to Superintendent, Estate Duty Office, Somerset House, re Will of late William Sutton. (William Sutton Trust, Head Office Archive (York) GN 421 Part 1 History of the Trust).
47 Chesterman suggests that at the turn of the century, 'it was coming to be felt that the increased role of the state ... demanded that supervision of charities, should, in some fields at least ... be partly or wholly carried out by the state agency actually responsible for providing the relevant social service'. *Charities*, p. 75.
48 M. Taylor, 'Voluntary Action and the State' in D. Gladstone (ed) *British Social Welfare. Past, Present and Future* (UCL Press, 1995), pp. 215–216.

CHAPTER 2: THE PERFORMANCE OF THE WILLIAM SUTTON TRUST 1900–2000

1 In 1994, the Trust had 53 estates in 33 English towns and cities. By December 1998, the number had risen to 57 estates in 38 towns.

2　The William Sutton Trust, *Report of Trustees*, 1994–1995, p. 7. and *ibid*, 1995–1996, p. 4.

3　CORE data is produced from Continuous Recording of Housing Association Lettings and Sales.

4　*The Builder* reported in 1908 that the Sutton Executors had agreed to purchase 'land in the vicinity of Marlborough Square' subject to the approval of the Court (Volume 95, July–December 1908).

5　The Sutton Model Dwellings in Chelsea comprised 674 flats with a population when occupied of 2,200. The next largest estate in London was that of the Guinness Trust in Pages Walk, Bermondsey, which had 457 tenements. In Chelsea, the Borough Council housed 1,580 people and other model dwellings companies including Peabody, Lewis and Guinness together housed 3,200. It was estimated that 25% of the working class population of Chelsea lived in 'industrial dwellings' in 1914 (Chelsea Borough Council, Annual Report, Medical Officer of Health 1912 and 1914.).

6　Chelsea Borough Council, Annual Report, Medical Officer of Health 1908–1914.

7　Richard Dennis, 'The Geography of Victorian Values: Philanthropic Housing in London 1840–1900', *Journal of Historical Geography* Volume 15 (1) (1989) pp. 40–54.

8　In Chelsea, for example, the Medical Officer of Health's 1919 report showed that, if the William Sutton dwellings are subtracted from the total, over 50% of housing trust or company accommodation in the borough was in the form of 'associated tenements' where WCs and washhouses were common to more than one tenement. (p. 17).

9　Sutton Dwellings Trust, *Report and Accounts 1950*, p. 3. Forty eight of the houses on the Birmingham estate were built without bathrooms.

10　The Sutton Dwellings Trust, *Report and Accounts for the Year Ended 31 December 1949*, p. 5. The significance of recreational and other Estate facilities is discussed further below pp. 159–167.

11　Letter to author, 18 September 1992.

12　Ibid.

13　The Sutton Dwellings Trust, *Report and Accounts for the Year Ended 31 December 1950*, p. 8.

14　Registers for all six London estates exist (Bethnal Green, Chelsea, City Road, Islington, Rotherhithe and St Quintin Park), together with those from eight provincial estates – Birmingham, Hull, Manchester, Newcastle (Barrack Rd), Salford, South Shields and Stoke on Trent (Trent Vale and Abbey Hulton) Because so little was known about the characteristics of tenants on the various estates it was decided not to sample from the available population. The internal arrangement of the tenancy ledgers was based on streets or blocks subdivided by dwelling size and would in any event have made drawing a sample extremely complex.

15   The Registrar General's Occupational Classification and Social Class Divisions from the 1931 and 1951 Census were used.

16   P. Johnson (ed), *Twentieth Century Britain. Economic, Social and Cultural Change,* (Longman, 1994) Table 1.2 Average earnings for an adult male semi-skilled worker, p. 6.

17   B. S. Rowntree, *Poverty. A Study of Town Life* (Macmillan, 1901) and ibid, *Poverty and Progress. A Second Social Survey of York* (Longman, 1941).

18   A. L. Bowley, *Wages and Incomes since 1860* (Cambridge University Press, 1937); L. Smith, ed., *The New Survey of London Life and Labour* (P. S. King, 1930) Vol. 1.

19   For fuller details on rents see Chapter 5, Tables 5.1 and 5.2.

20   43 per cent of new tenants had one child or none and the average per family was two. 62 per cent of tenancies went to families with children under 14.

21   Guinness and Peabody had virtually stopped building by 1939 and were even contemplating demolishing some of their original estates. They were in any event managing accommodation only in London.

22   In 1939, the Trust's head office at Victoria House, Southampton Row, London was staffed by a secretary and general manager, Andrew Kay and an assistant secretary, Charles Baker.

23   Letter to author, 18 September 1992.

24   The Sutton Dwellings Trust, Report and Accounts for the Year ended 31 December 1940.

25   Ibid 31 December 1950, p. 9.

26   P. Malpass, *Housing, Philanthropy and the State: A History of the Guinness Trust* (Bristol: University of West of England, 1998) p. 30. On the Guinness Trust's King's Road estate, 80 of the 160 dwellings were destroyed and the rest were damaged by 1944.

27   The Sutton Dwellings Trust, *Report and Accounts for the Year ended 31 December 1950*, p. 6.

28   Malpass, *Guinness,* p. 41.

29   Ibid p. 36.

30   The Sutton Dwellings Trust, *Report and Accounts for the Year ended 31 December 1950*, p. 8.

31   Malpass, *Guinness*, pp. 36–37.

32   The Sutton Dwellings Trust, *Report and Accounts for the Year ended 31 December 1955.*

33   PRO HLG 37/178 CHAC Advisory Committee on Housing Standards 1959–60: Evidence Submitted by the Sutton Dwellings Trust.

34   The Sutton Dwellings Trust, *Report and Accounts for the Year Ended 31 December 1949*, pp. 6–7.

35   Malpass, *Guinness*, p. 39. Malpass comments that in the 1970s, 'Guinness still owned the majority of its pre 1914 associated tenements – nearly 60% of its stock – and it still did not have a definite and feasible policy for their future'. (p. 44).

36 Butcher, *The Housing Sutton Trust*, pp. 44–45.
37 J. R. Short, *Housing in Britain. The Post-War Experience* (Methuen, 1982) p. 189.
38 The Guinness Trust took similar steps, setting up the Guinness Housing Association in 1962 to take advantage of the 1961 Housing Act. The Association did not, however, succeed in building anything and was wound up in 1973. Malpass, *Guinness*, p. 49–50.
39 In the event 1,117 houses were transferred to the William Sutton Trust, Stafford Borough Council preferring to acquire the estate there itself.
40 Malpass, *Guinness*, p. 46 and p. 50.
41 During interviews conducted in 1998, tenants on the ex-Kingsway estates in Rugby still spoke of their 'English Electric' houses. (Interview 2/8) Indeed, the interviewer failed to find the Rokeby estate until he began asking for it as 'English Electric'. Requests for directions to the Sutton Trust estate were not recognised, even by people living close by it. Some of the remaining ex-English Electric tenants on the estate regarded themselves as 'the stalwarts' and Sutton tenants as 'outsiders'. (Rugby interview 10).
42 See for example, Trustees' reports for 1942, 1949 and 1954.
43 *The Sutton Dwellings Trust Report and Accounts for the Year ended 31 December 1949*, p. 9.
44 Ibid, 31 December 1950, p. 8.
45 Butcher, *The Sutton Housing Trust*, p. 50.
46 Ibid, p. 54.
47 R. Best, 'Housing Associations: The Sustainable Solution' in P. Williams, ed., *Directions in Housing Policy* (Paul Chapman Publishing, 1997) pp. 107–109.
48 Malpass, *Guinness*, p. 55; The Sutton Housing Trust, *Report and Accounts for the Year ended 31 December 1974*, p. 5.
49 The Sutton Housing Trust, *Report and Accounts for the Year ended 31 December 1974*, p. 5.
50 Ibid, 31 December 1978, p. 5.
51 Ibid, 31 December 1981, p. 3.
52 Malpass, *Guinness*, p. 70.
53 Butcher, *The Sutton Housing Trust*, p. 57.
54 The Sutton Housing Trust, *Report and Accounts for the Year ended 31 December 1977*, p. 6.
55 Ibid *31 December 1974*, p. 6.
56 Ibid, *Year ended 31 December 1978*, p. 6.
57 Ibid, *Year ended 31 December 1981*, p. 3.
58 William Sutton Trustee, Interview with author, November 1998. The Guinness Trust by contrast was criticised for the nature of its board of trustees – throughout the 1970s and 1980s, it continued to be dominated by members of the Guinness family. Malpass, *Guinness*, p. 61.
59 Ibid, *Year ended 31 December 1980*, p. 3.

60 Ibid, *Year ended 31 December 1983*, p. 3.
61 Ibid, *Year ended 31 December 1985*, p. 3.
62 Ibid, *Year ended 31 December 1984*, p. 3.
63 Ibid, *Year ended 31 December 1982*, p. 4.
64 J. Blake, 'The New Providers' in J. Goodwin and C. Grant, *Built to Last? Reflections on British Housing Policy*, 2nd edition (Shelter, 1997) p. 175.
65 Best, 'Housing Associations', p. 111.
66 Communication with author, Mike Morris, Chief Executive, William Sutton Trust, November 1998.

CHAPTER 3:   PHILANTHROPY AND HOUSING IN ENGLAND SINCE 1900

1 E. Gauldie, *Cruel Habitations: A History of Working Class Housing, 1780–1918* (Allen and Unwin, 1974) p. 235.
2 D. Owen, *English Philanthropy 1660–1960* (Cambridge, Mass., 1964) p. 6.
3 J. N. Tarn, *Five Per Cent Philanthropy: An Account of Housing in Urban Areas between 1840 and 1914* (Cambridge: Cambridge University Press, 1973) p. xiv.
4 Housing histories which have stressed the importance of the growth of the local authority sector include A. S. Wohl, *The Eternal Slum. Housing and Social Policy in Victorian Britain* (Edward Arnold, 1977), and G. Stedman *Jones, Outcast London: A Study in the Relationship Between Classes in Victorian Society* (Oxford, 1971). Others who have challenged the notion that expansion of the state sector was inevitable include P. Kemp, 'The Origins of Council Housing', in J. Goodwin and C. Grant, eds, *Built to Last? Reflections on British Housing Policy* Second edition (Shelter, 1992) and M. J. Daunton, *Housing the Workers 1850–1914: A Comparative Perspective* (Leicester : Leicester University Press, 1990).
5 M. Daunton, 'Housing' in F. M. L. Thompson, ed., *The Cambridge Social History of Britain 1750–1950*, Volume 2 (Cambridge: Cambridge University Press, 1990), pp. 223–234.
6 For an analysis of the contrasting roles of the public, private and voluntary sectors see P. L. Garside, 'Modelling the Behaviour of Nonprofit Housing Agencies in Britain and France 1900–1939' in C. Zimmermann (ed), *European Housing Policy in Comparative Perspective 1900–1939* (Fraunhofer IRB Verlag, 1997) A. Power, *Hovels to High Rise: Social Housing in Europe since 1850* (Routledge, 1993), M. Harloe, *The People's Home? Social Rented Housing in Europe and America* (Oxford: Blackwell, 1995) and M. Kleinman, *Housing, Welfare and the State in Europe* (Cheltenham: Edward Arnold, 1996).
7 Recent works on British philanthropy include W. K. Jordan, *Philanthropy in England 1480–1660*, (New York, 1959); Owen, *Philanthropy;* F. K. Prochaska, *The Voluntary Impulse: Philanthropy in Modern Britain*, (Faber and Faber, 1988) and Prochaska, 'Philanthropy' in Thompson, *Social History*, Volume 3.

8   Prochaska, 'Philanthropy', p. 357.
9   Prochaska, *The Voluntary Impulse* .
10 Harloe, *People's Home*, pp. 16–17; A. Mayne, *The Imagined Slum: Newspaper Representation in Three Cities 1870–1914* (Leicester: Leicester University Press, 1993).
11 Tarn, *Five Per Cent Philanthropy*, p. 31.
12 Southwood Smith, *Results of the Sanitary Improvement* (1854) p. 16.
13 Peabody Trust, *Mr Peabody's Gift to the Poor of London* (1865) p. 1.
14 Metropolitan Association for Improving the Dwellings of the Industrious Classes, *Sixth Report of the Directors* (1850).
15 Artisans, Labourers and General Dwellings Company, *Prospectus* (n.d.) Lambeth Archives Centre, Acc IV/122/96.
16 David Clapham, 'A Woman of Her Time', in Goodwin and Grant (eds) *Built to Last*, p. 26.
17 Society for Improving the Condition of the Labouring Classes, *Eighteenth Annual Report*, p. 4.
18 The Guinness Trust's Deed of Trust for the London Fund stressed that this housing charity also was to be run on strictly non-sectarian, non-political lines (Minutes 4 February 1890).
19 Artisans, Labourers and General Dwellings Company, *Prospectus*, 1870.
20 London Metropolitan Archives, Acc 2983/008, 27 August 1906.
21 S. Morris, 'Private Profit and Public Interest: Model Dwellings Companies and the Housing of the Working Classes in London, 1840–1914' (PhD Dissertation, University of Oxford, 1999) p. 61.
22 Guinness Trust Minutes, 4 December 1889.
23 Octavia Hill played a leading role in the Charity Organisation Society which emphasised personal visiting of the poor and developed many of the methods of modern social work practice. See David Clapham, 'A Woman of her Time', p. 31, Anne Power, *Property Before People* (Allen and Unwin, 1997) and M. Brion, *Women in the Housing Service* (Routledge, 1995).
24 C. S. Loch, *The Dwellings of the Poor* (1882) p. 9.
25 Ian Emsley, 'The Development of Housing Associations With Special Reference to London and Including a Case Study of the London Borough of Hammersmith' (PhD Dissertation, University of London, 1985) p. 37.
26 Jerry White, 'Business Out of Charity', in Goodwin and Grant , eds, *Built to Last*, p. 13.
27 Morris, 'Private Profit and Public Interest', p. 63.
28 Clapham, 'Woman of Her Time', p. 30.
29 These loans were introduced by the Labouring Classes Dwelling Houses Act 1866.
30 Thirty Ninth Annual Report of Public Works Loan Board, 1913–14, pp. 93–5.
31 J. Burnett, *A Social History of Housing 1815–1970* (Methuen, 1978) pp. 175–6.

32   Emsley, 'Housing Associations', p. 61.
33   Ibid, p. 65.
34   Morris, 'Private Profit', p. 248.
35   Quoted in Emsley, 'Housing Associations', p. 53.
36   For a discussion of the experience of London, Birmingham, Manchester, Sheffield and Liverpool, see Jane Morton, *"Cheaper than Peabody" Local Authority Housing from 1890 to 1919* (Joseph Rowntree Foundation, 1991) Chapter 3, 'The Search for Models'.
37   M. Swenarton, *Homes Fit for Heroes,* (Heinemann, 1981) pp. 28–31. In 1913, the York Medical Officer of Health reported that 'There is no doubt that ... the City has become faced by something of a housing famine'.
38   Statutory definitions of Public Utility Society, housing cooperative, housing society and housing association are given in Appendix 6.
39   M. Daunton, *A Property Owning Democracy? Housing in Britain,* (Faber and Faber, 1987) p. 49 and K. J. Skilleter, 'The Role of Public Utility Societies in Early British Town Planning and the Garden City Movement', *Planning Perspectives* 10 (1995) pp. 329–358.
40   K. J. Skilleter, 'The Role of Public Utility Societies in early British Town Planning and Housing Reform 1901–1936', *Planning Perspectives* 8 (1993).
41   Local promoters of copartnership housing included labour co-partners, cooperators, philanthropists, employers, landowners, branches of the Garden City Association and 'city beautiful' movement, trade unionists and local authorities. See Johnston Birchall, 'Co-partnership Housing and the Garden City Movement', *Planning Perspectives*, 10, (1995) p. 341.
42   Skilleter, 'Public Utility Societies', pp. 129–132.
43   PRO, RECO 1/482, Bryce Leicester Report on Public Utility Societies, December 1917.
44   Daunton, for example, has argued that 'there was no inevitability in the acceptance of subsidised public housing as the end result of policy, as the experience of other countries makes perfectly clear'. *House and Home in the Victorian City: Working Class Housing 1850–1914* (Edward Arnold, 1983) pp. 2–3.
45   Morton, 'Cheaper than Peabody', p. 57. Jane Morton acknowledges the difficulty of assembling housing statistics for this period but estimates there were 25,000 local authority homes in England and Wales by 1917 and the voluntary sector had 'quite probably' twice that number.
46   PRO RECO 1/548 Memorandum from B. S. Rowntree to Bryce Leicester, 'Public Utility Housing', September 1917.
47   Birchall, 'Co-partnership Housing', Table 1, pp. 337–339.
48   PRO RECO 1/525 Housing (Financial Assistance) Committee – Correspondence with Housing Trusts.
49   The role of the Local Government Board in relation to the William

Sutton Trust and local authorities between 1900 and 1919 is discussed in detail below, Chapter 4.

50 Mark Swenarton's much debated work, *Homes for Heroes,* offered a radical reappraisal of the postwar housing programme. The interplay between state housing and the private rented sector is assessed by M. J. Daunton, *A Property Owning Democracy? Housing in Britain* (Faber, 1987) and by Kemp, 'Origins of Council Housing'.

51 Emsley, 'Housing Associations', p. 74.

52 Most of the evidence about the attitude of the trusts is taken from PRO RECO 1/525 Housing (Financial Assistance) Committee – Correspondence with the Housing Trusts 1918.

53 Ibid, Letter to Secretary, Housing (Financial Assistance) Committee from William Balmain, Secretary to the William Sutton Trustees, 9 October 1918.

54 Emsley, 'Housing Associations', p. 74.

55 Ibid, p. 80.

56 A. A. Nevitt, *Housing, Taxation and Subsidies* (Nelson, 1966) p. 82. In 1920, the rate was increased to 50% for the period up to 1927.

57 Emsley, 'Housing Associations', p. 83.

58 PRO RECO1/548 Memorandum by Bryce Leicester, *Public Utility Housing*, September 1917.

59 PRO RECO 1/526 Housing (Financial Assistance) Committee – Criticisms of Public Utility Societies Representatives of Draft Proposals.

60 PRO RECO 1/482 Report on Public Utility Societies December 1917.

61 The conversion to capitalism continued up to 1939 through individual sales and sales of entire estates out of the cooperative realm. The Bradford Property Trust, for example, bought Garden City Tenants in 1934 and Ealing Tenants in 1940, converting them into private limited companies. Birchall, 'Copartnership Housing', p. 353.

62 See below Chapter 5.

63 RECO 1/526 Criticisms ... of Draft Proposals 1918.

64 Commenting on the postwar situation, Parker Morris (then Town Clerk of Chesterfield) wrote that voluntary housing societies 'could not undertake the work of clearing large slum areas or the erection of large numbers of new houses. So far as they have been able to carry out such work, the state has assisted them, but it was obviously necessary for the State to delegate the bulk of the work to public bodies.' 'The Respective Spheres of Public Authorities and Voluntary Organisations in the Administration of Social Services.' *Public Administration,* 1927, p. 386.

65 P. L. Garside, "Unhealthy Areas": Town Planning, Eugenics and the Slums 1890–1945' *Planning Perspectives* 3 (1988) 24–46.

66 T. Speake, *War against the Slums Voluntary Housing Societies in the Front Line*, (Shrewsbury, Adnitt and Naunton, 1930) p. 45.

67 Ibid, p. 30.

68 Parker Morris commented, 'Moreover, when the State ... has under-

taken a service, however broad the basis of the scheme, there will be sure to be "gaps" which are not provided for. Here remains work for Voluntary Associations to undertake even when the service has been taken over by a Public Authority. They can also continue their propaganda with a view to the scheme being amended to close the "gaps". Ibid, p. 387.

69 Ibid, p. 38.
70 M. Bowley, *Housing and the State 1919–1945* (New York: Garland, 1945) Chapter 6.
71 The detailed analysis of this contest is to be found in P. L. Garside, 'Central Government, Local Authorities and the Voluntary Housing Sector 1919–1939' in A. O'Day, ed., *Government and Institutions in the Post 1832 United Kingdom* (Lampeter: Edwin Mellen Press, 1995) pp. 85–125.
72 *The Times* 20 July 1933.
73 J. R. Jefford, 'Reconditioning in Relation to Urban Housing', *Journal of the Royal Sanitary Institute*, 54 (1933–34) p. 451.
74 E. Macadam, *The New Philanthropy:: A Study of the Relations between the Statutory and Voluntary Social Services* (London, 1934) p. 149.
75 Ibid, p. 50.
76 Ministry of Health, *Report of the Departmental Committee on Housing* (the Moyne Committee) Cmd. 4397, July 1933 pp. 4–5.
77 Ibid, p. 12.
78 Ibid, pp. 29–33.
79 Macadam, *New Philanthropy*, p. 153.
80 PRO HLG 29/213 Notes of a Conference on the Report of the Moyne Committee 4/11/1933. The 1935 Housing Act susequently substituted the term 'housing association' for the previously used 'public utility society'. Details are given in Appendix 6.
81 Garside, 'Central Government' pp. 107–114.
82 T. S. Simey, *Principles of Social Administration* (London, 1937) p. 69.
83 In 1939, for example the housing management and housing associations subcommittee of CHAC produced a report, *The Operations of Housing Associations* (Ministry of Health).
84 Malpass, 'Guinness Trust', p. 35. Leigh Breese, Secretary to the Guinness trust, chaired the national Federation during World War Two.
85 P. Malpass, 'The Missing Years' in J. Goodwin and C. Grant, eds, *Built to Last?* p. 128.
86 PRO HLG 49/1467 1952–55 Housing Associations. Promotion and Assistance by Local Authorities.
87 R. Best, 'Housing Associations: The Sustainable Solution?' in Peter Williams (ed.) *Directions in Housing Policy. Towards Sustainable Housing Policies for the UK*, (Paul Chapman Publishing, 1996) p. 104. Best calculates that the employers' housing 'accounted for more than half' of the sectors' total stock in the 1960s. The Coal Board alone provided 111,000 properties.

88 1961 Housing Act. Section 7.
89 The William Sutton Trust's evidence to the Parker Morris Committee on housing standards (1960) related exclusively to housing for the elderly. PRO HLG 37/178.
90 M. Tims, *An Historical Survey of Selected Housing Associations* (Joseph Rowntree Memorial Trust, 1968).
91 Best, 'Housing Associations' p. 107.
92 Butcher, *The Sutton Housing Trust*, p. 56.
93 Macadam, *New Philanthropy*, p. 27.
94 J. Blake, 'The New Providers' in Goodwin and Grant, eds, *Built to Last?*, p. 175.
95 Ibid, p. 180.
96 Ibid, p. 182–3.
97 Trevor Hendy, 'David against Goliath', *Voluntary Housing*, 14 January 1994, pp. 10–11.
98 M. Warrington, paper presented to Institute of British Geographers, 6 January 1994, reported in *the Guardian*, and *Inside Housing*, 7 and 14 January 1994.

CHAPTER 4: GAME THEORY, NESTED GAMES AND VOLUNTARY HOUSING ORGANISATIONS

 1 For a recent comprehensive review of the field see G. Owen, *Game Theory* , 3rd ed., (San Diego, California: Academic Press, 1995).
 2 George Tsebelis, *Nested Games and Rational Choice in Comparative Politics* (Los Angeles: University of California Press, 1990) p. 239.
 3 Tsebelis, *Nested Games*, p. 62.
 4 E. Ostrom, *Governing the Commons: The Evolution of Institutions for Collective Action* (New York: Cambridge University Press, 1990) p. 6.
 5 Ostrom, *Governing the Commons*.
 6 See for example, E. Ostrom, *Crafting Institutions for Self-Governing Irrigation Systems* (San Francisco: Institute for Contemporary Studies Press, 1992).
 7 R. D. Putnam, for example, has used game theory to compare the quality of collective life in north and south Italy in *Making Democracy Work* (New Jersey, 1993). Gary Becker, *The Economic Approach to Human Behaviour* (Chicago/London, 1977) argued that macro-effects like public policy and social practices are best understood as the sum of self-interested choices by rational units. (Chapter 1).
 8 Douglass C. North, *Institutions, Institutional Change and Economic Performance* (New York: Cambridge University Press) pp. 100 and 140. See also E. Ostrom, 'An Agenda for the Study of Institutions', *Public Choice* 48 (1986): pp. 3–25.
 9 Tsebelis, *Nested Games*, p. 32.
10 B. Bengtsson, 'Housing in Game Theoretical Perspective', *Housing Studies*, 10 (2) (1995), p. 238.
11 Tsebelis, *Nested Games*, p. 64.
12 See C. E. Lindblom, *Politics and Markets* (New York: Cambridge

University Press, 1977) for the argument that in capitalist societies, business is the dominant player and not just another player in social and political decisions.

13   Putnam, *Making Democracy Work*, p. 166.
14   See below pp. 86–95.
15   Tsebelis, *Nested Games*, pp. 9–10.
16   Tsebelis, *Nested Games*, p. 46.
17   P. L. Garside, 'Modelling the Behaviour of Non-profit Housing Agencies in Britain and France' in C. Zimmermann, ed., *European Housing Policy in Comparative Perspective 1900–1939* (Stuttgart: Fraunhofer IRB Verlag, 1997) pp. 56–59.
18   On process tracing see A. L. George and T. J. McKeown, 'Case Studies and Theories of Organisational Decision Making' in L. Sproull and V. Larkey, eds, *Advances in Information Processing in Organisations*, Vol 2 (Santa Barbara: JAI Press, 1985).
19   B. Bengtsson, 'Housing', p. 232.
20   Ibid, p. 240.
21   The St. Quintin Park estate was acquired in two sections – one of eight acres in 1928 and another adjoining the first of one acre in 1933.
22   The full text of the Will can be found in Appendix 2.
23   London Metropolitan Archives, Acc 2983/010/1-8, Sutton *v.* Attorney General, 14 March 1906.
24   London Metropolitan Archives, Acc 2983/010/1-8 Transcript of Shorthand Notes, High Court, Chancery Division, before Mr Justice Warrington, In Re Sutton, Sutton *v* Attorney General, 14 March 1906, and 'The Sutton Dwellings Trust. Its Origin and History' Typescript, n.d. 1951? The William Sutton Trust, Head Office (York) Archive, GN421, Part 1, History of the Trust.
25   *The City Press*, 20 June 1900.
26   London Metropolitan Archives, Acc 2983, Executors' Minute Book 8 April 1902. The William Sutton Trust Head Office Archive, GN421 Part One History of the Trust 'Value of the Original Estate, 22 December 1947'. Subsequent affidavits raised the sum bequeathed as additional assets were discovered. See above, Chapter 1 note 1.
27   *The City Press*, 24 July 1901.
28   William Sutton Trust, Head Office (York) Archive GN421 Part 1 History of the Trust. Letter from Assistant Secretary, The William Sutton Trust, to Superintendent, Estate Duty Office, 19 August 1949. The case itself is reported at Ellis *v* Sutton, *Law Reports*, 1901 Chancery, p. 604. The legal grounds on which the will was challenged, including the private and public implications of charitable gifts are explored in Chapter 1.
29   *The City Press*, 27 July 1901.
30   London Metropolitan Archives, Acc 2983/010/1-8, Sutton *v* Attorney General, 14 March 1906. Transcript p. 16.
31   Ibid, p. 12, The Attorney General.

32 Ibid, pp. 7–8, Treasury Solicitor.

33 Ibid, p. 8, Sir Robert Finlay, Counsel for the Trustees.

34 Ibid, p. 10, Finlay for Trustees.

35 London Metropolitan Archives, Acc 2983, 014/112. Letter N. T. Kershaw, Assistant Secretary Local Government Board to the Solicitor to the Treasury, 27 August 1906.

36 On housing associations, local authorities and national housing policy see Patricia L. Garside in A. O'Day, *Government and Institutions in the Post-1832 United Kingdom* (Edwin Mellen Press, 1995).

37 H. Butcher and I. Butcher, *The Sutton Housing Trust – its foundation and history* (The Sutton Housing Trust, 1982) p. 15.

38 PRO HLG1\1032 Scheme for Regulating and Management of the Sutton Trust 1906–1913.

39 London Metropolitan Archives, Acc 2983/010/1-8 Appointment of Advisory Committee, Letter from Solicitor to Trustees to Treasury Solicitor, 7 February 1913.

40 London Metropolitan Archives, Acc 2983/010/1-8. Correspondence re Sutton Trust, Advisory Committee. In the High Court of Justice, Chancery Division, 26 June 1913, Sutton dec'd Sutton *v.* Attorney General.

41 London Metropolitan Archives, Acc 2983/052 Sutton Advisory Committee Minutes, 12 November 1914.

42 PRO HLG1\1032 Memo to Noel Kershaw from A. D. Adrian (LGB) 3 May 1906. Letter to Secretary to LGB from the Solicitor to the Treasury, including notes on draft Scheme, 23 February 1906.

43 London Metropolitan Archives Acc 2983 175(j) Local Government Board to Treasury Solicitor, 27 August 1906.

44 London Metropolitan Archives Acc 2983 175 (k) LCC on Draft Scheme, 13 November 1906.

45 PRO HLG49/1497 Letter from Balmain to E. R. Forber 9 January 1925.

46 London Metropolitan Archives, Acc 2983/052 Sutton Advisory Committee Minutes, 5 February 1914.

47 London Metropolitan Archives Acc 2983/010/1-8 Re Sutton, Sutton *v.* Attorney General.

48 London Metropolitan Archives Acc 2983/010/1-8 Letter from Messrs Lamb (Solicitors acting on behalf of trustees) to J. Rye, Solicitor to the Treasury, 3 November 1906.

49 PRO HLG1\1032 Note attached to letter from Treasury Solicitor to Secretary Local Government Board, 23 May 1913.

50 PRO HLG 49/1497 Sutton Draft Scheme 1906–1920. Towns with more than 200,000 population were London, Birmingham, Manchester, Sheffield, Leeds, Bristol, West Ham, Hull, Bradford, Newcastle-upon-Tyne, Nottingham, Portsmouth, Stoke-on-Trent, Leicester, Salford and Plymouth. (Trustees meeting, 12 November 1914. PRO HLG49/1497).

51 London Metropolitan Archives, LCC Minutes, 13 November 1906.

52 For a succinct account of the various contending interpretations see
    P. Kemp, 'The Origins of Council Housing' in J. Goodwin and C.
    Grant, eds, *Built to Last? Reflections on British Housing Policy*
    Second Edition (Shelter Publications, 1997) pp. 47–54).

53 M. J. Daunton, *A Property-Owning Democracy? Housing in Britain*
    (Faber and Faber, 1987) p. 116.

54 'Housing Problem Scheme of the Sutton Trustees. A Great Benefac-
    tion. Liverpool to Share in It'. *The Liverpool Courier*, 24 September
    1913.

55 City of Liverpool, Housing Committee Minutes, 3 December 1909;
    PRO HLG1/1536. Visit of William Sutton Trustees to Liverpool, 23
    September 1913.

56 'Scheme of Sutton Trustees and Liverpool's Share in it', *The Liver-
    pool Courier*, 23 September 1913.

57 *Daily Post and Mercury,* 7 October 1909 and *The Liverpool Courier*,
    28 October 1909.

58 Brigadier-General Kyffin-Taylor: obituary *The Liverpolitan*, March
    1937 p. 19.

59 City of Liverpool, Housing Committee Minutes, 8 September 1910;
    17 November 1910; 16 December 1910.

60 PRO HLG1/1536 Notes of J. A. E. Dickinson on meeting of
    Advisory Committee, 6 April 1916.

61 London Metropolitan Archives, Acc 2983/052, Minutes of Advisory
    Committee, 23 March 1916.

62 PRO HLG 1/1535 Note of interview between Balmain (Secretary)
    and J. A. E. Dickinson at Local Government Board (ibid) Dickinson
    was appointed to the Advisory Committee as the Board's nominee in
    June 1913.

63 Note from J. A. E. Dickinson on legal advice, Liverpool (Burlington
    Street) Scheme, 22 June 1916 (ibid).

64 Note from J. A. E. Dickinson following meeting with William E
    Hart, Town Clerk of Sheffield, 14 July 1914 (ibid).

65 Notes of J. A. E. Dickinson after meeting Liverpool Town Clerk and
    City Treasurer, 13 July 1914 (ibid).

66 Charles Sutton, *The Liverpool Courier*, 24 September 1913.

67 PRO HLG 1/1536 Letter from Liverpool Town Clerk to J. A. E.
    Dickinson, 19 July 1916.

68 PRO HLG 49/1497 'Sutton Dwellings Trust – Sutton Model Dwell-
    ings Scheme 1913–1926' Messrs Lamb, Son and Prentice to William
    Balmain re: Proposal for General Scheme, 27 March 1914.

69 For the deliberations of the Housing (Financial Assistance)
    Committee, see above Chapter 3.

70 PRO RECO 1/525 Housing (Financial Assistance) Committee –
    Correspondence with Housing Trusts 1918).

71 On the 'pragmatic short term' interpretation of housing policy in
    1919 see M. Daunton, *A Property Owning Democracy?* , pp. 116–7;
    on the 'lack of interest' by housing associations in cities like Liver-

pool, Birmingham, Manchester and Sheffield – all places that the Sutton Trust was actively involved with, see J. Morton, *"Cheaper than Peabody"*, pp. 60–61.

72 These flats were on the St. Quintin Park estate. The estate was built in two phases – the first, completed in 1930, had 540 flats. A further 102 were added in 1934.

73 See above Chapter 3, p. 19.

74 London Metropolitan Archives, Acc 2983/052, Minutes of Advisory Committee, 21 March 1914 and 12 November 1914.

75 The 1920 Draft Scheme is included in full as Appendix 3.

76 PRO HLG 49/1497 Sutton Dwellings Trust Sutton Model Dwellings Scheme 1913–1926. Letter, Lamb, Son and Prance to William Balmain, Secretary to the Trustees, 27 March 1914.

77 PRO HLG 49/1497 Sutton Model Dwellings Scheme. Annotated version 19 March 1920: Letter from Charity Commissioners to the Treasury Solicitor, 1 May 1926.

78 Ibid. Notes on a memo re Sutton and the Scheme, 10 March 1924.

79 Ibid. Letter from J. A. E. Dickinson to Edward Forber, 12 August 1923.

80 Ibid. Note from J. A. E. Dickinson to Edward Forber, 30 January 1920.

81 Ibid. Scheme of Management 1926. Comments of Kyffin-Taylor, 18 May 1926.

82 Ibid. Comments on Draft Scheme of Management, E. R. Forber, 1 May 1926.

83 Butcher, *The Sutton Housing Trust*, p. 29–31.

84 PRO HLG 49/1497 Sutton Dwellings Trust Sutton Model Dwellings Scheme 1913–1926. Note to E. Forber re discussions with Mr Macpherson, Charity Commission, 29 March 1924.

85 London Metropolitan Archives, Acc 2983 010/1-8 Letter from William Balmain to Lamb Son and Prance, 15 November 1923.

86 Ibid. Acc 2983 011/1 – 27 Claims for Trustees' Expenses 1920–1926.

87 For a description of housing development in North Kensington and its slum problems see *Survey of London Vol XXXVII, Northern Kensington* (Athlone Press, 1973) p. 303 and pp. 349–350.

88 A list of the housing associations active in North Kensington and the number of dwellings they were providing is given in Kensington Borough Council Minutes vol. 31 (1930–31) p. 350.

89 Lord Balfour of Burleigh was Chairman of the Kensington Public Health Committee and also of the Kensington Housing Trust.

90 On the reservation of tenancies on the LCC estate at Wormholt for tenants from Kensington see LCC Housing Committee Minutes, 28 January 1925 and 23 November 1927. For the mechanism of 'chains of relief' see Kensington Borough Council Minutes, 30 December 1930.

91 Kensington Borough Council Minutes, 28 June 1932, p. 279.

92 Kensington Borough Council, Medical Officer of Health Report, 1925, pp. 89–94.

93 Kensington Borough Council Minutes vol. 31, p. 273, confirming a minute of Public Health Committee, 11 January 1923.

94 LCC, Minutes of the Housing Committee, 22 July 1925 and 28 October 1925.
95 London Metropolitan Archives, Acc 2983 Minutes of Trustees, 2 March 1927.
96 Ibid, 6 April 1927.
97 Ibid, 4 May 1927.
98 The design of the St. Quintin Park estate and the amenities provided in individual flats are discussed in detail in Chapter 6.
99 Kensington Borough Council Minutes, 4 December 1928.
100 Kensington Borough Council Minutes, 30 December 1930.

CHAPTER 5: HOUSING THE POOR – RENTS, SUBSIDIES AND THE MARKET BEFORE 1939

1 H. Butcher, *The Sutton Housing Trust*, pp. 31–32: Sutton Model Dwellings, *Report*, 31 December 1920. Figures for 1920 exclude the Trust's Birmingham estate which was still requisitioned for Vickers' munition workers.
2 See above especially Chapter 2.
3 A conference held at the University of York in 1998 to celebrate the centenary of Rowntree's study of poverty attracted over fifty papers on various aspects of poverty.
4 On the standard of living in the industrial revolution see A. J. Taylor (ed.), *The Standard of Living in the Industrial Revolution* (Methuen, 1975); on the First World War see Lynda Bryder, 'The First World War: Healthy or Hungry?' in *History Workshop Journal* 18 (1987) and J. Winter and J.-L. Robert, *Capital Cities at War Paris, London, Berlin 1914–1919* (Cambridge: Cambridge University Press, 1997); on the 1930s, see C. Webster, 'Healthy or Hungry Thirties?', *History Workshop Journal*, 13 (1982).
5 P. Johnson (ed.), *20th Century Britain*, (Longman, 1994) p. 6.
6 T. J. Hatton and R. E. Bailey, *Poverty and the Welfare State in Inter-War London* (Centre for Economic Policy Research, 1997) p. 14–17.
7 B. S. Rowntree, *Poverty and Progress A Second Social Survey of York*, (Longmans, 1941), p. 456.
8 See A Sen, 'The Standard of Living 1' and 'The Standard of Living 11' in Geoffrey Hawthorn (ed.) *The Standard of Living* (Cambridge University Press, 1987).
9 Sen, ibid, pp. 15–17.
10 Ibid, p. viii.
11 See, for example, John Burnett, *A Social History of Housing 1815–1970* (Methuen, 1978) Chapter 8; Peter Kemp, 'The Origins of Council Housing' in *Built to Last? Reflections on British Housing Policy*, Second Edition (Shelter, 1997) and M. Daunton, 'Housing' in F. M. L. Thompson, *The Cambridge Social History of Britain 1750-1950* Vol 2 (Cambridge: Cambridge University Press, 1990).
12 G. Darley, *Octavia Hill – A Life* (Constable, 1990) and D. Clapham,

'Octavia Hill – A Woman of her Time' in *Built to Last? Reflections on British Housing Policy* Second Edition (Shelter, 1997).

13 J. N. Tarn, *Five Per Cent Philanthropy: An Account of Housing in Urban Areas between 1840 and 1914* (Cambridge: Cambridge University Press, 1973) p. 134.

14 G. C. M. M'Gonigle and J. Kirby, *Poverty and Public Health* (Gollancz, 1936) Chapter 7.

15 Mass Observation (on behalf of the Advertising Services Guild), *An Enquiry into People's Homes* (John Murray, 1943).

16 R. Dennis, ' "Hard-to Let" in Edwardian London', *Urban Studies*, 26 (1989) pp. 77–89.

17 Peter Malpass describes the Guinness Trust's growing problems in letting its 'associated tenements' in *Housing, Philanthropy and the State: A History of the Guinness Trust* (Bristol: The University of the West of England, 1998) pp. 24–26.

18 Interview, Bethnal Green 6.

19 Interview, Birmingham 17.

20 In 1927, the Sutton Trustees received a delegation from Kensington charities and elected bodies. It included Lord Balfour of Burleigh (Kensington Housing Trust), J. M. Rendell (Kensington Board of Guardians) Miss A. M. Alexander and Lady Maurice (Kensington Baby Clinic), Percy Bates, MP and Lady Trustam Eve (LCC). They 'urged the claims of the Kensington Housing Trust to be allowed to nominate tenants to occupy the (St Quintin Park) dwellings when built'. (London Metropolitan Archives Acc 2983/031 Trustees minutes 5 October 1927) In the following year, the LCC itself approached the Trustees with a view to recommending applicants for St Quintin Park tenancies (ibid, 7 March 1928) For agreement to rehouse tenants displaced by clearance schemes, see ibid, 6 January 1932. The St. Quintin Park estate was in many respects a special case, as Chapter 4 has shown.

21 London Metropolitan Archives, Acc 2983/031 Trustees' Minutes, 1 March 1933 and 5 April 1933.

22 Laisterdyke Local History Group, *Laisterdyke Roundabout*, (Bradford, 1992) p. 123. At St Quintin Park, also, a notice was erected 'inviting applications for accommodation'. London Metropolitan Archives, Acc 2983, Trustees' Minutes, 2 January 1929.

23 On choice and valuation in relation to standards of living see Amartya Sen pp. 12–13. On the importance of choice for the value ascribed to home, see A. Ravetz with R. Turkington, *The Place of Home English Domestic Environments, 1914–2000*, (E and FN Spon, 1995) pp. 206–7.

24 M. Swenarton and S. Taylor, 'The Scale and Nature of Owner-Occupation in Britain between the Wars', *Economic History Review*, 2nd ser., 38, 1985.

25 G. E. Arkell, 'Blocks of Model Dwellings' in C. Booth (ed.), *Labour and Life of the People Volume 11* (William and Norgate, 1891) Tables 1 and 2.

26 Jane Morton, *"Cheaper than Peabody" Local Authority Housing from 1890 to 1919* (Joseph Rowntree Trust, 1991) pp. 38–39.
27 M. Daunton, (ed.) *Councillors and Tenants in Local Authority Housing in English Cities 1919–1939* (Leicester: Leicester University Press, 1984) p. 19.
28 Morton, *"Cheaper than Peabody"*, p. 39.
29 S. Merrett, *State Housing in Britain* (Routledge and Kegan Paul, 1979).
30 Morton, *"Cheaper than Peabody"*, p. 40.
31 Dennis, 'Hard to Let', p. 80.
32 Harry Quelch, Social Democratic Federation member and LCC Councillor, *Justice*, 23 January 1889.
33 Dennis, 'Geography of Victorian Values' p. 13.
34 Ibid, pp. 49–51; see Figure above, Chapter 2.
35 London Metropolitan Archives, Acc 2983/010/1-8, Re Sutton. Sutton *v* Attorney General. Letter Messrs Lamb Son and Prance to J Rye, Treasury Solicitor, 3 November 1906.
36 Sutton Model Dwellings, *Report*, 1915, pp. 2–6.
37 M. S. Pember Reeves, *Round About A Pound A Week* (Bell, 1913) pp. 30 ff.
38 Dennis, 'Hard to Let' p. 87. The LCC was merely acting in line with its original principle of basing rents 'on the basis of comparability with similar private rented accommodation in the locality'. (W. Eric Jackson, *Achievement A Short History of the LCC*, Longman, 1965 p. 106).
39 Increase of Rent and Mortgage Interest (War Restrictions) Act, 1915.
40 Metropolitan Borough of Chelsea, Annual Report of Medical Officer of Health, 1912, p. 28.
41 Details of the William Sutton Trust's land transactions are given in Appendix 4.
42 Taking into account the rents from shops on the Chelsea estate, the William Sutton Trust achieved a return of 3.3% on capital expended. This was the highest return of any of the Sutton estates. See Table 2.2 Sutton Model Dwellings Account 1924 Chapter 2.
43 The Chelsea Metropolitan Borough Council Public Health Committee were informed in April 1913 that '25 occupiers had left the Council's dwellings during the last fortnight to take up tenancies in the Sutton Trust buildings'. Minute Book, volume 10, July 1911– April 1914.
44 Sutton Model Dwellings, *Report* (1915) p. 5.
45 Birmingham Reference Library Archives, *Jewel Baillie Collection Newspaper Cuttings 1910–1913*, Birmingham Housing Inquiry, Report of Special Committee, Interim Report, October 1914.
46 Birmingham Reference Library Archives, *Birmingham Town Planning Letter Book No.2 1912–May 1913*, Letters, Town Clerk to Local Government Board, 25 January 1913 and 8 February 1913.
47 Birmingham Reference Library Archives, *Jewel Baillie Collection*

Newspaper Cuttings 1910–1913, Birmingham Daily Post 19 November 1911 'Town Planning East Birmingham Scheme'. Ibid. 24 May 1912. 'Submission of Warwick and Worcester Committee of Surveyors' Institution'.

48 Seebohm Rowntree, while acknowledging the wide variation in rents in 1918 said that he 'took 6/- a week for a three-bedroom house as the predominant rental, including rates'. *Human Needs of Labour* (Longmans, Green and Co., 1937) p. 90.

49 Birmingham Reference Library Archives, *Jewel Baillie Collection Newspaper Cuttings 1910-1913 Birmingham Daily Post*, 31 July 1912, 'Town Planning in East Birmingham'.

50 Ibid, *Daily Post*, 12 July 1912, 'Town Planning in Birmingham Saltley and Stetchford Conference of Owners'.

51 Ibid, *Birmingham Daily Post*, 19 November 1910, 10 October 1911 and 12 July 1912.

52 City of Birmingham Reference Library Archives, *Reports of Town Clerk to Various Committees*, January–December 1913.

53 London Metropolitan Archives Acc 2983/052 Advisory Committee Minutes, 5 February 1914.

54 Sutton Model Dwellings, *Report*, 31 December 1920.

55 Robert Ryder, 'Council House Building in County Durham, 1900–39: The Local Implementation of National Policy', in M. Daunton (ed) *Councillors and Tenants : Local Authority Housing in English Cities, 1919–1939* (Leicester: Leicester University Press, 1984) p. 81.

56 Ibid, p. 82.

57 Daunton, *Councillors and Tenants*, p. 22.

58 London Metropolitan Archives, Acc 2983/252 Minutes of Advisory Committee, Matters attended to December 1914–December 1915.

59 See above pp. 62 PRO RECO1/525 Housing (Finance Assistance) Committee – Correspondence with Housing Trusts 1918.

60 PRO RECO1/525 Letter from William Balmain, Secretary, William Sutton Trust, dated 9 October 1918, p. 4.

61 Ibid, p. 5.

62 PRO RECO 1/525 Letter from William Balmain, 9 October 1918, Appendix, Estimated cost of building cottages at Gorton, Manchester.

63 London Metropolitan Archives, Acc 2983/052 Minutes of Advisory Committee, 10 November 1920.

64 London Metropolitan Archives, Acc 2983 010/1-8, William Balmain, Secretary to Trustees to Messrs Lamb and Prince, Solicitors, 15 November 1923.

65 Ibid. Lengthy negotiations for subsidy under the 1919 Housing Act were entered into over the Islington estate where some accommodation for blind women was proposed. The subsidy was withdrawn before agreement could be reached, and no such accommodation was in fact provided. PRO HLG/49/676 Sutton Trust, Upper Street Islington, Application for Financial Assistance. I am grateful to Tanis Hinchcliffe for this reference.

66 PRO HAG 29/129 1923 Housing etc Bill – Commons Amendments, Ministerial note.
67 Ibid.
68 The Chamberlain subsidy remained in force until 1929 when it was cancelled.
69 London Metropolitan Archives, Acc 2983 010/1-8, Correspondence William Balmain to Messrs. Lamb, Son and Prance, 15 November 1923.
70 Land and building costs at Islington were £166,622 and £91,993 at Manchester. London Metropolitan Archives, Acc 2983/055/1-11, Schedule of Capital of the Trust as at 1926.
71 *The Manchester Guardian*, 27 November 1926.
72 Medical Officer of Health, Leeds City Council, 1927. Quoted in R. Finnigan, 'Council Housing in Leeds, 1919–1939: Social Policy and Urban Change' in Daunton, *Councillors and Tenants*, p. 114.
73 Leeds City Council, *Annual Report of Finance and Parliamentary Committee*, 1929–30.
74 Finnigan, 'Council Housing in Leeds', p. 103.
75 *Yorkshire Evening News*, 29 May 1929.
76 *Yorkshire Post*, 20 May 1929.
77 *Yorkshire Evening Post*, 16 January 1930.
78 Finnigan, 'Council Housing in Leeds', p. 114.
79 The Sutton Dwellings Trust, *Report and Accounts*, 31 December 1948, p. 8.
80 Finnigan, 'Council Housing in Leeds' p. 115.
81 Leeds City Council, Engineer's Office Cutting Book, *Yorkshire Evening Post*, 30 April 1929, NHTPC in Leeds, H. Milner, Chairman of Housing Subcommittee.
82 Daunton, *Councillors and Tenants*, p. 13.
83 The significant pieces of legislation were the Housing Act, 1930 (Greenwood Act); Housing (Financial Provisions Act), 1933; Housing Act, 1935; Rent and Mortgage Interest Restrictions Act, 1933 and Rent and Mortgage Interest Restrictions Act, 1939.
84 P.P. 1930–31 XVII, Ministry of Health, Report of the Inter-departmental Committee on the Rent Restriction Acts.
85 London Metropolitan Archives. Acc 2983, Minutes of William Sutton Trustees, 1 March and 5 April 1933.
86 PRO HLG 49/1497, Sutton Model Dwellings Account, 1934.
87 London Metropolitan Archives. Acc 2983, Minutes of William Sutton Trustees, 2 November 1936.
88 Seebohm Rowntree, *Poverty and Progress*, p. 462.
89 A 1936 survey of overcrowding showed that in South Shields where the Trust built an estate in 1934–36, there was five times as much overcrowding in the private rented sector as in the Council sector.
90 Central Housing Advisory Committee, Housing Management Subcommittee, *First Report*, 1939.

91 Councillor the Rev. Charles Jenkinson, 'Leeds Housing Policy', *Labour Research*, 5 (1934) p. 148.

92 Peter Malpass, 'Rents within Reach', in J. Goodwin and C. Grant, *Built to Last* , 2nd edition (Shelter, 1997) p. 72.

93 The Trust's handbook for its superintendents contained a routine for accepting lodgers.

94 London County Council, Minutes of the Housing Committee, 23 November 1927: Ryder, 'Council House Building in County Durham 1900–39', p. 84.

95 J. Burnett, *A Social History of Housing 1815–1970* (Methuen, 1978) p. 233.

96 The reasons why the William Sutton Trust became involved in building in North Kensington are discussed above, Chapter 4.

97 Interview Chelsea 11; *Laisterdyke Roundabout*, p. 126.

98 Between 1930 and 1939, only 6% of local authority tenders approved by the Ministry of Health were one bedroom. In the private sector, small dwellings were increasingly to be found in older, poorly equipped properties, while market forces 'militated against the development of a housing stock with a range of house sizes which matches the range of household sizes'. V. Hole and M. T. Pountney, *Trends in Population, Housing and Occupancy Rates,* (BRS, HMSO, 1971) p. 31.

99 A. Briggs, *A Study of the Work of Seebohm Rowntree,* (Longmans, Green and Co., 1961) p. 318.

100 Hatton and Bailey, *Poverty and the Welfare State* , p. 13.

101 London Metropolitan Archives, William Sutton Trustees Minutes, 7 December 1932.

CHAPTER 6:   RESOURCES AND CAPABILITIES – LIVING ON WILLIAM SUTTON TRUST ESTATES 1909–1939

1 Malpass, *History of the Guinness Trust*, pp. 13 and 17.

2 Interview, Chelsea 3.

3 M. Girouard, *The Victorian Country House* (New Haven: Yale University Press, 1979) p. 75.

4 Louis de Soissons, 'Working Class Housing' in *Flats. Municipal and Private Enterprise* (Ascot Gas Water Heaters Ltd., 1938) p. 7; N. Pevsner and J. Nairn, eds, *The Buildings of England London 1 The Cities of London and Westminster* (Harmondsworth: Penguin, 1973) p. 391. See also A. Cox, ' "An Example to Others": Public Housing in London 1840–1914', *London and Middlesex Archaeological Society Transactions,* 46 (1995) pp. 145–152.

5 Interview, Bethnal Green, 6. 'We had a piece of concrete with a metal fencing round it and one tree in the middle. If you climbed over there, my goodness you got told off by the superintendent and the porters'.

6 Obituaries, *Newcastle Journal*, 11 May 1935, *Journal of the Royal Institute of British Architects*, November 1935 and *The Builder*, 24 May 1935.

7 London Metropolitan Archives, Acc 2983, William Sutton Trustees' Minutes, March 1914.

8 *Reports of the Medical Officer of Health*, Newcastle 1909–1913. In 1911, faced with 'a great number of houses standing empty' on its model cottage estate at Walkergate, one Alderman called for an end to more building. 'It is the most absurd thing that ever entered into the heart of any intelligent man'. He was supported by a petition from the Newcastle Property Owners Association. *Proceedings of Newcastle City Council*, 6 December 1911 and 1 May 1912.

9 Mr Cairns, *Proceedings of the Newcastle Council*, 4 March 1914, p. 451.

10 Interviews, Newcastle, Barrack Road, 7 and 5.

11 See above pp. *Proceedings of the Newcastle Council*, 4 March 1914, p. 450 (Mrs Bell).

12 See above pp. 120–122. The Birmingham Alum Rock scheme was the last designed for the Trust by E. C. P. Monson. From 1919, he designed housing for Islington Metropolitan Borough Council.

13 PRO, RECO 1/525, Letter from Balmain, Secretary to the Trustees, 9 October 1918.

14 London Metropolitan Archives, Acc 2983, For an example of Ministerial involvement at the layout stage see William Sutton Trustees' Minutes, 2 March 1927, Stoke on Trent.

15 London Metropolitan Archives, The William Sutton Trustees' Minutes, 2 September 1931.

16 Ibid, 4 May 1932.

17 *Manchester Guardian*, 27 November 1926. 'A New Housing Scheme in Manchester'.

18 London Metropolitan Archives, Acc 2983, 232–233, Plan of Middlesborough Estate.

19 Bridgeland, ed., *Laisterdyke Roundabout* , p. 124.

20 Ibid, p. 126.

21 *An Enquiry into People's Homes* Mass Observation (on behalf of the Advertising Service Guild), (John Murray, 1943) p. xviii.

22 London Metropolitan Archives Acc 2983, William Sutton Trust Minutes, 6 February 1929. Referring to design of flats in Salford, 'Mr Fairhurst (local architect) to be instructed and something along the lines of the LCC 3 storey tenements at White Hart Lane to be provided, the main feature being open work balconies for children's prams'.

23 London Metropolitan Archives Acc 2983/083 Private Ledger 1927–36, Islington.

24 Louis de Soissons, 'Working Class Housing', p. 9.

25 See pp. 104–107 for the circumstances of the development at St. Quintin Park.

26 London Metropolitan Archives Acc 2983 William Sutton Trustees' Minutes, 7 December 1927.

27 Ibid, 4 April 1928.

28 J. Fletcher, 'Kensington Builds for the Poor', *Architectural Review*, March 1934, p. 86.

28 Interview, Bethnal Green 6, quoting a parent in 1922.
30 Interview, Newcastle, Barrack Road 31.
31 *Enquiry into People's Homes*, Chapter XX111, 'Privacy', and p. xix.
32 Interview, Birmingham 14.
33 Rowntree, *Poverty and Progress*, pp. 462–465.
34 Interview, Birmingham 14.
35 Interviews, Newcastle Barrack Road 1, 11, 12.
36 Interview, Bethnal Green 6.
37 Interview, Bethnal Green 31.
38 *Laisderdyke Roundabout*, p. 126.
39 Rowntree, *The Human Needs of Labour*, p. 115.
40 Cox, "An Example to Others", p. 150.
41 Interview, Birmingham 13.
42 Cox, "An Example to Others", p. 149.
43 Quoted in J. Burnett, *A Social History of Housing 1815 to 1970* (Methuen, 1980) p. 229.
44 London Metropolitan Archives, Acc 2983,010/1-8 The William Sutton Trust, Balmain to Lamb, 15 November 1923.
45 London Metropolitan Archives, Acc 2983, The William Sutton Trustees' Minutes, 4 April 1928.
46 Fletcher, 'Kensington Builds for the Poor', p. 83.
47 London Metropolitan Archives, Acc 2983, The William Sutton Trustees' Minutes, 1 June 1927.
48 *An Enquiry into People's Homes* , p. xiv.
49 *Manchester Guardian*, 'A New Housing Scheme in Manchester', 27 November 1926.
50 London Metropolitan Archives, Acc 2983, Minutes of the William Sutton Trustees, 2 February 1927.
51 Ibid, 6 April 1927.
52 Ibid, 2 March 1927.
53 Ibid, 6 July 1927.
54 Ibid, 2 November 1936.
55 Ibid, 1 December 1930; 1 July 1931.
56 *An Enquiry into People's Homes,* pp. xii–xiii.
57 Interviews, Birmingham 6. On the Birmingham estate, only 30 out of 230 houses were 'parlour-type'.
58 G. M'Gonigle and J. Kirby, *Poverty and Public Health* (Gollancz, 1936).
59 Interviews, Birmingham 13.
60 Rowntree, *The Human Needs of Labour*, p. 41.
61 London Metropolitan Archives, William Sutton Trust Minutes, 4 May 1927. The Guinness Trust also provided blinds on some of its estates but costs were recouped from tenants through a small weekly charge. (Trustees' Minutes, 24 July 1891).
62 Ibid, 7 October 1931.
63 Butcher, *The Sutton Housing Trust*, p. 19, quoting an interview with the architects in the national press.

64 Mass Observation, *Enquiry into People's Homes*, p. xvii.
65 Guinness rules of tenancy explicitly forbad the taking in of washing 'from persons who are not living in the buildings'. (Rule Number 4, *General Rules of Tenancy*).
66 A. Ravetz with R. Turkington, *The Place of Home English Domestic Environments 1914–2000* (E and F N Spon, 1995) p. 123.
67 Ibid, p. 124.
68 J. Winter and J.-L. Robert, *Capital Cities at War London, Paris, Berlin 1914–1919* (Cambridge: Cambridge University Press, 1997) p. 359.
69 Mass Observation, *Enquiry into People's Homes*, p. xv.
70 Butcher, *The Sutton Housing Trust*, p. 19.
71 L. Hannah, *Electricity before Nationalisation* (The Electricity Council/Macmillan, 1979) p. 208.
72 Mass Observation, *Enquiry into People's Homes*, p. xii.
73 Interview, Bethnal Green 6.
74 London Metropolitan Archives, The William Sutton Trustees' Minutes, 5 December 1928.
75 Ibid, 2 July 1930.
76 Interview, Bethnal Green 6.
77 Interview, Chelsea 8.
78 Mass Observation, *An Enquiry into People's Homes*, p. xii and p. 141–142.
79 'Kensington Builds for the Poor', pp. 85–86.
80 Ravetz, *The Place of Home*, p. 122–123.
81 London Metropolitan Archives, The William Sutton Trustees' Minutes, 2 January 1929. The arrears were subsequently found to relate to mishandling of cash by the Superintendent. Ibid, 1 January 1930. Upgrading of lighting, coppers and ranges was carried out in the mid 1930s. Interview, Birmingham 1.
82 Ibid, 5 December 1928.
83 Ibid, 6 February 1929.
84 Ibid.
85 Ibid, 6 May 1931.
86 Interview, Chelsea 11.
87 Mass Observation, *Enquiry into People's Homes*, p. 135.
88 London Metropolitan Archives, Acc 2983, The William Sutton Trustees' Minutes, 2 May 1928.
89 London Metropolitan Archives, Acc 2983, The William Sutton Trustees' Minutes, 6 July 1932.
90 Ibid, 7 May 1930.
91 Ibid, 7 May 1930.
92 Ibid, 5 November 1930.
93 The Sutton Dwellings Trust, *Report and Accounts*, 1948. p. 13 table 5.
94 Interview, Bethnal Green 12.
95 Interview, Newcastle, Barrack Road, 9.
96 Interviews, Bethnal Green 12; Bethnal Green 4, Chelsea 3, Bethnal Green 6.

97 Interviews, Bethnal Green 3, Birmingham 17.

98 Interview, Chelsea 3.

99 Interview, Birmingham 1; London Metropolitan Archives, Acc 2983, The William Sutton Trustees' Minutes, 4 December 1929 and 1 January 1930.

100 Ibid, 6 March 1929; 4 September 1929; 2 September 1931; 2 December 1931.

101 Interview, Bethnal Green 12.

102 Ibid, Birmingham 1; Bethnal Green 31; Newcastle 8.

103 Ibid, Birmingham 1.

104 Interview, Chelsea 8.

105 Interviews, Newcastle 7, 11 and 12.

106 London Metropolitan Archives, Acc 2983/011/1-37, April 1919.

107 London Metropolitan Archives, Acc 2983/052; Ibid 2983/011/1-27 April 1919, March 1920 and March 1921; Balance Sheet and Accounts 1927; Acc 2983/032 The William Sutton Trustees' Minutes 1 March 1933.

108 The Sutton Dwellings Trust, *Annual Report 1915* gives the rent of pram sheds as 1d to 2d per week, and barrow sheds, 6d.

109 Rowntree, *Poverty and Progress*, p. 232; Interview, Chelsea 8.

110 Mass Observation, *Enquiry into People's Homes*, p. xvii.

111 London Metropolitan Archives, Acc 2983, The William Sutton Trustees' Minutes, 2 July 1930.

112 Mass Observation, *Enquiry into People's Homes*, p. 234.

113 Interview, Birmingham 9.

114 Interview, Birmingham 1.

115 Mass Observation, *Enquiry into People's Homes*, p. xviii.

116 London Metropolitan Archives, Acc 2983/083, Private Ledger 1927–1936, 4 September 1929.

117 Interview, Birmingham 1.

118 London Metropolitan Archives, Acc 2983 The William Sutton Trustees' Minutes, 6 May 1931.

119 Ibid, 1 January 1930.

120 Ibid, 6 May 1931.

121 London Metropolitan Archives, Acc 2983, 011/1-27 Trustees' Claim for Year 8 March 1924.

122 An early draft scheme for the management of William Sutton's bequest in 1906 included a clause allowing for the 'fitting up' of libraries, school rooms, infant nurseries, laundries, baths and washhouses, reading rooms, gymnasiums, 'and any other (necessary) ... to promote the health and moral welfare (of tenants) including open space, gardens, playgrounds and places of rest'. The clause was dropped on advice from the Local Government Board that local authorities were already making such provisions. London Metropolitan Archives, Acc 2983, 010/1-8, 26 March 1906; 27 August 1906.

123 A. Olechnowicz, *Working Class Housing in England between the Wars. The Becontree Estate* (Oxford: Clarendon Press, 1997) The

New Estates Community Committee was established in 1928 by the National Council of Social Service, itself one of the most prominent inter-war voluntary associations whose founders had close links with the university settlement movement.

124 Interview, Birmingham 4.
125 London Metropolitan Archives, The William Sutton Trust Minutes, 6 July 1929.
126 Ibid, 4 March 1931.
127 Ibid, 6 July 1932.
128 Bridgeland, *Laisterdyke Roundabout*, p. 127.
129 Ibid, p. 128.
130 Ibid, pp. 128–129.
131 London Metropolitan Archives, The William Sutton Trustees' Minutes, 6 November 1929.
132 The William Sutton Trust, Head Office (York) Archive File Benwell Tenants' Association, Superintendent to Secretary, 23 January 1947.
133 Ibid, Records of the Leeds York Road Tenants' Association, File KB 82.
134 Bridgeland, *Laisterdyke Roundabout*, p. 130.
135 London Metropolitan Archives Acc 2983/226 Stoke on Trent (Trent Vale) Tenants Association Minutes, 27 August 1939.
136 London Metropolitan Archives, Acc 2983/226 Stoke on Trent (Trent Vale) Tenants' Association Minutes 31 October 1939.
137 Interviews, Birmingham 4, 6 and 7. Barrack Road 4, 11 and 12, Bethnal Green 12.
138 Interviews, Newcastle, Barrack Road 7 and 9.
139 London Metropolitan Archives, Acc 2983, The William Sutton Trustees' Minutes, 6 May 1931, 6 April 1932 and 5 October 1932.
140 The William Sutton Trust Head Office (York) Archive, File 82, Leeds York Road Tenants' Association; Interviews, Newcastle, Barrack Road 11, Birmingham 11.
141 Interviews, Newcastle, Barrack Road 7 and 9, Birmingham 3, 9 and 14, Chelsea 11. *Laisterdyke Roundabout*, p. 127.
142 The William Sutton Trust Head Office (York) Archive, Tenants' Associations, Manchester – Gorton. Letter from Secretary to Trustees to Superintendent, 7 November 1945.
143 Interviews, Birmingham 4 and Newcastle, Barrack Road 9
144 *An Enquiry into People's Homes*, pp. 208–9, p. xxii.

CHAPTER 7: NEW GAMES IN OLD ARENAS – POVERTY, CHARITY AND HOUSING AFTER 1945

 1 National Adult School Council, *Living in the 'Sixties* (Headley Bros., 1964), p. 1.
 2 Chesterman, *Charities*, pp. 83–84.
 3 This segmentation of the newly discovered poor persisted even though Brian Abel-Smith and Peter Townsend calculated that 7.5

million people were living below the official poverty line. B. Abel-Smith and P. Townsend, *The Poor and the Poorest* (Bell, 1967).

4   W. H. Beveridge, *Voluntary Action* (Allen and Unwin, 1948); Report of the Committee on the Law and Practice Relating to Charitable Trusts (Nathan Committee) Cmd 8710, HMSO, 1952; Lord Nathan, 'The Charitable Trusts Committee. Some Notes on its Recommendations', *Social Service* (Spring 1953): 149–155.

5   Evidence presented to CHAC, Subcommittee on Housing Associations and Societies, by Rt Hon Douglas Houghton, C.H., M.P.

6   Marilyn Taylor, 'Voluntary Action', citing Richard Crossman. p. 219.

7   Archbishop of Canterbury speaking in the House of Lords Debate on the Nathan Report, 22 July 1953, Col. 761.

8   See pp. 33–37.

9   M. Taylor, 'Voluntary Action', pp. 225–227.

10   Chesterman, *Charities*, argues this in relation to the activities of the Charity Organisation Society. Chapter 15.

11   Hansard, House of Lords, 13 May 1959, Col. 395.

12   Ibid, col 368–369.

13   Hansard, House of Lords, Debate on Charitable Trusts, 22 July 1953, Col. 826.

14   Nathan, 'Charitable Trusts', p. 153.

15   House of Lords, Debate on Charitable Trusts, 22 July 1953, Col 788

16   House of Lords, Debate on Charitable Trusts, 13 May 1959. Lord Nathan, Col 370.

17   Ibid, Col 371.

18   Ibid.

19   Ibid, Col 386 Viscount Samuels and Lord Hylton.

20   Ibid, Col 390, Lord Hawke.

21   Ibid, 22 July 1953, Lord Rennell.

22   *Charitable Trusts in England and Wales*, Cmd 9358. July 1955.

23   House of Lords, Debate on Charitable Trusts, 13 May 1959, Cols 400–409. The Lord Chancellor. The re-enactments were achieved in the 1960 Charities Act.

24   The William Sutton Trust, Head Office (York) Archive, GN 428, 'Committee on Charities'.

25   Ibid. The Sutton Dwellings Trust, Report of the Law and Practice relating to Charitable Trusts, 'Secretary's Memorandum' 3 March 1953.

26   Charles V. Baker, communication with the author, January 1993.

27   The William Sutton Trust, Head Office (York) Archive, GN 428, 'Extracts from letters from Sir Edward Forber to the Secretary dated 21 February and 9 March 1953'.

28   Ibid.

29   The William Sutton Trust, Head Office (York) Archive, GN428, 'Secretary's Memorandum'.

30   Ibid.

31   Chesterman, *Charities*, p. 91. Of the charities registered before 1970, 47% had relief of poverty as their object. Between 1960 and 1970, the percentage with this purpose fell to 18, and by 1975 it had fallen to 6.

32   Ibid. p. 100. A survey of a sample of registered charities in 1975 showed 80.7% with incomes of less than £10,000.

33   Nathan Committee Report, para 106.

34   House of Lords Debates, 22 July 1953, Col 762.

35   The William Sutton Trust, Head Office (York) Archive, GN 575 *Housing Charity, Legal Status and Rents* 'Notes of an Exchange of Views with Inland Revenue on the Review of the Work of Charitable Housing Agencies', ? May 1969.

36   Ibid. H.M. Inspector of Taxes to Leeds Jewish Housing Association Ltd, 23 January 1969.

37   The William Sutton Trust, Head Office (York)Archive, York GN 575 Housing Charity, Legal Status and Rents 'Notes of an exchange of views Between Waddilove and the Inland Revenue on the Review by the Department of the Work of Charitable Agencies'. ? May 1969.

38   Ibid. Lewis E. Waddilove to C. V. Baker, 26 March 1969 The Cohen Committee was an advisory body set up in 1968 under the Central Housing Advisory Committee. It was chaired by Sir Karl Cohen, but produced neither a report nor recommendations. A summary of the evidence presented to it was published in 1971 by the Department of the Environment as *Housing Associations. A Working Paper of the Central Housing Advisory Committee.*

39   'Some Clarity on Charity' *Voluntary Housing* 2 (4) (21 July 1970); (10 November 1970).

40   Chesterman, *Charities* Chapter 7. The Legal Definition of 'Charitable'.

41   Ibid, p. 137.

42   Chesterman, *Charities*, p. 140.

43   Ibid, pp. 142–143.

44   'Some Clarity' *Voluntary Housing*, 10 November 1970.

45   Housing associations which were charities within the meaning of the Charities Act 1960 had been excluded from applying fair rents, introduced into the private sector by the Rent Act of 1965. The exemptions were withdrawn in 1972. See Appendix 6 for details of changing statutory definitions of voluntary housing agencies.

46   The William Sutton Trust, Head Office (York) Archive, GN575, Lewis Waddilove to C. V. Baker 16 January 1970 and 18 January 1971.

47   Ibid. Marginal note (CVB) on correspondence, 18 January 1971.

48   Ibid. GN575 Letter L. Waddilove to W. E. A. Lewis, Charity Commission, 5 May 1969.

49   Ibid. Letter Lewis Waddilove to Charles Baker, dated 17 December 1969.

50   Ibid. 'Notes on an Exchange of Views with the Inland Revenue by the Department on the Work of Charitable Housing Societies', para 3.

51 Ibid. Inland Revenue to Lewis Waddilove, 22 April 1969.
52 M. Smith, *Guide To Housing*, 3rd ed. (Housing Centre Trust, 1989), p. 228.
53 The William Sutton Trust, Head Office (York) Archive GN575, Memorandum from Rt. Hon. Douglas Houghton, C.H., M.P. 'Charitable Housing'.
54 *Guardian*, 8 January 1969, 'Shelter's First Million' and subsequent correspondence, 18, 21 and 24 January 1969.
55 The William Sutton Trust, Head Office (York) Archive, GN575, Houghton, 'Charitable Housing'.
56 Ibid. GN575, Martin Bond, Peabody Trust to Charles Baker, 2 December 1969.
57 Ibid, GN561, *Housing in the English Electric Group*.
58 Ibid, GN536a. A schedule of subsidies for the Kingsway dwellings showed a total of £24, 004. They had all been paid under post-1945 legislation and were for 60 years.
59 Ibid, GN564, Kingsway Housing Association Ltd. Lettings Policy.
60 Ibid, GN559 Kingsway Housing Association – Statistical and Financial Information.
61 Ibid, Director, Kingsway Housing Association to Charles Baker, 13 March 1969.
62 Ibid, GN536a Memorandum on practical points, 7 November 1969.
63 Ibid, GN563b Agenda Item No 9, June 1969, Kingsway Housing Association Ltd.
64 Ibid, Document 126 (September 1969). Kingsway Housing Association Ltd.
65 Ibid, GN563b Agenda Item June 1969, Appendix 'B', General Manager's Note on the broad considerations involved in the proposed acquisition of houses from Kingsway Housing Association Ltd.
66 Ibid, GN536 Agenda Item No 9, June 1969, Kingsway Housing Association Ltd.
67 Ibid, GN563b Agenda Item No 9, June 1969, Kingsway Housing Association Ltd.
68 Ibid, GN558A, Note from Charles Baker to Charity Commissioners, 13 January 1970.
69 Ibid, GN564, Notes of Meeting, Charles Baker and Director Kingsway Housing Association Ltd., 27 January 1970.
70 Ibid, GN558A, Letter Charles Baker to S.P. Grounds, Charity Commission, 15 August 1969.
71 Ibid, 558A Kingsway Acquisition – Correspondence with Charity Commissioners, 13 January 1970.
72 Ibid, 20 January 1970.
73 Ibid, 6 February 1970.
74 Ibid, GN5636, Appendix B.
75 Ibid, GN564, Letter Charles Baker to L. G. Larke, Kingsway Housing Association Ltd., 11 December 1969.

76 Ibid.
77 Ibid, GN558A 25 August 1969.
78 Ibid, GN563b Appendix B, General Manager's note on proposed acquisition of Kingsway, June 1969.

CHAPTER 8: THE WILLIAM SUTTON TRUST AT THE END OF THE TWENTIETH CENTURY

1 P. Allen, 'The Role of Housing Associations in Britain', (MSc dissertation, University of Bristol, 1981), p. 223.
2 Ibid, pp. 156–158.
3 Interview with Keith Curtis, July 1998 and with Chris Edwards, November 1997.
4 Interview with Richard Dally, January 1997.
5 Butcher, *The Sutton Housing Trust*, p. 54.
6 Keith Curtis interview.
7 Charles Baker, letter to the author, 18 September 1992.
8 In 1993, the Trust employed 550 people, 75% of whom worked on estates 'delivering front line services to customers' through a local estate office. Many of the staff lived on the estates where they worked. *The William Sutton Trust Corporate Plan*, p. 4–5.
9 The William Sutton Trust, Extract from edited proceedings of staff conference, September 1978.
10 Philip Mayo, Chair of Trustees, 1985-1994, 'Tenant Participation', typescript, no date, ?1993.
11 *Sutton Housing Trust. A Political Audit*. A Report by GJW Government Relations, August 1993.
12 Ibid, p. 3.
13 Butcher, *The Sutton Housing Trust* p. 73.
14 Interview with Mike Morris, 20 November 1998.
15 *Inside Housing* 22 August 1997, p. 4.
16 This account of the Trust's most recent period relies heavily on an interview with Mr M. Morris, 20 November 1998.
17 See N. Johnson, *The Welfare State in Transition: The Theory and Practice of Welfare Pluralism* (Brighton: Welfare Books, 1987); J. Wolch, *The Shadow State: Government and the Voluntary Sector in Transition* (New York: The Foundation Centre, 1990; J. Le Grand and W. Bartlett, eds, *Quasi-markets and Social Policy* (Macmillan, 1993 and M. J. Warrington, 'Welfare Pluralism or Welfare State? The Provision of Social Housing in the 1990s', *Environment and Planning (A)*, 27 (9) (1995): pp. 1341–1360.
18 House of Commons, Environment Committee, *The Housing Corporation*, Second report, Volume 1, 1993.

Appendix 1

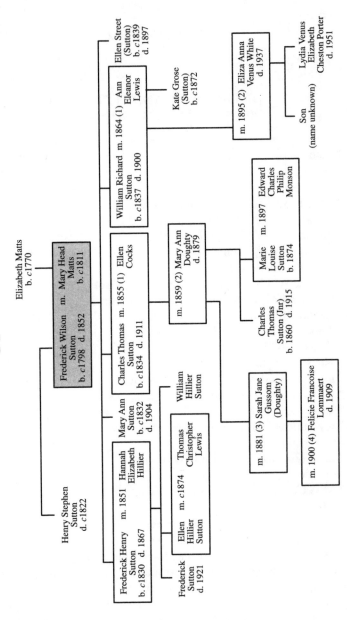

Appendix 2

THE LAST WILL AND TESTAMENT
OF WILLIAM RICHARD SUTTON

Name	Amount per annum
To my brother Charles Thomas Sutton	£ 5,000
" my nephew Charles Thomas Sutton Junior	£ 250
" my nephew William Hillier Sutton	£ 250
" my sister Mary Ann Sutton	£ 500
" my sister Ellen Street	£ 500
" my late Wife's adopted daughter Kate Grose	£ 200
" my friend Mrs Dunning of Fitzroy House Upper Norwood	£ 52
" Thomas Christopher Lewis of Brixton Organ Builder	£ 500
" Nelly Lewis his wife and my niece	£ 500
" my old friend Miss Eliza Barret of Brixton	£ 100
" my Coachman George Dolby if in my service at my death	£ 78
" my butler George Turner if in my service at my death	£ 78
" my Cook Lucy Nash if in my service at my death	£ 52
" Miss Cracknell of Camberwell my late Wife's Dressmaker	£ 26

I DIRECT that the above mentioned life annuities shall be paid free from duty quarterly the first quarterly payment to be made at the expiration of three months from my decease and none of such annuitants are to be entitled to receive the value of his or her annuity in lieu thereof or to anticipate his or her annuity I

BEQUEATH to Thomas Watson the Manager of my business of a Carrier at Golden Lane aforesaid all my horses carts vans and other effects used in my said carrier's business and the Goodwill thereof for his own use and benefit absolutely and I DIRECT that the said Thomas Watson shall provided he shall within three calendar months from my death give notice in writing of such desire to my Trustees hereinafter named be entitled to a lease of the premises in Golden Lane aforesaid now used for the purposes of my said business such lease to be for the term of twenty one years from my death at the yearly rent of Five thousand pounds and subject to all usual and ordinary covenants and conditions including full repairing and insurance covenants and a provision for re entry on nonpayment of rent for thirty days or non performance of covenants and I EMPOWER my Trustees (hereinafter named) to grant to the said Thomas Watson such lease accordingly.

I APPOINT my brother CHARLES THOMAS SUTTON CHARLES EDWARD TRANTER LAMB of 53 Moorgate Street in the City of London and the said THOMAS WATSON to be EXECUTORS and TRUSTEES of this my Will and they and the survivors and survivor of them and the executors and administrators of such survivor and other the Trustees or Trustee for the time being hereof and hereinafter included in the expression "my Trustees" I GIVE DEVISE AND BEQUEATH all my real estate of any tenure and the residue and remainder of my personal estate and effects whatsoever and wheresoever unto my Trustees their heirs executors and administrators respectively according to the nature thereof UPON TRUST to sell convert into money and get in the same at such time or times as my Trustees shall think fit (but as to reversionary property not until it falls into possession unless it shall appear to my Trustees that an earlier sale would be beneficial) and so that they shall have the fullest power and discretion to postpone for such period as they shall think fit the sale conversion or getting in of all or any part of my trust estate and effects whether of a wearing out nature or otherwise and to continue for so long as my Trustees shall think advisable all or any investments whatsoever existing at my death without incurring any responsibility or liability whatsoever for any loss or damage incurred or sustained by reason of such postponement or continuance or in anywise relating thereto.

I DIRECT that my Trustees shall stand possessed of the net moneys to arise from the sale conversion and getting in my real estate and residuary personal estate and effects (after payment of all my just debts funeral and testamentary expenses) and of the rents dividends income and produce therefore in the meantime and of any moneys to be received by them as herein after mentioned (all hereinafter referred to as "the trust premises") UPON the following trusts namely.

1. UPON trust to purchase or acquire from time to time freehold or copyhold land in London or any other populous place or Town in England as sites for the erection of the model dwellings and houses hereinafter mentioned (with power to enfranchise at any time and copyhold land so purchased or acquired) and to pay all monies required for any of the purposes aforesaid out of the trust premises.

2. AND UPON FURTHER TRUST to build upon the sites so to be purchased or acquired as foresaid model dwellings and houses for use and occupation by the poor and from time to time to repair and rebuild the same with power to enter into any contracts and to employ any persons necessary in the sole judgement of my Trustees for such purposes and to pay all moneys required for any of the purposes aforesaid and all taxes rates assessments and outgoings whatsoever (including the premiums on any policies of insurance against loss or damage by fire) which at any time be taxed rated charged or assessed or be payable upon or in respect of such dwellings out of the trust premises.

3. AND UPON FURTHER TRUST to let the said dwellings and houses when so erected to the poor in the several districts in which they are erected at such rents (being below the full rents which could be obtained for the same) as my trustees shall in their uncontrolled discretion in each case and from time to time determine but so that the rents received by my Trustees therefore shall be held by them for the general purpose of the trust intended to be hereby created and shall form part of the trust premises.

4. AND I EMPOWER my said Trustees in their uncontrolled discretion from time to time to sell any part or parts of the land so to be purchased by them together with all buildings thereof and to raise any sum or sums of money upon Mortgage thereof and generally deal with the same as if they were absolute owners thereof but so that all moneys to arise by any of the means aforesaid shall be held by my Trustees for the general purposes of the trust intended to be hereby created and form part of the trust premises.

5. AND I ALSO EMPOWER my Trustees to employ all Architects, Builders, Workmen, Clerks, Accountants Agents and Servants whatsoever necessary or expedient in their discretion to carry out or assist in the work required by the trusts of this my Will and to pay them out of the trust premises such remuneration salaries and wages and recompense as they shall think fit.

6. The model dwellings and houses when erected to be called "The Sutton Model Dwellings".

7. I DIRECT that my Trustees shall if they in their absolute discretion think necessary have power to raise money for all or any of the purposes aforesaid from any Bank Insurance Office or other financial or public office or institution by way of loan upon security of all or any part of my property and estate it being my will desire and intention by the means aforesaid to create a continuing Trust for the purpose of supplying the poor in London and other populous places or Towns in England with proper and sufficient dwelling houses or lodgings at such rents (however low) as my Trustees shall in each case in their absolute discretion consider the tenants can afford to pay and see fit to charge them (but I wish that some rent however small shall be paid and no-one shall be allowed to live in the said dwelling houses or lodgings rent free) but so nevertheless that my Trustees are to be left in complete control of the said trust and to have the amplest and fullest powers and discretions as to the methods by which the same shall be carried into effect and in applying the trust premises in the execution thereof.

I DESIRE that my Trustee and Executor Charles Edward Tranter Lamb shall act as the Solicitor in all matters relating to the trust and execution of this my Will and the administration of my estate and shall notwithstanding his acceptance of the offices of Trustee and Executor of my Will and his acting in the execution thereof be entitled to make the same professional charges to receive the same pecuniary remuneration for all business done by him or any partner of his and all attendances time and trouble bestowed by him or any partner of his in or about the execution of the trusts and powers of my Will or the management or administration of my trust estate real or personal as if he not being himself a Trustee or Executor of my Will were employed by the Trustees or Executors thereof as Solicitor to such Trustees or Executors and shall be entitled to retain out of my estate or the property for the time being subject to the trusts of this my Will or to be allowed and to receive from his Co-trustees or Co-executors (if any) out of such trust estate or property aforesaid the full amount of such charges any rule of law or equity to the contrary notwithstanding nevertheless without prejudice to the right or competency of the said Charles Edward Tranter Lamb to exercise the authority control judgement and discretion of a Trustee and Executor of my Will.

LASTLY I REVOKE all prior wills and declare this alone to be my last Will and Testament IN WITNESS whereof I the said William Richard Sutton the Testator have to this my last Will and Testament set my hand this fifteenth day of August One thousand eight hundred and ninety four.

Signed by the said William
Richard Sutton the Testator as
and for his last Will and
Testament in the presence of
us who at his request in his
presence and in the presence of
each other (all being present at
the same time) have hitherto
subscribed our names as Witnesses

H.H Turner   } Clerks to Armstrong & Lamb
Chas. J. Mann   } Solrs. 53 Moorgate Street, E.C.

THIS IS A CODICIL to the last Will and Testament of me

WILLIAM RICHARD SUTTON of Golden Lane in the County of Middlesex and Sunnydene Sydenham Hill in the County of Kent Carrier which Will bears date the 15th day of August 1894 WHEREAS by my said Will I have bequeathed an annuity of £200 to my late Wife's adopted daughter Kate Grose an annuity of £500 to Thomas Christopher Lewis of Brixton Organ Builder and an annuity of £500 to my niece Nelly Lewis the wife of the said Thomas Christopher Lewis NOW I ABSOLUTELY REVOKE the gift of the said annuities and revoke my said Will so far as the said William Hillier Sutton, Kate Grose, Thomas Christopher Lewis, and Nelly Lewis. AND I confirm my said Will in all other respects IN WITNESS whereof I have hereunto set my hand this tenth day of October. One thousand eight hundred and ninety five.

SIGNED by the said William Richard }	
Sutton the testator as and for a }	
Codicil to his last Will and }	
Testament in the presence of us who }	
at his request in his presence and } W.R. Sutton	
in the presence at the same time) }	
have hereunto subscribed our names }	
as witnesses }	

Chas J. Mann	) Clerks to Armstrong and Lamb
E.W. Oxlade	) 53 Moorgate Street, E.C. Solicitors

THIS IS A SECOND CODICIL to the last Will and Testament of me WILLIAM RICHARD SUTTON of Golden Lane in the County of Middlesex and Sunnydene Sydenham Hill in the County of Kent Carrier which Will bears date the 15th day of August 1894 and the first Codicil whereto bears date the 10th day of October 1895 I GIVE and BEQUEATH to my Wife Eliza Anne Venus Sutton a life annuity of Five thousand pounds to commence from my death and to be payable in priority to all other Annuities and gifts by expiration of three calendar months from my decease AND in all other respects I confirm my said Will as varied and altered by the said First Codicil thereto and I confirm such first Codicil and I direct that my said Will as varied and altered by the said First Codicil thereto and I confirm such first Codicil and I direct that my said Will and first day of April One thousand eight hundred and ninety six AND immediately thereafter on the same day had reexecuted the said first Codicil thereto IN WITNESS whereof I have hereunto set my hand this tenth day of April One thousand eight hundred and ninety six.

SIGNED by the said William Richard }
Sutton the testator as and for a   }
Codicil to his last Will and   }
Testament in the presence of us who }
at his request in his presence and   } W.R. Sutton
in the presence of each other (all   }
being present at the same time)   }
have hereunto subscribed our names }
as witnesses   }

H.H. Turner   ) Clerks to Mr. C.E.T.
                                           Lamb
E.W. Oxlade   ) 17 Ironmonger Lane,
                                           E.C. Solicitor

Appendix 3

1. The Charity shall be known as "The Sutton Model Dwellings" and shall be governed and managed in accordance with the trust of the Will of William Richard Sutton (the "Testator") as explained by this Scheme.

2. The objects of the Charity are as follows:- To acquire land and buildings of freehold or copyhold tenure situated in or in the immediate neighbourhood of any populous place in England (a populous place up to the present has been defined as a place with 200,00 inhabitants or over) for the purpose of the erection or construction there on or on the sites thereof of Model Dwellings for the poor and to sell exchange let or otherwise deal with the same or any part thereof. To erect there on buildings either tenements or cottages or partly both suitable for the poor (including if thought fit) any shops or other profit earning build-ings and to have conspicuously inscribed thereon "Sutton Model Dwellings" and for that purpose to pull down or alter convert reconstruct and adapt existing buildings and for the carrying out of these purposes to take all necessary and proper steps and to enter into all necessary contracts.

To enfranchise any copyhold land acquired and to redeem any land tax or tithe rent charge payable in respect of any land acquired.

To lease or let any premises temporarily in hand until a site is cleared for building tenements or cottages.

To fit up the Dwellings with baths, sinks, shelves, and such fittings and appliances and maintain same as are necessary and expedient for the health and comfort of the occupants.

To provide Infant Nurseries laundries drying rooms reading rooms and gymnasium and to make any provision tending in the opinion of the Trustees to promote the health and moral welfare of the occupants.

To reserve open spaces in and about the Dwellings for playgrounds or places of rest and to provide allotments for tenants desirous of cultivating same.

To let the tenements or cottages to poor persons at rents to be settled by the Trustees, bearing in mind the return of 2½% on the capital outlay in each case, but leaving the Trustees free in particular cases of poverty or misfortune to charge any rent however small and for any period necessary to meet the circumstances of the case.

The tenants to be selected from the poor of good character preference to be given to married men with families for the larger tenements, tenements and cottages to be allotted according to the number in family the larger, the family, the more accommodation; the smaller the family the less the accommodation. Single room tenements not to the occupied by more than 2 adults of the same sex, newly married couples to be given 2 rooms where possible.

The principle laid down by the Trustees at the opening of the 1st Block dwellings was:

1 Room	tenement	to be occupied by man wife and 1 child under 4 or 2 adults (same sex).
2 "	"	to be occupied by man wife and 2 children or 5 adults.
3 "	"	to be occupied by man wife and 5 children or 5 adults.
4 "	"	to be occupied by man wife and 6 children or 6 adults.

(adults all over 14)

The wage limits of applicants

for	1 room tenements	£1	to	25/- per week
	2 " "	25/-	"	27/6 " "
	3 " "	30/-	"	33/- " "
	4 " "	35/-	"	37/6 " "

These limits owing to the increased cost of living and the rise in wages were increased to:-

25/-	and later to	55/-
30/-	"	50/-
40/-	"	60/-
50/-	"	70/-

with slight increases where the family was larger was larger than usual.

The administration of the Trust to be wholly unsectarian and non-political and all influences tending to impart to it any bias or distinctive character sectarian or political or to favour persons professing any particular views religious or political shall be at all time excluded.

To make and enforce such regulations for the good government of the Model Dwellings and for the preservation of order therein as the Trustees may think fit and to repeal and alter these regulations from time to time.

To supply coals or other necessaries of life at or about cost price but so as to make no loss.

To subscribe by annual or other payments or by donation or otherwise to any hospitals dispensaries or charitable institutions for the benefit of the poor our tenants or others.

To enter into arrangements for co-operating with any other Trustees person or Company or public body engaged in carrying out any like objects and to delegate any of the powers of the Trustees to any person or persons or public body but subject to the control and supervision of the Trustees.

To expend money in obtaining Reports and information in regard to undertakings institutions works and Schemes in Great Britain and abroad having for their object the amelioration and improvement of the condition of the poor.

To borrow money on any terms as to repayment and as to interest thereon and with or without mortgage or pledge of any of the lands hereditaments or other assets or income of the Trust and apply the money so raised to any of the objects of the Trust.

To employ and pay out of the Trust funds a secretary clerks Officers and other persons solicitors accountants surveyors architects and other as may be deemed expedient and hire or otherwise acquire general or other offices for the purposes of the Trust.

To invest funds in hand, pending application to the objects of the Trust, in securities authorized by law for investment of Trust funds and to vary the same at discretion.

Any Trustee may resign office by notice in writing to the other Trustees or to their Secretary.

Bankruptcy insolvency or absence from the United Kingdom for a continuous period of calendar months or incapacity to act shall be sufficient to cause a vacancy, a vacancy to be deemed to have occurred when it is so declared by the other Trustees and not before.

Trustees to have power to grant leave of absence.

The Trustees to consist of the present Trustees of the Will, viz: James Barnes Collin, Henry Joseph Wakefield with new Trustees to be appointed from the present Advisory Committee. If at any time the number of Trustees be reduced the remainder to appoint another in his place. The first chairman to be James Barnes Collin and the Deputy Chairman to be

The functions and powers of all additional or new Trustees so appointed shall be the same as if they were named Trustees herein.

The Trustees may act in all things in relation to the Trusts and exercise all or any of their powers either by Joint concurrence of all of them or by Resolution of a meeting of the Trustees duly convened.

Meetings of the Trustees may be held at any time without notice when all are present and may be convened by any one Trustee or by the Secretary or by any other person authorized for that purpose by the Trustees, meetings so convened to be held at the office of the Trust unless the Trustees otherwise determine. Notice of meetings may be given personally or sent by post to the usual or last known address of the Trustees and may be for the day following that on which the Notice is given or posted or for any subsequent day. Default of receipt of notice by any Trustee shall not invalidate a meeting and no notice shall be required to be given to any Trustee absent abroad.

(At any meeting) shall be a quorum. Each Trustee shall have one vote and all questions before a meeting shall be determined by a majority of votes. The Chairman in the event of an equality of votes for and against shall have a casting vote.

Every resolution duly passed at a meeting of the Trustees as hereinbefore provided, entered in the Minute Book of such meeting and signed by the Chairman of that or the following meeting shall bind the whole of the Trustees.

(?) Any Trustee to have the right to have any objection entered on the Minutes.

The Trustees shall make and publish an annual Report for each year ending the 31st December of their operations and administration of the Trust during the year together with a Balance Sheet and Statement of Accounts showing receipts and expenditure and assets and liabilities. The first Report shall be for the year ending on the 31st December 1923.

The remuneration of each Trustee to be one hundred and fifty guineas per annum with an additional one hundred guineas for the Chairman.

The reasonable expenses of any Trustee engaged on the business of the Trust necessitating travelling to and from any of the Buildings or Sites in London and provincial cities scheduled as suitable for Sutton Model Dwellings to be borne out of the Trust Funds.

It shall be lawful for the Trustees by the unanimous concurrence of all of them, with the sanction of an Order of the High Court of Justice in England from time to time to cancel or vary all or any of the powers Trusts and provisions for the general objects or purposes pointed out by this Deed or the management or administration thereof for those objects or purposes and in any manner which may seem desirable to the Trustees.

Appendix 4

THE WILLIAM SUTTON TRUST: SITE PURCHASES 1900–1950

Date of purchase	Site	Vendors	Acreage	Cost £	Cost per acre £
1907	**London:** Bethnal Green (James Street)	John Samuel Davis and William Readhead Smith	1	11,000	11,000
1908	City Road	Ecclesiastical Commissioners and James Bigwood	2	96,000	48,000
1910	Chelsea	Piza Barnet	4.5	85,000	18,888
1913	Rotherhithe	Elizabeth Ram	2.16	12,650	5,856
1919	Islington	Church Missionary Trust (site is former Church Missionary College)	3.13	16,000	5,111
1928	St Quintin Park	Not given. Sutton Land adjacent to Peabody	8.00 1.32	15,000 4,084	

continued ...

THE WILLIAM SUTTON TRUST: SITE PURCHASES 1900–1950 (CONTINUED)

Date of purchase	Site	Vendors	Acreage	Cost £	Cost per acre £
1912	**Provinces:** Birmingham	Various individuals	21.4	8,300	388
1914	(Barrack Road) Newcastle Upon Tyne	NE Banking Co. of 1st part and Mr RT & AW Lambert of 2nd part	2.2	10,915	4,961
1926	**ditto**	Lord Mayor, Alderman and Citizens	0.98	3,166	3,231
1915	(Broomwell House Site) Bristol	George Samuel Gerrish	15.46	7,000	452
1920	Manchester	Charles Hesketh Fleetwood Hesketh	29.9	10,462	350
1920	Sheffield	Frederick Fowler	29.5	8,990	304
1922	Leicester (Gypsy Lane)	William Parker	20.0	5,000	250

continued ...

THE WILLIAM SUTTON TRUST: SITE PURCHASES 1900–1950 (CONTINUED)

Date of purchase	Site	Vendors	Acreage	Cost £	Cost per acre £
1924	Leeds (Killingbeck, York Road)	Lord Mayor, Alderman and Citizens of 1st part, Rt Hon Lindley Wood MP of 2nd part	20.26	2,500	123
1926	Stoke-on-Trent	(a) Lord Mayor & Citizens	10.36	5,675*	547
1926	(Trent Vale)	(b) Thomas Swinnerton Pilkington (Baronet)	8.056	1,000	124
1929	ditto	(c) Arthur Swinnerton Pilkington	8.925	1,000	112
1930	Hull	Trustees of Mrs Ann Watson's Charity	25.9	3,700	143
1930	ditto	W & G England, pt of Bilton Grange Farm	13.7	1,100	80
1931	Bradford	Various individuals	9.464	2,839	300

continued ...

THE WILLIAM SUTTON TRUST: SITE PURCHASES 1900–1950 (CONTINUED)

Date of purchase	Site	Vendors	Acreage	Cost £	Cost per acre £
1931	Bradford	Liquidators of Eagle Insurance Co	15.644	3,911	250
1931	Salford	The King in the County Palatine of Lancaster	4.66	2,550	504
1935	ditto		6.65	6,250	939
1931	Leeds (Selby Road)	Rt Hon Edward Linley Baron Irwin	27.5	4,400	160
1932	South Shields	Robert Chapman (land encircled by Eccles Commissioners)	32.89	3,980	121
1935	ditto		1.59	771	434
1932	Stoke (Abbey Hulton)	Lord Mayor, Alderman & Citizens, land known as Greasley Side Farm	34.93	3,900	112

continued ...

The William Sutton Trust: Site purchases 1900–1950 (Continued)

Date of purchase	Site	Vendors	Acreage	Cost £	Cost per acre £
1933	Newcastle (Benwell)	Margaret Peacock (High Cross Lodge)	3.795	6,750	1,178
1934	Plymouth (St Budeaux)	John Trelawny-Ross and 1 other	28.022	9,000	321
1936	Middlesborough	George Curry and 1 other	31.576	5,525	175
1939	(Linthorpe)	Barbara Emerson	6	1,050	175
1940	Hartlepool	Mayor Alderman & Bargesses – W View Housing Estate	29.643	4,400	148
1940	Sunderland	Francis Bury	36	8,600	238
1946	Bethnal Green (Extension)		0.66	10,000	15,000

*Sum includes cost of street works already carried out.
Source: London Metropolitan Archives, Acc 2983/231 (Accounts 1931).

Appendix 5

THE WILLIAM SUTTON TRUST: NEW SCHEMES, ACQUISITIONS,
INFILL AND EXTENSIONS 1900–1974[1]

Location	Estate	Flats	Houses
1900–19 NEW SCHEMES			
London:	Bethnal Green	160	–
London:	City Road	284	–
London:	Chelsea	674	–
London:	Rotherhithe	194	–
Birmingham:	Alum Rock	64	230
Newcastle:	Barrack Road	177	–
Total		1,553	23
1900–1919 Total		**1,553**	**230**
1920–1940 NEW SCHEMES			
London:	Islington	199	–
London:	St. Quintin Park, Kensington	629	–
Manchester:	Gorton	72	340
Salford:	Seedley Road	365	–
Leeds:	Killingbeck, York Road	220	–
	Halton, Selby Road	87	179
Sheffield:	Hillsborough	–	336
Bristol:	Brislington	16	176
Leicester:	Belgrave	–	246
Stoke-on-Trent:	Trent Vale	–	310
Stoke-on-Trent:	Abbey Hulton	36	365
Hull:	Marfleet Lane	24	476
South Tyneside:	Cleadon	52	404
Bradford:	Dick Lane	87	221

Location	Estate	Flats	Houses
1920–1940 NEW SCHEMES (CONTINUED)			
Newcastle:	Benwell	276	–
Plymouth:	St. Budeaux	60	277
Middlesborough:	Linthorpe	44	321
Total		2,147	3,871
1920–40 ACQUISITIONS			
Tower Hamlets:	Bethnal Green	15	–
Total		15	–
1920–1940 Total		**2,172**	**3,871**
1945–74 NEW SCHEMES			
Plymouth:	Miles Mitchell Village, Crownhill	24	137
Bolton:	Platt Hill	144	212
Halton:	Widnes	78	283
Tamworth:	Glasgote	129	217
Total		375	849
1945–74 ACQUISITIONS			
1966 ACQUISITION FROM PLYMOUTH HOUSING IMPROVEMENT SOCIETY			
Plymouth:	Valletort Place	21	–
1970 ACQUISITION FROM KINGSWAY HOUSING ASSOCIATION			
Preston:	Lea	–	229
Rugby:	Bilton & Rokeby	42	325
Chelmsford:	Great Baddow	77	193
Luton:	Stopsley	–	62
Newcastle:	Kidsgrove	24	57
St. Helens:	Newton-le-Willows	48	75
Total		212	941

Location	Estate	Flats	Houses
1945–74 INFILL AND EXTENSIONS TO EXISTING SCHEMES			
Tower Hamlets:	Bethnal Green	31	–
Birmingham:	Alum Rock	60	–
Southwark:	Rotherhithe	48	–
Manchester:	Gorton	4	2
Leeds:	Killingbeck	27	–
Sheffield:	Hillsborough	4	2
Leicester:	Belgrave	20	–
Stoke-on-Trent:	Trent Vale	–	7
Hull:	Marfleet Lane	12	18
South Tyneside:	Cleadon	16	17
Salford:	Seedley Road	112	–
Leeds:	Selby Road	–	80
Bradford:	Dick Lane	34	31
Plymouth:	St. Budeaux	60	6
Middlesborough:	Linthorpe	16	88
Total		444	251
1945–1974 Total[1]		**1,031**	**2,041**

[1](This information relates to total number of dwellings that the Trust has either built or acquired by the end of each period. These figures may differ from the total number of dwellings let at the end of each period)

Appendix 6

1. PUBLIC UTILITY SOCIETY

Section 4(2) of the *Housing, Town Planning Act 1909* stated that:

> "for the purposes of this section a public utility society means a society registered under the *Industrial and Provident Societies Act 1893*, or any amendment thereof, the rules whereof prohibit the payment of any interest or dividend at a rate exceeding five pounds per centum per annum".

Section 40 of the *Housing, Town Planning Act 1919* revised the definition slightly as follows:

> "the expression 'public utility society' means a society registered under the Industrial and Provident Societies Acts 1893 to 1913, the rules whereof prohibit the payment of any interest or dividend at a rate exceeding six per cent per annum."

The term 'public utility society' was superseded by the term 'housing association' in the *Housing Act 1935*.

2. HOUSING TRUST

Section 40 of the *Housing, Town Planning Act 1919* stated that:

> the expression 'housing trust' means a corporation or body of persons which, by the terms of its constituent instrument is required to devote the whole of its funds, including any surplus which may arise from its operations, to the provision of houses for persons the majority of whom are in fact members of the working classes, and to other purposes incidental thereto."

This definition was repeated in Section 188 of the *Housing Act*

1935 and in Section 189 of the *Housing Act 1957*. However in the *Housing Repairs and Rents Act 1954*, which excluded housing association and housing trust tenancies from the provisions of the Rent Acts, a modified definition of 'housing trust' was used. Section 33 Paragraph 9 of this Act stated that:

"in this section the expression 'housing trust' means a housing trust as defined in the *Housing Act 1936*, or a corporation or body of persons which, being required by the terms of its constituent instrument to devote the whole or substantially the whole of its funds to charitable purposes, would be a housing trust as so defined if the purposes to which it is so required to devote its funds were restricted to those to which it in fact devotes the whole or substantially the whole thereof."

This cumbersome definition was re-enacted in the *Rent Act 1968* which stipulated (Section 5 Paragraph 2g) that it is only the tenancies of housing trusts which are charities within the meaning of the *Charities Act 1960* which are excluded from the Rent Acts. The expression 'housing trust' itself is then defined (Section 5 Paragraph 3) as:

"a corporation or body of persons which:
(a) is required by the terms of its constituent instrument to devote the whole of its funds, including any surplus which may arise from its operations to the following purposes, that is to say, the provision of houses for persons the majority of whom are in fact members of the working classes, and other purposes incidental thereto;
or
(b) is required by the terms of its constituent instrument to devote the whole or substantially the whole of its funds to charitable purposes, and in fact devotes the whole or substantially the whole of its funds to the purposes set out in paragraph (a) above."

It is this fuller definition that has been used in subsequent legislation and the 1957 Act definition is thus redundant.

3 HOUSING ASSOCIATION

Section 26 of the *Housing Act 1935* stated that:

> "for references in the Act of 1925 and in the Act of 1930 to a
> public utility society there shall be substituted references to a
> 'housing association' that is to say any society, body of trustees
> or company established for the purpose of, or amongst whose
> objects or powers are included those of, constructing, improv-
> ing, or managing, or facilitating or encouraging the construc-
> tion or improvement of houses for the working classes being a
> society, company or body of trustees who do not trade for
> profit or whose constitution or rules prohibit the issue of any
> capital with interest, or dividend exceeding the rate for the time
> being prescribed by the Treasury, whether with or without dif-
> ferentiation as between share and loan capital".

This definition was repeated in Section 188 of the *Housing Act
1936* and in Section 189 of the *Housing Act 1957* although in the
latter case the phrase "for the working classes" was dropped from
the definition. Section 189 of the *Housing Act 1957* was amended
by paragraph 6 of Schedule 13 of the *Housing Act 1974* and the
definition of a housing association was then as follows:

> "a society, body of trustees or company established for the
> purpose of, or amongst whose objects or powers are included
> those of, providing, constructing, improving or managing or
> facilitating or encouraging the construction or improvement of
> houses, or hostels (as defined in Section 129(1) of the Housing
> Act 1974) being a society, body of trustees or company who do
> not trade for profit or whose constitution or rules prohibit the
> issue of any capital with interest or divident exceeding the rate
> for the time being prescribed by the Treasury, whether with or
> without differentiation as between share and loan capital."

4 HOUSING SOCIETY

Section 1 subsection 7 of the *Housing Act 1964* states that:

> "the expression 'housing society' means a society:
> (a) which is registered under the *Industrial and Provident Socie-
>   ties Act 1983* and

(b) which does not trade for profit; and
(c) which is established for the purpose of, or amongst whose objects or powers are included those of, constructing, improving or managing houses, being:
    (i)   houses to be kept available for letting, or
   (ii) where the rules of the society restrict membership of the society to persons entitled or prospectively entitled (whether as tenants or otherwise) to occupy a house provided or managed by the society, houses for occupation by members of the society..."

The following paragraph of the Act stipulated that such 'housing societies' could not have any supplementary purpose other than providing land or buildings for purposes connected with the requirements of the people occupying the society's houses, encouraging the formation of other housing societies and giving advice on the running and formation of them.

5   REGISTERED HOUSING ASSOCIATION
Section 13 of the *Housing Act 1974* provides that:

(1) there shall be a register of housing associations which shall be established and maintained by the Housing Corporation and in which the Corporation may register any housing association which:
    (a) is a registered charity and not an exempt charity; or
    (b) is a society registered under the Industrial and Provident Societies Act 1965 and fulfills the conditions in subsection (2) below
(2) The conditions referred to in subsection (1)(b) above are that the housing association does not trade for profit and is established for the purpose of, or has among its objects of powers those of, providing; constructing, improving or managing:
    (a) houses to be kept available for letting, or
    (b) where the rules of the association restrict membership of the association to persons entitled or prospectively entitled (whether as tenants or otherwise) to occupy a house provided or managed by the association, houses for occupation by members of the association, or
    (c) hostels

and that if the association has any additional purposes or objects, it has none which are not mentioned in subsection (3) below.

(3) The additional purposes or objects referred to in sub-section (2) above are those:

    (a) of providing land or buildings for purposes connected with the requirements of the persons occupying the houses or hostels provided or managed by the association.

    (b) of providing amenities or services for the benefit of those persons either exclusively or together with other persons.

    (c) of encouraging and giving advice on the formation of other housing associations which would be eligible for registration by the Housing Corporation; and

    (d) of providing services for, and giving advice on the running of registered housing associations.

Section 129(1) of the *Housing Act 1974* then provides that:

"In the application of this Act in England and Wales...

'registered' except in the register of housing associations established under section 13 of this Act and 'registration' and 'unregistered' shall be construed accordingly.

6 HOUSING CO-OPERATIVE

In the Final Report of the Working Party on Housing Co-operatives (HMSO 1975) the term 'housing co-operative' is defined as:

"a society which corporately owns a group of houses or flats in which each member occupies a dwelling."

The term did not, however, receive a clear statutory definition although it appeared on the Statute Book. The *Housing Finance Act 1972*) referred to a certain type of housing co-operative without actually using those words. Section 104 of that Act describes housing associations which are, or are deemed to be, duly registered under the Industrial and Provident Societies Act 1965 and whose rules restrict membership to persons who are tenants or prospective tenants of the association and preclude the granting or assigning of tenancies other than to members.

Paragraph 9, Schedule 1 of the *Housing Rents and Subsidies Act 1975* uses the term 'housing co-operative' to mean 'a society, company or body of trustees for the time being approved by the Secretary of State for the purpose of this paragraph." Paragraph 9 then provides that if with the approval of the Secretary of State an agreement is made between a local authority and a housing co-operative whereby the co-operative exercises certain housing functions, the authority does not lose its entitlement to Exchequer subsidies, as it would if it had disposed of the properties in any other way. The ability for local authorities to set up such 'management co-operatives' was reaffirmed under the provisions of Schedule 20 of the *Housing Act 1980*.

It is important to note that a housing co-operative as defined by Paragraph 9 of the Housing Rents and Subsidies Act 1975 does not need to be a housing association. It seems probable, however, that any organisation which is approved by the Secretary of State will have a constitution which brings it within the statutory definition of a housing association. Furthermore, such a body may very well be a housing association registered as such under Part 2 of the *Housing Act 1974*.

Section 6 of the *Housing Rents and Subsidies Act 1975* altered the provisions of Sections 29 and 32 of the *Housing Act 1974* that had excluded from eligibility for Housing Association Grant, associations which have a full mutuality of tenants and members. These Sections had been inserted to prevent co-ownership societies that had already benefited from option mortgage subsidy claiming further grants, but in the process had also excluded co-operatives where there was no individual stake in the equity. Section 6 of the *Housing Rents and Subsidies Act 1975* thus made Housing Association Grant and Revenue Deficit Grant available to housing co-operatives that became registered housing associations.

Bibliography

SOURCES CONSULTED

The place of publication is London unless otherwise stated.

Arranged as follows:

1. Interviews
2. Manuscripts
3. Unpublished Theses
4. Parliamentary Papers
5. Miscellaneous Printed Sources
6. Newspapers and Periodicals
7. Articles
8. Books and Pamphlets

1. INTERVIEWS
   Baker, Charles
   Best, Richard
   Curtis, Keith
   Dally, Richard
   Edwards, Christopher
   Howell, Peter
   Morris, Mike
   Stallybrass, Mrs.
   Sutton, Reginald

In addition, short questionnaires and anonymous interviews based on a prepared schedule were completed with a total of fifty six tenants. They were mostly people who had lived on Sutton estates for lengthy periods and who were resident on the following estates in 1996, Bethnal Green, Chelsea, Birmingham, Stoke (Trent Vale), Rugby, Bolton (Platt Hill) and Hemel Hempstead

2. MANUSCRIPTS
Brewers' Company
  List of Freemen 1723–1886
  Scrapbooks and Memoranda 1880–1891
Brewers' and Licensed Retailers Association
  Notes and Correspondence 1860–1900
British Library of Political and Economic Science
  HD6/D267 Statistics of Middle Class Expenditure (nd ? 1896)
Business Archives Council
Charity Commissioners
  Central Register
  Regional Office (Liverpool) Register
City of Birmingham Reference Library Archives
  Birmingham Town Planning Letter Book No. 2 1912–May 1913
  Jewel Baillie Collection Newspaper Cuttings
City of London
  Alphabet of Freedoms 1842–1914
City of London School
  Register of Pupils Volume 1 1837–1860
Companies House
  Index of Companies Registered 1856–1920
  Liquidation Accounts 1890–1932
  Lists of Shareholders and Directors, Carriers, Brewers,
  Distillers
Distillers' Company
  List of the Court of Assistants and Livery of the Worshipful
  Company of Distillers Volume 5 1872–1901
Grand Lodge Library and Museum
  Members' Registers
House of Lords Record Office
  House of Commons Select Committee on the London and
  North Western Railway (Additional Powers) Bill and Midland
  Railway (Additional Powers) Bill, 4 April 1879
London Metropolitan Archives
  Acc 2983 (The William Sutton Trust)
        001/1–5
        002/1–5
        003/1–19
        004–006
        007/1–8

008/1–13
009/1–11
010/1–18
011/1–27
014/1–2
020–030
031–034
052
055/1–11
056/1–7
060–067
083–084
088
100
166–169
175(j)
175(k)
200
226–227
231
232–233
234/1–29
242
Public Record Office
BT31/14848/23534
BT31/3689/22944
BT31/14372/2087c
BT31/457/1763

CAB27309 CB30(26)
CAB24/202 CP100(29)

HLG1/1–32
HLG1/14A1–3
HLG1/37/178
HLG1/1032
HLG1/1535–1539
HLG1/4590/601/1
HLG1497
HLG29/129

HLG29/213
HLG32/3121–3128
HLG32/3146
HLG36/6
HLG37/4 B16–B18
HLG37/5 B1–B6
HLG37/178
HLG48/12
HLG49/1497
HLG49/7
HLG49/909
HLG49/1467
HLG49/1497
HLG49/92033/1/3A
HLG52/201
HLG52/790–794

RECO1/474
RECO1/482
RECO1/525–526
RECO1/531
RECO1/548

William Sutton Trust Head Office (York) Archives (selected material is being deposited with the London Metropolitan Archives)
GN33
GN104
GN228
GN232–234
GN393
GN421
GN434
GN451
GN459
GN501
GN558–559
GN563–564
GN575
H3/12–14
H16/SF13

H21/SH82
H57/BLB13
H72/BNM13
H190/MC417(2)
H199/MC12(3)
H199/MC13–14
H200/MC13–14
H251 SR13–14
Parish of Sydenham
Register of Baptisms October 1869–February 1883

3. UNPUBLISHED THESES

Allen, P. 'The Role of Housing Associations in Britain'. M.Sc. Thesis. University of Bristol, 1981

Cook, G. 'The Development of the Four Principal Housing Trusts in London.' M.A. Thesis. University of Manchester, 1974

Emsley, Ian. 'The Development of Housing Associations with Special Reference to London and including a Case Study of the London Borough of Hammersmith.' Ph.D. Thesis. University of London, 1985

Hole, W. Vera. 'Housing of the Working Classes in the Metropolis.' Ph.D. Thesis. London School of Economics, 1965

Morris, Susannah. 'Private Profit and Public Interest: Model Dwellings Companies and the Housing of the Working Classes in London, 1840–1914.' Ph.D. Thesis. University of Oxford, 1999

Whittle, M. 'Philanthropy in Preston: The Changing Face of Charity in a 19th Century Provincial Town.' Ph.D. Thesis. University of Lancaster, 1990

4. PARLIAMENTARY PAPERS

Endowed Charities (County of London) Return Volume VII, 1904

Board of Trade, Cost of Living of the Working Classes: Report of an Enquiry by the Board of Trade into Working Class Rents, Housing and Retail Prices, LXVI, 1913

Public Works Loans Board, 39th Annual Report , 1913–1914

The Land: Report of the Land Enquiry Committee, Volume 2, 1914

Housing (Financial Assistance) Committee, Interim Report on Public Utility Societies, Cmnd 9223, 1918

Ministry of Health. *Annual Reports.* 1919–1936

Ministry of Health. *Housing.* July 1919–June 1921

Ministry of Health. *Housing: House Production, Slum Clearance etc.* 1919–1939

Ministry of Health, Local Taxation Returns, England and Wales, Part 11 (LCC, metropolitan borough councils and county borough councils) 1919–1939

Ministry of Health, Report of the Interdepartmental Committee on the Rent Restriction Acts, XVII, 1930–1931

Ministry of Health, Report of the Departmental Committee on Housing (Chairman Lord Moyne) Cmd 4397, July 1933

Ministry of Health, Central Housing Advisory Committee, Housing Management and Housing Associations Subcommittee, First Report, The Operations of Housing Associations, 1939

Charitable Trusts, Report of the Committee on the Law and Practice relating to Charitable Trusts (Chairman The Rt Hon Lord Nathan) Cmd 8710, 1952

Government Policy on Charitable Trusts in England and Wales Cmd 9538, 1955

Old Houses into New Homes, Cmnd 2838, 1965

Ministry of Housing and Local Government, Housing Associations (Working Paper of the Central Housing Advisory Committee, Chairman Sir Karl C. Cohen) 1971

Housing Finance Act 1972: Memorandum on Housing Associations, 1972

Widening the Choice: The Next Steps in Housing Cmnd 5280, 1973

Department of the Environment, Final Report of the Working Party on Housing Cooperatives, 1975

Housing Policy – A Consultative Document Cmnd 6851, 1977

Central Policy Review Staff (Cabinet Office), Relations between Central Government and Local Authorities, 1977

Housing Associations and the Housing Corporation, Fifth Report of Session, 327, 1978–1979

The Future of Voluntary Associations, Wolfenden Committee, 1978

Department of the Environment, Housing Services Advisory Group, Housing Associations and their Part in Current Housing Strategies, 1978

Department of the Environment, Housing Services Advisory

Group, Housing Action Areas and the Role of Housing Associations, 1981

House of Commons, Environment Committee, The Housing Corporation, Second Report, Volume 1, 1993

Central Statistical Office, Annual Abstract of Statistics, 132–135, 1996–1999

5. MISCELLANEOUS PRINTED SOURCES

Central Committee on Post-War Reconstruction, *Looking Ahead: Foundations for Housing.* Interim Report of the Conservative Sub-Committee on Housing. Conservative Party, 1944

Council for Research on Housing Construction, *Slum Clearance and Rebuilding.* 1934

Council for Research on Housing Construction, *Housing Standards and Statistics.* 1935

Council for Research on Housing Construction, *Housing Finance: Report on Subsidies for Rehousing in Urban Areas.* 1935

Court of Exchequer Reports. 21 November 1865. Sutton v. South Eastern Railway Company

Sutton Housing Trust. A Political Audit. A Report by GTW Government Relations, August 1993

Local Collections (i) London

Chelsea Metropolitan Borough Council.
    Minutes of Public Health Committee. 1911–1914
    Medical Officer of Health, Annual Reports, 1908–1919
Finsbury Library
    Local History Collection
Kensington Metropolitan Borough Council
    Minutes of Proceedings 1919–1935
    Medical Officer of Health, Annual Reports 1919–1935
Lambeth Metropolitan Borough Council
    Lambeth Borough Archives
Lewisham Metropolitan Borough Council
    Archives and Local History Collection
London Metropolitan Archives
    London County Council Minutes
    London County Council Annual Reports
    London County Council Statistical Abstract

London County Council London Statistics
London County Council Clerks Department Records
London County Council Housing Department Records
Sutton Dwellings Trust Estates in London prior to 1951
London County Council, *The Housing Question in London: Being an Account of the Housing Work done by the Metropolitan Board of Works and the London County Council between the Years 1855 and 1900.* London County Council: 1901
London County Council, *Housing of the Working Classes in London ... with Special Reference to the Action taken by the London County Council between the Years 1889 and 1912.* London County Council: 1913
Southwark Metropolitan Borough Council
    Local Studies Library

Local Collections (ii) outside London

Brighton
    Reference Library
City of Birmingham Reference Library
    Reports of Town Clerk to Various Committees, 1913
Croydon
    Croydon Borough Reference Library
Hertfordshire
    Record Office
Leeds City Council
    Annual Reports of Finance and Parliamentary Committee
Liverpool City Council
    Proceedings 1906–1919
    Housing Committee Minutes. 1909–1919
Manchester Housing Committee Minutes.
    Report of the Director of Housing on the Housing Schemes of the City Council of Birmingham. 5 May 1926
Manchester and Salford Council of Social Service.
    Social Welfare: Notes and News Quarterly 1930
    Public Utility Societies and the Housing Problem 1934
Morden Reference Library
    Local History Collection
Newcastle on Tyne Central Library, Local Studies Unit
    Proceedings of the Newcastle Council. 1911–1914

Reports of the Medical Officer of Health 1909–1913
City and County of Newcastle upon Tyne.
   Housing. A Statistical Survey of Municipal Housing to 31 March 1955

Digests, Directories etc

Charities Digest
City of London Directory, 1871–1900
Clarks Crystal Palace District Handbook and Directory, 1875
St Pancras Directory, 1862
Directory of British Architects, 1884–1900
Kelly's Directory of the Wine and Spirit Trades, 1884–1898
Kelly's Islington Directory, 1887–1888
Kelly's Post Office London Directory, 1820–1822
Kelly's Post Office London: Streets and Commercial 65th ed., 1864
Kelly's Post Office London Directory, 1900
Kelly's Post Office London Suburban Directory. Southern Suburbs, 1864
The London Assurance Policy Registers, 1856–1892
The Municipal Year Book 1902
Peabody Trust, Annual Reports, from 1896
Stock Exchange Year Books 1885
The William Sutton Trust, Annual Reports, from 1914

6. NEWSPAPERS AND PERIODICALS
Architects Journal June–October 1933
The Builder
Estates Gazette
Inside Housing
Voluntary Housing
Birmingham Daily Post
The City Press 1850–1920
The Liverpolitan
Liverpool Daily Post and Mercury
The Liverpool Courier 1906–1919
The Manchester Guardian
Newcastle Journal
Sydenham, Forest Hill and Penge Gazette
The Sydenham Times

The Times
Yorkshire Evening News
Yorkshire Post

7. ARTICLES

———— "Some Clarity on Charity", *Voluntary Housing*. 2 (4) (21 July 1970 and 10 November 1970)

Bengsston, Bo. "Housing in Game Theoretical Perspective", *Housing Studies* 10 (2) (1995): 229–243

Ben-ner, A. and Ven Hoomissen,T. "Non Profit Organisations in the Mixed Economy: A Demand and Supply Analysis", *Annals of Public and Cooperative Economics* 62 no. 4 (1991): 519–550

Birchall, J. "Co-partnership Housing and the Garden City Movement", *Planning Perspectives* 10 (1995): 329–358

Bryder, Lynda. "The First World War: Healthy or Hungry?", *History Workshop Journal* 18 (1987): 141–157

Cox, Alan. "'An Example to Others': Public Housing in London 1840–1914", *London and Middlesex Archaeological Society Transactions* 46 (1995): 145–165

Daunton, M. J., "House-ownership from Rate-books", *Urban History Yearbook* (1976): 21–27

Davis O. and Whinston A., "Economics of Urban Renewal", *Law and Contemporary Problems* 26 (1961): 105–117

Dennis, Richard. "The Geography of Victorian Values: Philanthropic Housing in London, 1840–1900" *Journal of Historical Geography* 15 (1989): 140–154

Dennis, Richard. "'Hard to Let' in Edwardian London", *Urban Studies* 26 (1989): 77–89

Errington, C. S. "Dwellings for the Poor", *Journal of the Royal Sanitary Institute* 40 (1919–1920)

Finlayson, G. "A Moving Frontier: Voluntarism and the State in British Social Welfare 1911–1949", *Twentieth Century British History* 1 (2) (1990): 183–206

Fisher, D. "The Role of Philanthropic Foundations in the Reproduction and Production of Hegemony: Rockefeller Foundation and the Social Sciences", *Sociology* 17 (1983): 206–233

Fletcher, Janet. "Kensington builds for the Poor", *The Architectural Review* LXXV (Jan–June 1934): 82–86

Foster, J. "How Imperial London Preserved its Slums", *International Journal of Urban and Regional Research* 3 (1) (1979): 93–114

Garside, Patricia L. "'Unhealthy Areas': Town Planning, Eugenics and the Slums 1890–1945", *Planning Perspectives* 3 (1988): 24–46

Harris, Jose. "Political Thought and the Welfare State 1870–1940: An Intellectual Framework for British Social Policy", *Past and Present* 134–135 (1992): 116–141

Harrison, Brian. "Philanthropy and the Victorians", *Victorian Studies* 9 (1966): 353–374

Jefford, J. R. "Reconditioning in Relation to Urban Housing", *Journal of the Royal Sanitary Institute* 54 (1933–34)

Jenkinson, Charles. "Leeds Housing Policy", *Labour Research* 5 (1934)

Kidd, Alan J. "Charity Organisations in Manchester 1870–1914", *Social History* 9 (1984): 45–66

Kirby, A. "The Housing Corporation 1974–79: An Example of State Housing Policy in Britain", *Environment and Planning A* 13 (1981): 1299

McKenna, M. "The Suburbanisation of the Working Class Population of Liverpool between the Wars", *Social History* 16 (1991): 173–189

Marshall, J. L. "The Pattern of Housebuilding in the Inter-war Period in England and Wales", *Science Journal of Political Economy* 15 (2) (1968): 184–205

Meller, H. "Philanthropy and Public Enterprise: International Exhibitions and the Modern Town Planning Movement 1889–1913", *Planning Perspectives* 10 (3) (1995): 295–310

Moore, M. J. "Social Work and Social Welfare. The Organisation of Philanthropic Resources in Britain 1900–1914", *Journal of British Studies* (1977): 85–104

Nathan, Lord. "The Charitable Trusts Committee: Some Notes on its Recommendations". *Social Service* (Spring 1953): 149–155

Ostrom, Elinor. "An Agenda for the Study of Institutions". *Public Choice* 48 (1986): 3–25

Parker, Morris. "The Respective Spheres of Public Authorities and Voluntary Organisations in the Administration of Social Services", *Public Administration* (1927)

Paton, Mona. "Corporate East End Landlords. The Example of the London Hospital and the Mercers Company", *The London Journal* 18 (1993): 113–128

Raynsford, Nicholas. "The Role of Voluntary Organisations in Housing", *Housing and Planning Review* 36 (1980): 10–12

Skilleter, K. J. "The Role of Public Utility Societies in Early British Town Planning and the Garden City Movement", *Planning Perspectives* 10 (1995): 329–358

Skilleter, K. J. "The Role of Public Utility Societies in Early British Town Planning and Housing Reform, 1901–1936", *Planning Perspectives* 8 (1993): 125–165

Swenerton, Mark and Taylor, Sandra. "The Scale and Nature of Owner-Occupation in Britain between the Wars", *Economic History Review* 2nd ser. 38 (1985): 373–392

Waddington, Keir. "Bastard Benevolence: Centralisation, Voluntarism and the Sunday Fund 1873–1898", *The London Journal* 19 (2) (1994): 151–167

Warrington, M. J. "Welfare Pluralism or Shadow State? The Provision of Social Housing in the 1990s", *Environment and Planning A* 27 (9) (1995): 1341–1360

Webster, Charles. "Healthy or Hungry Thirties?", *History Workshop Journal* 13 (1982): 110–129

Webster, C. "Health, Welfare and Unemployment during the Depression", *Past and Present* 46 (1985): 204–9

8. BOOKS AND PAMPHLETS

Abel-Smith, B. and Townsend, P. *The Poor and the Poorest. A New Analysis of the Ministry of Labour's Family Expenditure Surveys of 1953–54 and 1960.* Bell, 1967

Allen, J. and McDowell, L. *Landlords and Property: Social Relations in the Private Rented Sector.* Cambridge: Cambridge University Press, 1989

Arkell, G. E. "Blocks of Model Dwellings." In *Labour and Life of the People*, 2. Edited by Charles Booth. Williams and Norgate, 1891

Armstrong, W. A. "The Use of Information about Occupation." In *Nineteenth Century Society.* Edited by E. A. Wrigley. 191–310. Cambridge: Cambridge University Press, 1972

Banks, J. A. "The Social Structure of Nineteenth Century England as seen through the Census." In *The Census and Social Structure.* Edited by R. Lawton. 179–223. Cass, 1978

Barlow, J. and Dundan, S. *Success and Failure in Housing Provision. European Systems Compared.* Pergamom, 1994

Becker, Gary. *The Economic Approach to Human Behaviour.* Chicago: University of Chicago Press, 1977

Belcher, V. *The City Parochial Foundation 1891–1991 A Trust for the Poor of London.* Aldershot: Scolar Press, 1991

Best, Richard. "Housing Associations: The Sustainable Solution?" In *Directions in Housing Policy.* Edited by Peter Williams. Paul Chapman Publishing, 1997

Beveridge, W. H. *Voluntary Action A Report on Methods of Social Action.* Allen and Unwin, 1948

Blake, J. "The New Providers." In *Built to Last? Reflections on British Housing Policy.* Second edition. Edited by J. Goodwin and C. Grant. Shelter, 1997

Booth, Charles. *The Housing Question in Manchester: Notes on the Report of the Citizens Association* 1904.

Bowley, A. L. *Wages and Incomes Since 1860.* Cambridge: Cambridge University Press, 1937.

Bowley, M. *Housing and the State 1919–1944.* New York: Garland Publishing, 1945

Bremner, R. H. *American Philanthropy.* Second edition. Chicago: University of Chicago Press, 1988.

Bridgeland, Gina. *Laisterdyke Roundabout.* Bradford: Laisterdyke Local History Group, 1992

Briggs, Asa. *Seebohm Rowntree 1871–1954.* Longman, 1961

Brion, Marion. *Women in the Housing Service.* Routledge, 1995

Buck, Nicholas H. "The Analysis of State Intervention in 19th Century Cities: The Case of Municipal Labour Policy in East London 1886–1914." In *Urbanization and Urban Planning in a Capitalist Society.* Edited by M. Dear and A. J. Scott. 501–535. Methuen, 1981

Burnett, John. *A Social History of Housing 1815–1970.* Methuen, 1978

Butcher, H. *The Sutton Housing Trust. Its Foundation and History.* Tring: The Sutton Housing Trust, 1982

Caradog Jones, D. *The Social Survey of Merseyside.* Liverpool: Liverpool University Press, 1934

Checkland, Olive. *Philanthropy in Victorian Scotland: Social Welfare and the Voluntary Principle.* Edinburgh, 1980

Chesterman, M. *Charities, Trusts and Social Welfare.* Weidenfeld and Nicholson, 1979

Clapham, David. "A Woman of Her Time." In *Built to Last? Reflections on British Housing Policy* Second edition. Edited by J. Goodwin and C. Grant. Shelter, 1992

Curti M., Green J. and Nash R. "Anatomy of Giving: Millionaires in the late Nineteenth Century." In *Sociology and Historical Methods*. Edited by J. M. Lipset and R. Hofstedter. New York: Basic Books, 1968

Cunningham, H. *The Volunteer Force: A Social and Political History 1859–1908*. Croom Helm, 1975

Darley, G. *Octavia Hill – A Life*. Constable, 1990

Daunton, M. J. *A Property Owning Democracy? Housing in Britain*. Faber and Faber, 1987

Daunton, M. J. *Councillors and Tenants in Local Authority Housing in English Cities 1919–1939*. Leicester: Leicester University Press, 1984

Daunton, M. J. *House and Home in the Victorian City: Working Class Housing 1850–1914*. Edward Arnold, 1983

Daunton, M. J. "Housing." In *The Cambridge Social History of Britain 1750–1950*. Volume 2. Edited by F. M. L. Thompson. Cambridge: Cambridge University Press, 1990

Daunton, M. J. *Housing the Workers 1850–1914: A Comparative Perspective*. Leicester: Leicester University Press, 1990

de Soissons, Louis. "Working Class Housing", *Flats, Municipal and Private Enterprise*. Ascot Gas Water Heaters Ltd., (1938)

Donajgrodzki, A. P., ed. *Social Control in Nineteenth Century Britain*. Croom Helm, 1977

Englander, David. *Landlord and Tenant in Urban Britain 1838–1918*. Oxford: Clarendon Press, 1983

Finnigan, Robert. "Council Housing in Leeds, 1919–1939: Social Policy and Urban Change." In *Councillors and Tenants: Local Authority Housing in English Cities 1919–1939*. Edited by M. J. Daunton. Leicester: Leicester University Press, 1984

Forrest, R., Murie, A. and Williams, P. *Home Ownership: Differentiation and Fragmentation*. Unwin Hyman, 1990

Foucault, M. *Discipline and Punish: The Birth of the Prison*. Translated from the French. Harmondsworth: Penguin, 1979

Garside, Patricia L. "Central Government, Local Authorities and the Voluntary Housing Sector 1919–1939." In *Government and Institutions in the post 1832 U.K.* Edited by A. O'Day. Lampeter: Edwin Mellen Press, 1995.

Garside, Patricia L. "Modelling the Behaviour of Non-Profit Housing Agencies in Britain and France 1900–1939." In *European Housing Policy in Comparative Perspective 1900–1939.* Edited by C. Zimmerman. Stuttgart: Freunhofer IRB Verlag, 1997

Garside, Patricia L. and Morris, Susannah. *Building a Legacy. William Sutton and his Housing Trust.* Tring: The William Sutton Trust, 1994

Gauldie, E. *Cruel Habitations: A History of Working Class Housing 1780–1918.* Allen and Unwin, 1974

George, A. L. and McKeown, T. J. "Case Studies and Theories of Organisational Decision Making." In L. Sproull and V. Larkey (eds). *Advances in Information Processing in Organisations.* Volume 2. Santa Barbara: J.A.I. Press, 1985

Gidron, B., Kramer, R. M. and Salamon, L. M. "Government and the Third Sector in Comparative Perspective: Adversaries or Allies?" In *Government and the Third Sector: Emerging Relationships in Welfare States.* Edited by B. Gidron, R. M. Kramer, and L. M. Salamon, Jossey-Bess, San Francisco, 1992

Girouard, Mark. *The Victorian Country House.* New Haven: Yale University Press, 1979

Gladstone, F. J. *Voluntary Action in a Changing World.* Bedford Square Press, 1979

Gooderson, P. J. *Lord Linoleum. Lord Ashton, Lancaster and the Rise of the British Oilcloth and Linoleum Industry.* Keele: Keele University Press, 1997

Habermas, J. *The Structural Transformation of the Public Sphere.* (M.I.T. Press, 1991). German edition, 1962

Hannah, Leslie. *Electricity before Nationalisation.* The Electricity Council: Macmillan, 1979

Harloe, M. *The People's Home? Social Rented Housing in Europe and America.* Oxford: Blackwell, 1995

Harris, Jose. *Private Lives, Public Spirit. A Social History of Britain 1870–1914.* Oxford University Press, 1993

Harrison, B. *Peacable Kingdom: Stability and Change in Modern Britain.* Oxford University Press, 1983

Hatton, T. J. and Bailey, R. E. *Poverty and the Welfare State in Inter-War London.* Discussion Paper No. 1686. Colchester: Centre for Economic Policy Research, 1991

Hole, V. and Poutney M. T. *Trends in Population, Housing and Occupancy Rates.* HMSO, 1971

Jackson, W. Eric. *Achievement: A Short History of the London County Council.* Longman, 1965

Jevons, R. and Madge, J. *Housing Estates: A Study of Bristol Corporation Policy and Practice between the Wars.* Bristol: Arrowsmith, 1973

Johnson, N. *The Welfare State in Transition: The Theory and Practice of Welfare Pluralism.* Brighton: Welfare Books, 1987

Johnson, Paul. *Saving and Spending: The Working Class Economy in Britain 1870–1939.* Oxford University Press, 1985

Johnson, Paul. *Twentieth Century Britain. Economic, Social and Structural Change.* Longman, 1994

Kemp, Peter. "The Origins of Council Housing." In *Built to Last? Reflections on British Housing Policy.* Second edition. Edited by J. Goodwin and C. Grant. Shelter, 1992

Kirkman Grey, B. *A History of English Philanthropy.* P. S. King and Son, 1905

Kleinman, Mark. *Housing, Welfare and the State in Europe.* Cheltenham: Edward Arnold, 1996

Kramer, R. *Voluntary Agencies in the Welfare State.* Berkeley: University of California, 1981

Le Grand, J. and Bartlett, W., eds. *Quasi-Markets and Social Policy.* Macmillan, 1993

L'Hopital, Winifrede De. *Westminster Cathedral and its Architect.* Hutchinson, 1919

Lindbolm, C. E. *Politics and Markets.* New York: Cambridge University Press, 1977

Loch, C. S. *The Dwellings of the Poor.* 1882

Macadam, Elizabeth. *The New Philanthropy. A Study of the Relations between the Statutory and Voluntary Services.* 1934

Malpass, Peter. *Housing, Philanthropy and the State: A History of the Guinness Trust*. Bristol: University of the West of England, 1998

Malpass, Peter. "The Missing Years." In *Built to Last? Reflections on British Housing Policy*. Second edition. Edited by J. Goodwin and C. Grant. Shelter, 1997

Malpass, Peter. "Rents within Reach." In *Built to Last? Reflections on British Housing Policy*. Second edition. Edited by J. Goodwin and C. Grant. Shelter, 1997

Manchester University Settlement, *A Survey of Housing and Social Amenities on Belle Vue Gorton New Housing Estate 1942–43.* 1943

Mayhew, Henry. *The Morning Chronicle Survey of Labour and the Poor in the Metropolitan Districts*. Horsham: Caliban Books, 1980–1982

Mayne, A. *The Imagined Slum: Newspaper Representation in Three Cities 1870–1914*. Leicester: Leicester University Press, 1993

Mass Observation, *An Enquiry into People's Homes*. John Murray, 1943

M'Gonigle, G. C. M. and Kirby, J. *Poverty and Public Health*. Gollancz, 1936

Merrett, Stephen. *State Housing in Britain*. Routledge and Kegan Paul, 1979

Merrett, Stephen. *Owner Occupation in Britain*. Routledge and Kegan Paul, 1982

Mitchell, B. R. and Deane, P. *Abstract of British Historical Statistics*. Cambridge: Cambridge University Press, 1962

Morris, Mary. *Voluntary Organisations and Social Progress*. 1955

Morris, Mary. *Voluntary Work in the Welfare State*. Routledge and Kegan Paul, 1969

Morris, Robert J. *Class, Sect and Party*. Manchester: Manchester University Press, 1990

Morton, Jane. *'Cheaper than Peabody'. Local Authority Housing from 1890 to 1919*. York: The Joseph Rowntree Foundation, 1991

Nash, D. and Reeder, D. *Leicester in the Twentieth Century*. Stroud, Alex Sutton Publishing, 1995

Nevitt, A. A. *Housing, Taxation and Subsidies*. Nelson, 1966

North, Douglass C. *Institutions, Institutional Change and Economic Performance*. New York: Cambridge University Press, 1990

Olechnowicz, Andrej. *Working Class Housing in England between the Wars. The Becontree Estate*. Oxford: Clarendon Press, 1997

Ostrom, Elinor. *Crafting Institutions for Self-Governing Irrigation Systems*. San Francisco: Institute for Contemporary Studies Press, 1992

Ostrom, Elinor. *Governing the Commons: The Evolution of Institutions for Collective Action*. New York: Cambridge University Press, 1990

Owen, A. D. K. *A Survey of the Standard of Living in Sheffield*. Sheffield: 1933

Owen, David. *English Philanthropy 1660–1960*. Cambridge, Mass. and London: Cambridge University Press, 1964

Owen, Guillermo. *Game Theory*. Third Edition. New York: Academic Press, 1995

Parsons, J. *Housing by Voluntary Enterprise*. 1903

Peabody Trust, *Mr. Peabody's Gift to the Poor of London*. 1865

Pember Reeves, M. S. *Round About a Pound a Week*. Bell, 1913

Pevsner, Nicholas and Nairn, John. *The Buildings of England: London 1. The Cities of London and Westminster*. Hermondsworth: Penguin, 1973

Power, Anne. *Hovels to High Rise: Social Housing in Europe since 1850*. Routledge, 1993

Prochaska, Frank K. "Philanthropy." In *Cambridge Social History of Britain 1750–1950*. 3. Edited by F. M. L. Thompson. Cambridge: Cambridge University Press, 1990

Prochaska, Frank K. *Royal Bounty: The Making of a Welfare Monarchy*. New Haven: Yale University Press, 1995

Prochaska, Frank K. *The Voluntary Impulse: Philanthropy in Modern Britain*. Faber, 1988

Prochaska, Frank K. *Women and Philanthropy in Nineteenth Century England*. Oxford: Clarendon Press, 1980

Putnam, R. D. *Making Democracy Work: Civic Traditions in Modern Italy*. Princeton, New Jersey: Princeton University Press, 1993

Ravetz, Alison with Turkington, Ralph. *The Place of Home*.

English Domestic Environments 1914–2000. E. and F.N. Spon., 1995

Rose, Michael., ed. *The Poor and the City: The English Poor Law in its Urban Context.* Leicester: Leicester University Press, 1985

Rowntree, B. Seebohm. *The Human Needs of Labour.* Longman, 1937

Rowntree, B. Seebohm. *Poverty and Progress. A Second Social Survey of York.* Longman, 1941

Rowntree, B. Seebohm. *Poverty. A Study of Town Life.* Macmillan, 1901

Rubin, K. D. "The Four Per Cent Industrial Dwellings Company Ltd. Its Function and its East End Development 1885–1901." In *The Jewish East End 1840–1939.* 193–204. Edited by A. Newman. Jewish Historical Society of England, 1981

Rubinstein, W. D. *Men of Property.* Croom Helm, 1981

Russell, C. E. B. *Social Problems of the North, London and Oxford.* 1913 (Facsimile edition, New York: Garland, 1980)

Ryder, Robert. "Council House Building in County Durham, 1900–1939." In *Councillors and Tenants: Local Authority Housing in English Cities, 1919–1939.* Edited by M. J. Daunton. Leicester: Leicester University Press, 1984

Scott-Moncreiff, W. W. *John Francis Bentley.* Ernest Benn, 1924

Sealander, J. *Private Wealth and Public Life. Foundation Philanthropy and the Reshaping of America from the Progressive Era to the New Deal.* Johns Hopkins University Press, 1997

Sen, Amartya. "The Standard of Living I." and "The Standard of Living II." In *The Standard of Living.* Edited by Geoffrey Hawthorn. Cambridge: Cambridge University Press, 1987

Short, John R. *Housing in Britain. The Post-War Experience,* Methuen, 1982

Shubik, M. *Game Theory in the Social Sciences: Concepts and Solutions.* Cambridge, Mass: MIT Press, 1982

Simey, Margaret. *Charity Rediscovered.* Liverpool: Liverpool University Press, 1992

Simey, T. S. *Principles of Social Administration.* Oxford University Press, 1937

Smith, H. Llewellyn. *New Survey of London Life and Labour.* 9 volumes. P. S. King, 1930–1935

Smith, M. *Guide to Housing*. Third edition. Housing Centre Trust, 1989

Smith, Southwood. *Results of the Sanitary Improvement, Illustarated by the Operation of the Metropolitan Societies for Improving the Dwellings of the Industrious Classes, the Working of the Common Lodging Houses Act, Etc.* 1854

Speake, Thomas. *War against the Slums. Voluntary Housing Societies in the Front Line.* Shrewsbury: Adnitt and Naunton, 1930

Stedman Jones, Gareth. *Outcast London: A Study in the Relationship between the Classes in Victorian Society.* Peregrine Books, 1984

Survey of London. Volume XXXVII. Northern Kensington. Athlone Press, 1973

Swenarton, Mark. *Homes Fit for Heroes.* Heinemann, 1981

Tarn, J. N. *Five Per Cent Philanthropy: An Account of Housing in Urban Areas Between 1840 and 1914.* Cambridge: Cambridge University Press, 1973

Taylor, A. J. *The Standard of Living in the Industrial Revolution.* Methuen, 1975

Taylor, G. H. *A Review of Housing in London 1966–1976.* Greater London Council. Research Memorandum 534. 1978

Taylor, Mary. "Voluntary Action and the State." In *British Social Welfare Past, Present and Future.* Edited by D. Gladstone. University College London Press, 1995

Tims, M. *An Historical Survey of Selected Housing Associations.* York: Joseph Rowntree Memorial Trust, 1968

Trout, H. *The Standard of Living in Bristol.* Bristol: 1938

Tsebelis, George. *Nested Games and Rational Choice in Comparative Politics.* Los Angeles: University of California Press, 1990

Vernon, R. V. and Mansergh, N. *Advisory Bodies: A Study of their Uses in Relation to Central Government 1919–1939.* Allen and Unwin, 1940

Vicinus, Martha. *Independent Women: Work and Community for Single Women 1850–1920.* Virago, 1985

Victoria County History of Kent. Edited by William Page, F. S. A. Archibald Constable and Co. Ltd, 1908

Waller, P. J. *Democracy and Sectarianism: A Political and Social*

History of Liverpool 1868–1939. Liverpool: Liverpool University Press, 1981

Ward, Stephen. *The Geography of Interwar Britain: The State and Uneven Development*. Routledge, 1988

White, Jerry. "Business out of Charity." In *Built to Last? Reflections on British Housing Policy*. Second edition. Edited by J. Goodwin and C. Grant. Shelter, 1992

Winter, Joy. and Robert, Jean-Louis. *Capital Cities at War. Paris, London, Berlin 1914–1919*. Cambridge: Cambridge University Press, 1997

Wohl, Anthony. *Eternal Slum. Housing and Social Policy in Victorian Britain*. Edward Arnold, 1977

Wohl, Anthony. "The History of the Working Classes in London 1815–1914." In *The History of Working Class Housing*. Edited by S. D. Chapman. Newton Abbot: David and Charles, 1871

Wolch, J. *The Shadow State: Government and the Voluntary Sector in Transition*. New York: The Foundation Centre, 1990

Yelling, J. *Slums and Redevelopment. Policy and Practice in England 1918–1945*. University College London Press, 1992

Index